RATE A DATE

About the author

I've always loved puzzles from history. For example: was there a 'real' Arthur? Many people believe there was. Over the years I've read lots of books about Arthur – some of them very learned, some of them crazy.

What I've learnt is that if there had been a 'real' Arthur, he wouldn't have been a king in shining armour. He would have been a British warlord some time around the late 5th century who fought against the Saxons and other invaders at the end of the Roman Empire.

These are stories of what Arthur might have been like, told by an older man to a young boy, in just the same way that the ancient bards – and the Druids – passed on their ancestral stories and memories.

miss – you know, coming here – and talking."

"I'll miss it too, Anthony," said Mr Rhys.

"But now..." Mr Rhys stood up and pulled together the shutters on one of the big bay windows. "It's time to lock up this house and go home."

Gawain checked for a breath, then a heartbeat. Nothing. He placed the cauldron and knife in the bottom of the boat, next to Arthur. Then he took Caledfwlch from its scabbard, raised it high and plunged it through the bottom of the coracle. He waited to make sure that the boat was sinking. Finally, as the little boat began to tilt backwards, Gawain placed Caledfwlch into his dead leader's hands, then slipped over the side and began to swim through the darkness towards the shore.

"And that's the end of the story, Anthony," said Mr Rhys. "And the end of your babysitting."

There was a moment's silence.

"Thanks for telling me all that," said Anthony. "It's been really good. And I'll

Arthur. "I've got one last thing to do as Duke of Battles. I must get rid of these baubles forever. They've destroyed my army. Row out to the middle of the lake, Gawain. I'm going to throw the whole lot overboard."

Gawain pushed off, and clambered into the tiny boat just as the sun began to set. Slowly, he steered the small boat with its single oar into the middle of the lake. And there, as darkness fell, Arthur died.

Gawain took the bag.

"Now leave us, Bedwyr," murmured Arthur. Bedwyr turned and walked slowly back to join the rest of Arthur's army who were standing a little way off, watching.

"Don't let them see me like this, Gawain," whispered Arthur. "Dying slowly like a sick, old dog. Lift me up. Let them see me walking one last time."

Gawain lifted Arthur to his feet. They turned their backs on the crowd of soldiers, and as slowly as a toddler or a grandfather, Arthur walked, supported by Gawain, towards the lake.

Pulled up on the lake shore was a small round peasant's boat made of goatskin stretched over wooden basket-work.

"I've heard, Gawain, that when their leaders die, the Saxons put their bodies in a boat, set it on fire, and push it out to sea! Help me into that little boat."

Gawain helped Arthur into the boat.

"Pass me the bag of treasures," said

scything swipe cut Medrod's head clean off his neck.

Arthur's army charged forward, howling with rage.

"Spare no one!" screamed Gawain, waving the blood-stained Caledfwlch above his head. "Kill them all!"

By late afternoon the battle was over. Arthur sat slumped in the middle of the field, supported by Gawain, and surrounded by the wreck of his great army. It was silent once again, apart from the occasional groan as a wounded man was either carried from the battlefield or given a merciful death.

"Arthur!"

Wearily, Arthur lifted his head to see who had spoken. It was Bedwyr.

"Look." Bedwyr held out a simple leather bag. Inside were the stolen treasures, the broad-bladed knife and the small cauldron.

unite our two armies and all of Britain against the Saxons!"

Then Medrod stepped forward. His helmet had a beaten faceplate of his own features. From behind the burnished metal, his voice sounded blurred and indistinct. "I agree, Uncle. We'll meet in the middle with just one spear carrier to serve us."

"Gawain, be my carrier," said Arthur. Gawain grabbed a second spear from the man behind him and followed Arthur to the middle. Medrod strode forward too. Beside him was his carrier, also wearing a helmet with an elaborate faceplate.

The four men stopped, a pace apart. Then Medrod's spear carrier suddenly lunged forward and stabbed Arthur in his left side. Then he tore off his helmet. It was Medrod. "The wound is mortal!" he yelled in delight. "I am the victor!"

As the wounded Arthur slumped against him, Gawain tore Caledfwlch from its scabbard and with a great, upward

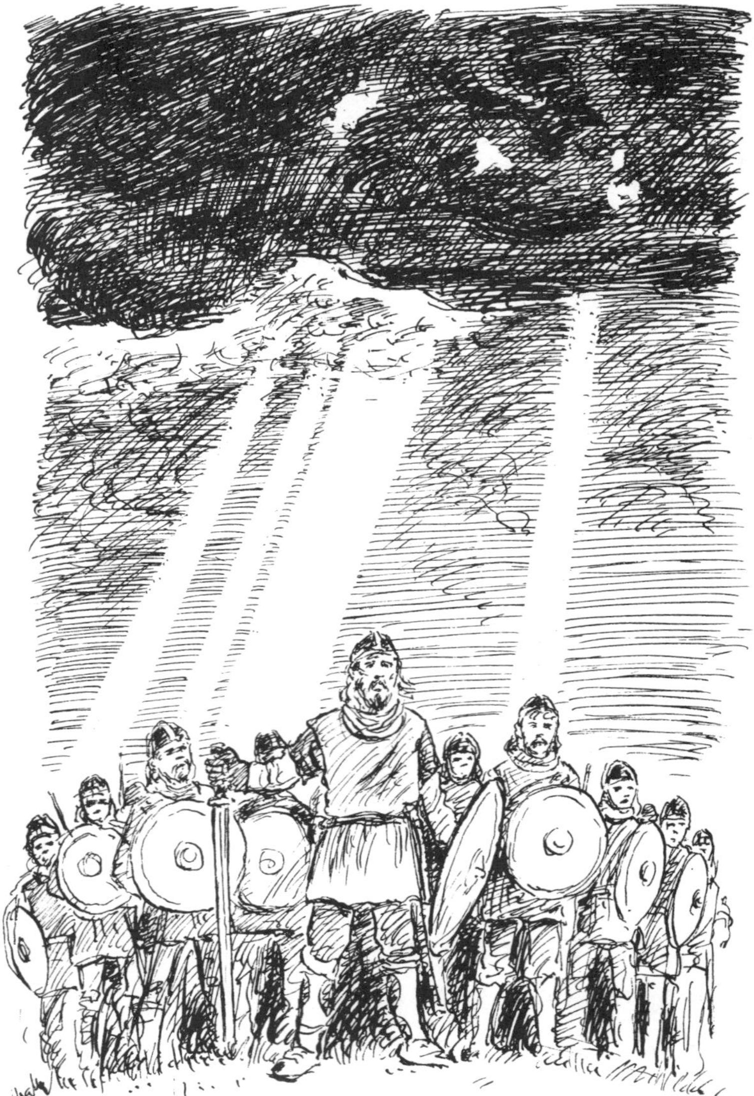

shouldn't need the death of anyone else. If only we could meet man to man, in single combat."

At noon, Arthur's men lined up as he'd commanded, pig snout formation with Arthur as the tip of the pig's snout.

Slowly, the two shield walls walked towards each other. But for once there was no chanting, no name-calling, no cursing. Men looked across the battle ground and saw their own brothers or fathers in the opposing line.

In the eerie silence, Arthur stepped forward from the line. He was wearing an open-faced helmet. Every man on that field could see clearly who he was. His voice carried easily across the marshy space between the two armies.

"Medrod! This is our quarrel! It could be settled with one death, no more. Let us fight this out between us. Single combat to the death. Let the gods decide. Whichever of us lives shall be the Duke of Battles, and

three sides by water. There was no way Arthur's heavy horsemen could attack from the sides or the rear. And the ground was too marshy. The cavalrymen would get bogged down.

"We'll fight on foot," he told Gawain. "In the old way. We'll form a shield wall in the shape of a pig's snout." He picked up a stick and scraped a rough diagram in the ground. "I'll be in the centre. Then on each side of me – but a pace behind – you and Bedwyr. Behind you two, four of our finest hand-to-hand fighters. Behind them another eight, behind them sixteen – and behind them the rest of the shield wall."

Gawain was appalled at the plan. "But that means you'll be exposed – visible – right in the centre. It'll be an invitation to any young tearaway to try his luck, and get quick fame with a lucky blow."

"I'm only interested in one young tearaway," replied Arthur. "Medrod. This is a quarrel between him and me. It

for the battle to come – forging swords, carving shields, casting spearheads, and sending out spies.

In early spring, Arthur heard that Medrod and his army had left their hill fort and were marching south. Arthur marched his men north to try to cut Medrod off.

Arthur knew that his army would be outnumbered, but he still had his cavalry. And Medrod could never see the point of cavalry, except to take messages and run errands.

Then Arthur's spies told him that Medrod had stopped. He'd made his final camp and was waiting for Arthur to come to him.

As Arthur's army got within sight of Medrod's, Arthur must have realized he was beaten. Medrod had lined his men up on the marshy ground beside a lake, and in the crooked arm of the river that fed the lake. Medrod's men were protected on

a dog's leg, doesn't it? It's very like the place where the last battle was fought.

"It took Arthur more than a year to catch up with Medrod, and it was a dreadful year. Every day, another couple of men would slip away to join Medrod's rebel army. And you couldn't really blame them."

Arthur was an old man. Medrod had two of the great, imperial treasures of Britain. The youngest of the fighters couldn't remember the days when Arthur had been a hero. Many of them hadn't even been born when the Saxons had been massacred on Badon Hill. Joining Medrod must have seemed the clever thing to do – a good career move for an up and coming young soldier.

For a whole year both armies prepared

Mr Rhys walked over to the window and stared out. "Come over here, Anthony. You can see the lake and the river. Can you see that curved bank down there? It looks a little like a bent elbow or

Chapter Five

"It's getting very near the end of the story of Arthur," said Mr Rhys, when Anthony arrived at Pendine House the next evening for his last babysitting session. "So I thought the best place to finish it would be in the library."

He led the way up the staircase, opened the door, and led Anthony into a large oval shaped room. The room was full of light. Thousands and thousands of old, leather-bound books filled three walls of the room from floor to ceiling. Large bay windows looked out across the grounds behind the hall.

"And that," said Mr Rhys, "is enough for tonight. It's time to be cycling back."

"Oh, no!" protested Anthony. "I've got to know what happened next."

"I thought you didn't like *history and stories and stuff*," said Mr Rhys in a voice that sounded rather like Anthony's.

"I don't," said Anthony.

"No," agreed Mr Rhys with a smile. "I can see you don't."

"It was a test to show to all the kings and chiefs that you have the courage and determination to lead the armies of Britain in the Saxon Wars which will come soon. Here…"

Arthur removed Gawain's belt and sword and tied Caledfwlch on its green and gold belt around Gawain's waist.

"When we return, I want all the troops to see who is to be their new leader."

But no one noticed Gawain was wearing Caledfwlch when they reached the camp that night. While Arthur and Gawain had been away, Medrod had declared himself Emperor of Britain. He had seized the remaining treasures – the cauldron, and the knife – and left the camp, taking with him many of Arthur's best troops.

standing on the ridge above him. "You've done well, Gawain, better than any other man I can think of. You faced certain death with courage, and fought a creature from the Other World – except, of course, he isn't!"

As Arthur clambered down the sloping bank, Gawain turned and looked hard at the Green Giant. He was big, but he no longer looked like the giant Gawain remembered from the feasting hall. And the green of his skin, was streaked and patchy, as if it was a stain.

"But how was he – were you…? I cut your head off."

"It's not as difficult as you think," said Arthur, with a smile, "to make strange things happen in a dark, smoke-filled room. Give men enough strong drink, or frighten them, and it's not hard to make them believe almost anything. Ask Myrddin."

"But why?"

Trying to control his fear, Gawain knelt on the stony ground of the river bank. He heard the swish of the upstroke of the sword, and flinched.

"What's this?" demanded the Green Giant. "Are you afraid, Gawain? I never showed any fear when you struck off my head."

"Strike now!" yelled Gawain. "I'm ready!"

The sword went up, and hurtled down. But, as it came to within a hair's breadth of Gawain's neck, it stopped dead, and all Gawain felt were two gentle taps – one on each shoulder.

"Get up, Gawain. You have received my blow!"

Gawain sprung to his feet, sword in hand. "Enough of these games! Now fight! Whoever, whatever you are!"

"*Stop!*" called a familiar voice from behind him.

Gawain turned and saw Arthur

Gawain didn't see a trace of any living creature until near nightfall, when he saw smoke rising in the distance. He crossed the river by the old Roman stone bridge. Following the plume of smoke, he approached a sharp bend in the river bank. As he got closer, he could hear a high-pitched scraping.

In a hollow, standing beside a spluttering fire, was the Green Giant. He was turning a great round grindstone to sharpen his enormous double-handed sword.

"Greetings, Gawain!" he bellowed. "Welcome to my humble home! I won't bother to show you around, you won't be here long!" And he swung the enormous sword above his head and brought it swishing down in a practice stroke. "Perfect! Won't you join me?"

Gawain dismounted.

"Kneel!" commanded the Green Giant. "And receive what you deserve!"

He slipped from the camp before dawn, unable to face saying his final goodbyes to his friends.

It was the bitterest winter in a century. As Gawain rode north he passed sheep frozen to death in the fields. He spent the night in an abandoned farm where the farmer and his family had fled south when their stocks of food and firewood had run out.

next spring, summer and autumn too, he was haunted by what was certain to happen to him when he met the Green Giant.

Death was his first thought on waking, and his last thought at night before he fell into a fitful sleep. But even when he was asleep Gawain was plagued by nightmares of the dreadful moment when the Green Giant swung the terrible sword and... off would come his head!

Just before Christmas a small war-band of Picts, desperate for food in the bitter weather, sailed south and raided some of the small villages on the west coast of Britain. So, as luck would have it, Arthur's men were camped only a few miles south of the Great West River when it was time for Gawain to set off in search of the Green Giant.

It took all Gawain's courage and determination to saddle his horse and collect together a bag of meagre rations.

He held out the head towards Gawain.

"Now it's your turn to receive my blow. But not here, and not now. Come and find me a year and a day from now, by the crooked bank on the north side of the Great West River." He took his sword from Gawain and thrust it back into its scabbard. Then, still holding his head by the hair, the Green Giant remounted his horse.

"If you don't keep your word and find me, I will find you, Gawain. Then you'll die a coward's death, instead of dying like a brave man and a true warrior." He turned his horse and rode towards the great double doors of the feasting hall. As he reached the door, he turned and bellowed: "A year and a day, Gawain – just ask anyone north of the Great West River, they'll show you where to find me. Meet me, Gawain, or be hunted down like a rat!"

Poor Gawain. All that winter, and the

Both men stood in the centre of the hall glaring at each other.

Then, without a word, the Green Giant gave his sword to Gawain and knelt down.

Gawain hesitated, uncertain what to do next.

"Come on!" roared the Green Giant. "Or has your courage failed you too? Your best blow – *now*!"

Gawain swung the sword high and brought it down on the Green Giant's neck.

The huge sword sliced through bone, muscle and sinew and the head fell to the ground with a great thud.

There was a ragged cheer, that quickly faded as Arthur's men realized that the Green Giant's body hadn't toppled forward. It remained kneeling, headless, beside the hearthstone in the middle of the hall. There was a gasp, as the Green Giant reached out his hand, picked up his head by its green hair, and clambered to his feet.

and you must accept the blow, unresisting just as I did."

He glared around the room. No one moved.

"You cowards! Is there no one with the courage to accept my challenge? Is there no one who'll trade me blow for blow?"

Arthur glanced to his left, where Gawain was sitting, and then to Medrod on his right. Slowly and deliberately, Arthur started to get to his feet. But before he could challenge the Green Giant, a voice from his left called: "I, Gawain, accept your challenge!"

Gawain stepped forward. The Green Giant jumped from his horse, sword in hand, and strode to meet Gawain.

Some had rabbits' feet, and one had a monkey's paw from a far away land near the edge of the world. Everyone in the hall knew that green was the colour of magic, the colour of creatures from the Other World: the world of spirits, monsters and ghosts; fiends that no man-made weapon could harm.

"If there's anyone among you with any courage," boomed the Green Giant, "I challenge him to a duel."

Hanging from his side was an enormous two-handed sword. He lifted the sword high in the air and whirled it around his head, like one of those mad, naked Saxon warriors who were always the first to charge into battle, and always the first to die.

"I challenge any man here to trade me blow for blow. And you weaklings may have the first blow. I won't resist. You may strike as hard as you're able, but make sure you strike well. For then it'll be my turn,

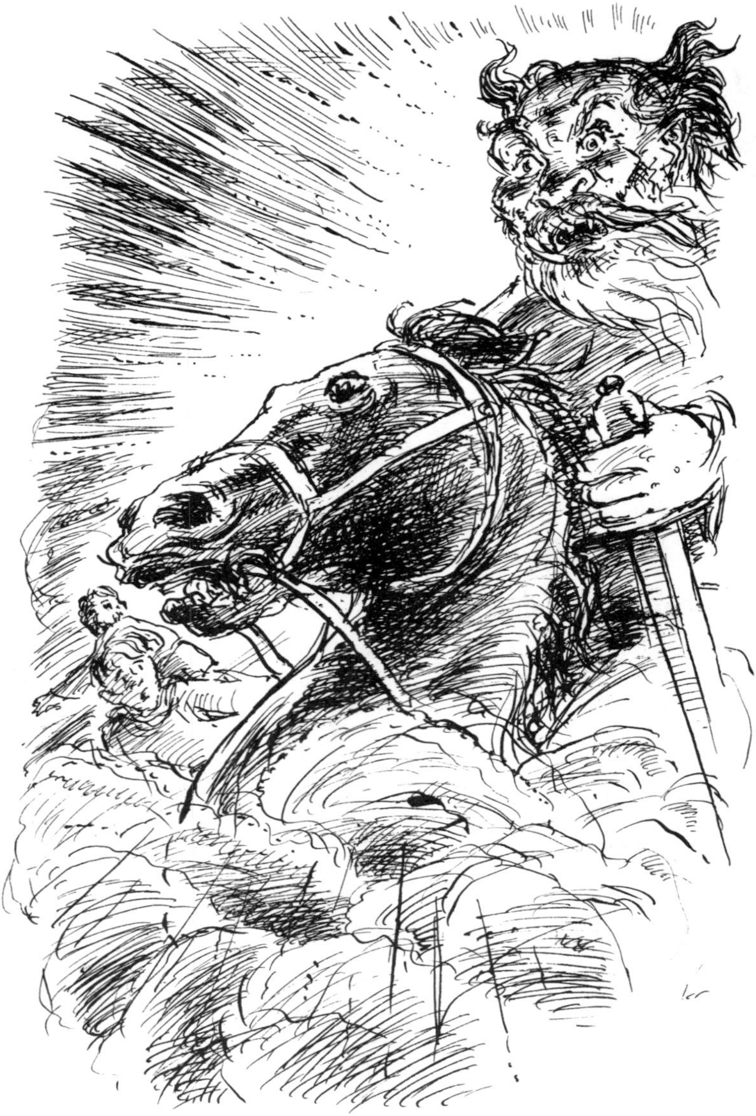

Into the smoke and darkness, rode an enormous man on a huge warhorse. Both man and horse were green. Not only were the man's clothes and the horse's tack green, but the skin of the man and the hide of the horse were bright green too.

"So this is Great Arthur's hall?" bellowed the Green Giant. "And these are his brave companions?" The Green Giant's voice was a great thundering, rumbling, boom. It seemed to come not from his throat, but from deep within his body.

He gave a great, mocking laugh. "You aren't men! You aren't soldiers! You're nothing but beardless boys, milksops – all of you! Look at how you shake and shiver with fear at the mere sight of me!"

It was true. Even the bravest soldier was afraid. Some were crossing themselves, or spitting on the ground for good luck, or making the sign to keep away the Evil Eye. Those that had them, grabbed for the lucky charms that hung on their belts.

"If that fellow from Gwynned looks at me again, I'll go over there and smash his face in!"

"I'm sure that Powys bloke's laughing at me. One more snigger out of him, and I'll stick me knife in him so fast he'll have a second mouth to laugh with!"

Suddenly the huge double doors at the end of the hall were flung open. Hearing the crash and feeling the sudden chill wind blowing, everyone turned to see who had burst in.

enormous wooden barn. There was a great double door at one end, with a row of wooden pillars in front to make it look more Roman and impressive. But it still looked like a barn.

Inside it was dark and foul-smelling. There were no glass windows, just square openings in the wall, covered with heavy wooden shutters. The only light came from dried rushes dipped in pig fat, which gave a poor light and stank. In the centre of the hall was the cooking fire. A hole had been knocked in the roof to let the smoke out, but the strong winter wind wasn't drawing the smoke out, but was blowing it back down the hole. Smoke and cooking smells and the stink of unwashed bodies mingled in a foul fug.

Although it was Christmas, the season of goodwill, tempers were short. Warlords glared at each other across the wooden tables in the smoky gloom, and their men muttered:

they'd built an enormous wooden feasting hall.

Arthur didn't need a feasting hall, but building it was a good way to keep the soldiers busy. Arthur could see how bored his soldiers had become, and he knew how quickly bored soldiers forget the enemy and start fighting each other. This was the Roman way to keep soldiers busy and fit – get them building something.

But to call what they built a hall probably makes it sound a lot grander than it was. It looked more like an

commander who would lose a war against the Saxons. If I choose Gawain, my legacy could be a civil war between him and Medrod."

"What it needs," said Myrddin slowly, "is some way to prove to everyone – Medrod as well – that Gawain is the better choice. I suggest we look, once again, to the old ways..."

It was Christmas in the City of The Legions, but there wasn't much left of the great Roman town. The great temples had been knocked down and the stone taken by local farmers to build field walls. All the roads and the forum were choked with thistles, hogweed and nettles, and in places sturdy young trees were growing out of cracks in the pavements.

But since the late summer, Arthur's troops had been clearing an area of rubble in the middle of the town, near where the old Roman town hall had been. Then

time."

"I know, I know," said Arthur, irritably.

"You need to name someone to succeed you as Duke of Battles."

Arthur said nothing.

"Follow the old ways, Arthur, the ways that the clans and tribes understand and respect. Name an heir – your sister's son, Gawain."

"I only wish I could," said Arthur. "But you seem to have forgotten, Myrddin, that I have two sisters. Gawain is Morgause's son. But what about my other sister, Morgana's son, Medrod? Gawain would be the better general, without question. But Gawain would never seek to take command. Yet, Medrod, who's half the soldier and leader Gawain is, would do anything to succeed me."

Myrddin sighed deeply. "Yes, it's always the way."

"So what should I do, Myrddin? If I choose Medrod, the army gets a poor

denying it. His thick red beard was going grey, and maybe – in training – he wasn't as quick with a lance or a sword as he used to be.

Myrddin put it to him straight: "There's a lot of men in your army who're beginning to mutter about what'll happen when you're no longer Emperor."

"Myrddin!" Arthur was on the point of loosing his famous temper. "How many times do I have to tell you? I am *not* an Emperor!"

"Of course you're not, of course you're not," agreed Myrddin, shaking his head vigorously. "You just tell everybody what to do, and they do it. That's nothing like an Emperor at all – no, no, perish the thought!" He paused. "But you and I can remember what things were like when Ambrosius died. And we also know that the Saxons are getting stronger every year. There's another war coming, and – well, you may not be able to lead the armies this

"The cord, please, Anthony."

Anthony placed the cord onto Mr Rhys's outstretched palm.

"Thank you," he said. "And now, I think, it's time to tell you about Gawain and the challenge of the Green Giant."

It was nearly twenty years since the Battle at Badon Hill. There had been the odd skirmish with Saxons, and with rebel chiefs and warlords, but for the most part, it had been twenty years of peace.

Many of the Roman ways had been saved. On feast days and Holy days, several of Arthur's men now wore togas. But many of the even older customs were coming back too. It was one of these older customs which was giving Arthur big problems.

Arthur was getting older, there was no

knuckles of his right hand, in and out, over and under, between his fingers.

"Things are not always how they seem," he said.

Mr Rhys stretched his hands to reveal a cat's cradle in the shape of a five pointed star.

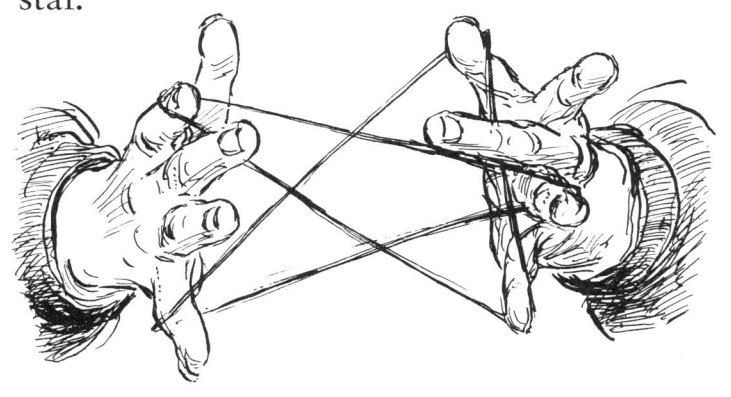

"Now you see it," he took one end and flicked the twisted cord into the air, "and now you don't!" A straight length of unknotted cord landed at Anthony's feet. Anthony picked up the cord. It was soft – not like string, more like a dressing-gown girdle – and twisting through it was a thin golden thread.

"Very underrated plants, nettles," said Mr Rhys. "You can make delicious soup with them. It's terribly good for you, full of iron. Just the thing to keep you warm on a cold day. And you can use them to dye cloth a lovely shade of green. It needn't just be cloth – fur, leather, anything. If you had enough nettles you could dye a horse green!"

Anthony shivered.

"You look frozen, boy. We'd better go inside before you turn blue!"

Mr Rhys led the way indoors, up the stairs and through the Grand Saloon. But as they were passing through the Saloon he stopped at a small glass-fronted display case.

"Ah, there it is."

He lifted the lid and took out a piece of green cord.

When they were seated once again in the small Keeper's room, Mr Rhys twisted the piece of green cord around the

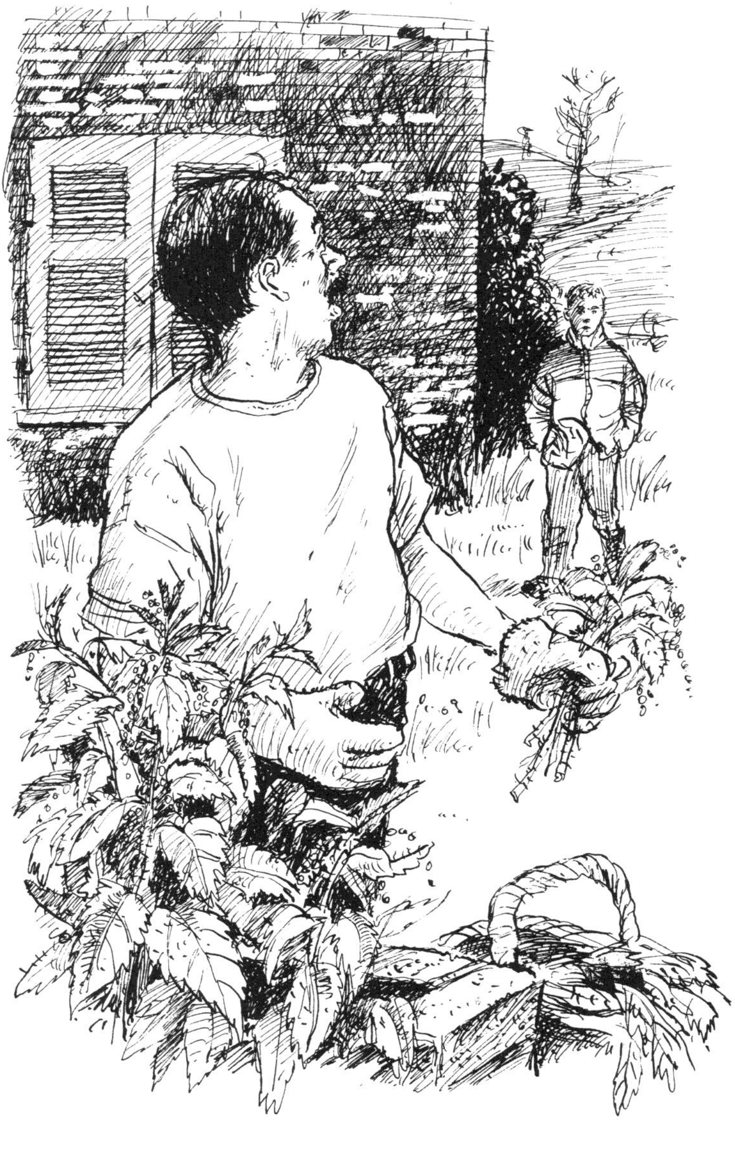

Then he noticed an empty bottle on the step beside the door. A scrap of paper stuck out of the top – like a note left for the milkman, but Anthony knew it couldn't be. The empty bottle had a garish red label: Kelliwac Cherry Cola.

Anthony pulled the scrap of paper out of the bottle:

I'm in the Kitchen Garden. Follow the path around the house to your right. It was signed: *R.*

Anthony followed the gravel path around the side of the house. About fifty metres away to his right, Anthony could see the bent back of Mr Rhys, stooped over a raised vegetable bed. Even in the biting north-easterly wind he was only wearing a thin T-shirt.

Mr Rhys straightened up. He was pulling up stinging nettles and carefully putting them into a basket on the path behind him as if they were flowers or vegetables.

Chapter Four

When Anthony arrived at Pendine Hall the next day, the front door was shut and locked. He rapped on the door expecting to hear footsteps coming down the great stairway and echoing along the lobby.

He waited and waited.

Nothing.

Anthony stepped back and gazed up at the shuttered windows, hoping to see a chink of light, or maybe Mr Rhys's face gazing down. He'd really enjoyed the gory battle story, and was hoping to hear more about Arthur's wars.

means 'Land of the Angles' – which is another name for the Saxons. But it wasn't the Saxons who defeated Arthur, it was his own men, the British. But that's another story for another day. It's time to lock up the house and go home."

said Mr Rhys. "If you'd ever tried riding a horse without your feet in the stirrups, you'd know. It's really difficult to stay in the saddle; you spend most of your time just trying to balance and grip with your legs. With stirrups you have something to brace yourself again; something to support you. You can lean left, or right. You can turn in the saddle. You can push a spear in and pull it out. You can swing a sword or a club without fearing that if you swing too hard, you'll simply fall off the horse and be at the mercy of the enemy troops."

And he started to sing again:

"For want of a nail, the shoe was lost.
For want of a shoe, the horse was lost..."

Swinging the leather stirrup backwards and forwards in time to the music.

"So did Arthur win the war?" Anthony asked, when Mr Rhys had finished his song.

"No, Anthony. In the end, I'm afraid, the Saxons won. The name 'England'

leader in the red cloak. "Kill them all!"

There's one terrible second of silence, then the British leader yells: "Charge!"

"And that," said Mr Rhys, "was the battle of Badon Hill. Five Saxon kings died that day, and their great invading army was destroyed – over nine hundred were said to have died in that last charge alone. It took the Saxons twenty years to rebuild the army they lost that day. The man in the red cloak was, of course, Arthur. And this was the secret of his success."

Mr Rhys held up the stirrup. "This enabled his cavalry to control their horses and fight the way did. Sometimes it's the littlest things that make all the difference."

"How?" asked Anthony. "I don't understand."

"It's easy to show, but hard to explain,"

The Saxons turn to run back up the hill, but from the woods on the other side of the lake, gallops another squadron of mounted soldiers, whirling great battle axes. The weight of the axes should drag them from their saddles, but it doesn't. The Saxons are dumbstruck. They never dreamed that men could fight like this!

Half way up the hill, the tattered remnants of the great Saxon army form a circle, locking shield to shield. But their spears were dropped after the first charge at the bottom of the hill. They have only swords, short-handled axes and knives to fend off the dreadful long spears of the British.

The leader of the British horsemen, a man in a scarlet cloak, signals his men to form a circle around the Saxons.

In silence, and with an awful, deliberate slowness, the horsemen level their terrifying lances at the Saxon circle.

"Spare no one!" shouts the British

horsemen charging towards them, armed with enormous lances. As they gallop into the panicking Saxons, they fight like no horseman has ever fought before. Their skill is inhuman, supernatural. These horsemen from hell can plunge a long spear into one man, pull it out and plunge it into another – over and over again!

turn and run, leaving the Saxon victors waving their swords, axes and clubs in the air and screaming with delight, and relief at being alive.

And then...

Out of the slanting sun, from behind a thick coppice of trees, come hundreds of stamping their feet in time to the curses:

"*Saxon cowards!*"

"*British scum!*"

For more than two hours they stand and taunt each other, beating their shields and stamping their feet. Then, without warning, a horn sounds and suddenly both lines are running at each other as fast as they can go. Some men trip and fall, others throw down their shields and spears and run away in blind panic.

With a deafening crash, both armies smash into each other, long spears plunging, shields colliding.

Many men are now lying on the floor, terribly wounded, screaming, but there's no time to help them. Out come the swords, axes and clubs, and the survivors are trampling on the wounded, hacking and chopping and beating at each other in a frenzy of fury and hatred.

The Britons realize they're losing. As if they'd been practising the manoeuvre, they panic. Some men are so drunk they can hardly walk – it's the only way they can find the courage to fight. Other men are being sick with fright.

Slowly, as the sun rises behind the lake, the two armies begin to walk towards each other. Their terrible, long spears are lowered.

They get within a few metres of each other... and stop.

Neither side wants to make the first move. So, like two crowds of rival football fans, they start to call out to each other – insults, curses: "*Your mother's a pig and your father's a leper!*" The worst insults they can think of.

Then one insult or curse takes the army's fancy, and they all start to chant it:

"*Saxon cowards!*"

"*British scum!*"

Over and over again. Someone starts pounding on the back of his shield, and the others join in. Then another group starts

from the enemy spears that were plunging at your chest, or throat or stomach. Or their swords and axes hacking at your arms and legs. It didn't matter how brave you were, or how skilled a fighter, if the man to your right in the shield wall failed, you were a dead man.

"Look up at Pendine Hill, Anthony and try to imagine it."

It's day break. Cold and damp. There's a mist in the air. A huge Saxon army is lined up on the side of a slope similar to Pendine Hill. Below them, in front of the lake, is a much smaller army of Britons. At a signal, both armies get ready to charge. Every soldier is praying to whatever god he believes in that the man next to him won't fall, or faint with fear, or drop his shield in

made Arthur's army unbeatable in battle for twenty years.

"Battles have always been dreadful things, full of fear and panic; the screams of the wounded and dying, and the most dreadful sights imaginable. But there was something especially frightening about the way battles were fought in Arthur's time.

"They were almost like rituals, blood sacrifices. As day broke, two armies would line up, facing each other, and form two human walls. Every soldier had a long spear and a shield. The nobles and chiefs had swords at their sides as well. Other men had axes tucked into their belts. The poorest had only a wooden club.

"But the battle always started with the dreadful long spears, with both lines crashing into each other – your spear stabbing into the enemy, or the enemies' spears stabbing into you. Your only protection was the shield of the man next to you – that was all that could save you

really be called a hill at all. It's an ancient fort. It was built long before the Romans came. There are lots of these old forts scattered around the country, nobody knows for certain who built them. But Arthur used them as bases to fight the Saxons from. It was at a fort called Badon Hill that Arthur trapped the great Saxon army and destroyed it."

"When was that?" asked Anthony.

"Oh, several years after Arthur took the sword from Myrddin and became the Duke of Battles," replied Mr Rhys.

"It was just as Arthur feared. Many of the British kings refused to accept him as their new leader. Some of them did, but for the first few years, for every battle he fought against the Saxons or the Picts, he had to fight one against a British warlord.

"Fortunately, Arthur had a secret weapon: this." Mr Rhys dangled the leather stirrup from the thumb of his right hand. "It may not look like much, but it

"Oh, don't worry about that," said Mr Rhys. "I don't need conversation, I can amuse myself. You carry on staring at Pendine Hill."

He pulled a loop of something out of his pocket, and dangled it between his fingers.

"What's that?" asked Anthony.

"Pendine Hill? It's a large lump of rock and soil that was built thousands of years ago, and it's supposed to be haunted."

"No, I meant that thing in your hand."

"What, this? It's a leather stirrup."

"What? For horse riding?"

"That's right."

There was a long pause.

"Mr Rhys...?"

"Yes, Anthony?"

"What was that you just said – about Pendine Hill?"

"Oh, you mean about it being *built* thousands of years ago?"

"Yes,"

"It's true," said Mr Rhys. "It shouldn't

He began singing again:

"For want of a nail, the shoe was lost.
For want of a shoe, the horse was lost.
For want of a horse, the King was lost.
For want of a King, the battle was lost.
For want of a battle, the war was lost.
For want of a war, the land was lost.
And all for want of a horseshoe-nail."

The nursery rhyme made no sense to Anthony, so he ignored Mr Rhys and looked down the long avenue of elm trees to the lake. Beyond the lake, the land rose steeply up to the top of Pendine Hill.

There was something very weird about Pendine Hill. Anthony had been told stories about strange sounds coming from the hill at night, and ghostly lights moving up and down the steep slopes in the darkness.

"You're not listening to me are you, Anthony?" said Mr Rhys.

"Err, no... I mean, yes," said Anthony, flustered.

Anthony followed the sound all the way around the side of the house. He found Mr Rhys sitting on a wooden garden bench on the terrace behind Pendine Hall.

"Hullo, Anthony."

Chapter Three

The sun was still shining when Anthony arrived at Pendine Hall the next evening. As he cycled along the gravel drive, Anthony found – to his surprise – that he was actually looking forward to seeing Mr Rhys again. Maybe Mr Rhys could tell him a bit more about this unfamiliar Arthur.

Anthony leaned his bike against one of the stained stone pillars beside the door. Then he tried the door handle. The front door was locked. Anthony was about to start knocking when he heard the distant sound of a man singing.

He glanced at Arthur to see if the flattery was working.

"Take the sword, Arthur, but use it as *you* wish: to lead an army that will push the Picts back over the wall and drive the Saxons into the sea!"

Arthur didn't move.

"Go on, Arthur! Take the sword, Arthur – take it!"

Arthur found himself behind the altar stone, with Myrddin at his side.

He hesitated for a moment, then grasped the sword, and with one smooth movement drew it from the earth.

"Arthur," said Myrddin softly. "Come with me, I need to talk to you."

He led Arthur to the far side of the circle of stones.

"Arthur," said Myrddin in a soft, persuasive whisper. "Look at them: petty tyrants, bandits, thugs. They can be brave enough when led, but they've got brains as dense as these stones.

"Britain needs a leader. Be their leader. Be their Emperor. Lead them against the Saxons and the Picts who are trying to destroy us."

"No, Myrddin. I said no, and I mean it. I'm not a king. They'd never accept me as their so-called Emperor. I'd have to fight every one of them, and what good would that do?"

"All right, not Emperor," said Myrddin, quickly, trying not to provoke Arthur's quick temper. "But I could make you their war leader – their Duke of Battles. You've got a clever mind and a soldier's cunning."

you – so you must be the Emperor."

Arthur turned to Myrddin. "Stop this madness, Myrddin. Britain doesn't need an Emperor. Why make enemies of men who should be fighting side by side? While the kings of Britain squabble over a meaningless title, our enemies – the Saxons and the Picts – steal and murder where and when they please."

"Spoken like a common upstart!" sneered Marcus.

"Spoken like a true Emperor," declared Myrddin.

"Myrddin! Didn't you hear what I said?" yelled Arthur. "Here! This is what I think of your Imperial sword!"

And with all his strength, Arthur plunged Caledfwlch into the soft ground behind the altar stone.

There was another gasp from the men in the stone circle. The Christian kings crossed themselves; the pagans made the sign to keep against the Evil Eye.

from its scabbard in one smooth movement.

There was a moment of silence, then a gasp of astonishment from all the kings and petty tyrants standing in the stone circle.

"That's the sword of the Emperor," murmured the little man. "It hasn't burnt

of what? I've spent all day trying to fight off three boatloads of Saxons, with a handful of men. And there's a *whole army* here, sitting around doing nothing!"

"Oi! It's my turn to try and draw the sword!" the short ugly king interrupted.

Myrddin turned to Arthur. He was still holding Caledfwlch by its scabbard.

"Whoever can draw Caledfwlch shall be the Emperor of All Britain," intoned Myrddin.

"You want a sword? Here, take mine!" shouted Arthur. He pulled his sword from its scabbard. Below the hilt, only a few centimetres of jagged, broken iron remained. He threw the sword onto the ground at the little man's feet. "That was broken fighting Saxons!"

Then Arthur grabbed the hilt of Caledfwlch in his mailed fist. "A good, British sword should be given to someone who's prepared to use it as it should be used – for killing Saxons!" He pulled it

jangling of harness, as a troop of mounted soldiers burst into the circle. Their horses were steaming, and lathered with sweat. Some of the men had fresh gashes down their cheeks and blood still flowing from wounds on their arms and legs.

Their leader, a tall man dressed in the tattered red cloak of a Roman cavalry officer, leapt from his horse. He tore off his leather helmet. His face was scarlet with rage.

"Myrddin! What are you doing? There are two hundred soldiers here, sitting on their backsides or fighting each other. Doesn't anybody realize there's a war on?"

"Show some respect, boy," snapped King Marcus.

"Yes, Arthur," said Myrddin. "You may be a good soldier, but you are in the presence of kings. We have met to decide on who should be Emperor."

That seemed to enrage Arthur even more. "*Emperor!*" he shouted. "Emperor

with a great shout. Crimson burns had appeared on the palm of his right hand the moment he tried to draw Caledfwlch from its scabbard.

One by one, each of the kings came forward. Some were blessed as Christians, others were blessed in the names of the old gods. But each man who tried to draw the sword got nothing but a burnt hand for his trouble.

By late afternoon, fights had started to break out between the supporters of the rival kings. Eventually, only one king remained to be tested. He was an ugly little warlord from a tiny kingdom of three half-deserted villages on the edge of a particularly unpleasant bog in the Far West.

"Step forward!" commanded Myrddin. "Are you a Christian or do you follow the old–"

The ritual was suddenly interrupted by a great clattering of horses' hooves and

As Marcus strode away from the altar stone rubbing his burned palm, King Urien of Rheged stepped forward. "I'll have none of your Christianity, Abbot. I live by the old gods, and my holy man has told me that it is their will that I am to be Emperor."

"Give me your hands," said Myrddin. "I bless you with water from the holy spring of the goddess Sulis." He sprinkled Urien's hands.

Urien grasped the sword. But just like King Marcus before him, he dropped it

my rightful place as Emperor."

"You're a Christian, aren't you, Marcus?" Myrddin said.

"I am."

The abbot stepped forward. "Hold out your hands, my son. In the name of Jesus Christ, St Michael and Saint George." As he spoke, the abbot sprinkled the upturned palms of King Marcus with holy water.

"Now, if you would be Emperor: draw the sword!" commanded Myrddin.

Holding the scabbard with his left hand, Marcus grasped the handle of the sword.

He immediately let out a cry and dropped the sword.

"Myrddin!" he bellowed. "What Druid's trick is this? Look!"

He held out his right hand. The palm was scorched red and the skin was already starting to blister.

"No trickery," said Myrddin smoothly. "It simply proves that you are not the one your God has chosen to be Emperor."

"Behold! The treasures of the Emperor of Britain. The sword, Caledfwlch, to defend his people. The cauldron of Annfwyn, to give him strength and heal his wounds. And the knife, Camwennan, to show that if he should fail in mind or body, he will willingly give his blood to save the Land of Britain.

"This sword, Caledfwlch, is not of this world. It was made from a star which fell burning from the heavens. It will never break, it will never blunt or rust. But only its true owner – the destined Emperor – can take it from its scabbard. It will burst into flames and destroy anyone else who tries to draw it.

Let the Gods show us who is to be Emperor of Britain!"

There was a pause as the Kings of Britain looked at each other, waiting to see who would make the first move, then Marcus of Kernow marched forward and stood in front of the altar stone. "I claim

procession who called themselves kings, but were just thugs or petty warlords who only ruled over one or two wretched villages.

As each King approached he laid down his weapons and entered the circle, alone and unarmed, as Myrddin had insisted.

"There will be only one sword within the circle, the sword belonging to the regalia of the Emperor," Myrddin had said.

One stone lay on its side within the circle, like an altar. On the stone lay a sword in a scabbard attached to a thin, green belt. Beside the sword was a small bronze cooking pot on three stumpy legs, and a sharp, broad-bladed knife.

To one side of the altar stone stood Myrddin dressed in a white robe. On the other side of the stone stood the Abbot of Glastonbury.

When all the Kings were inside the circle, Myrddin spoke.

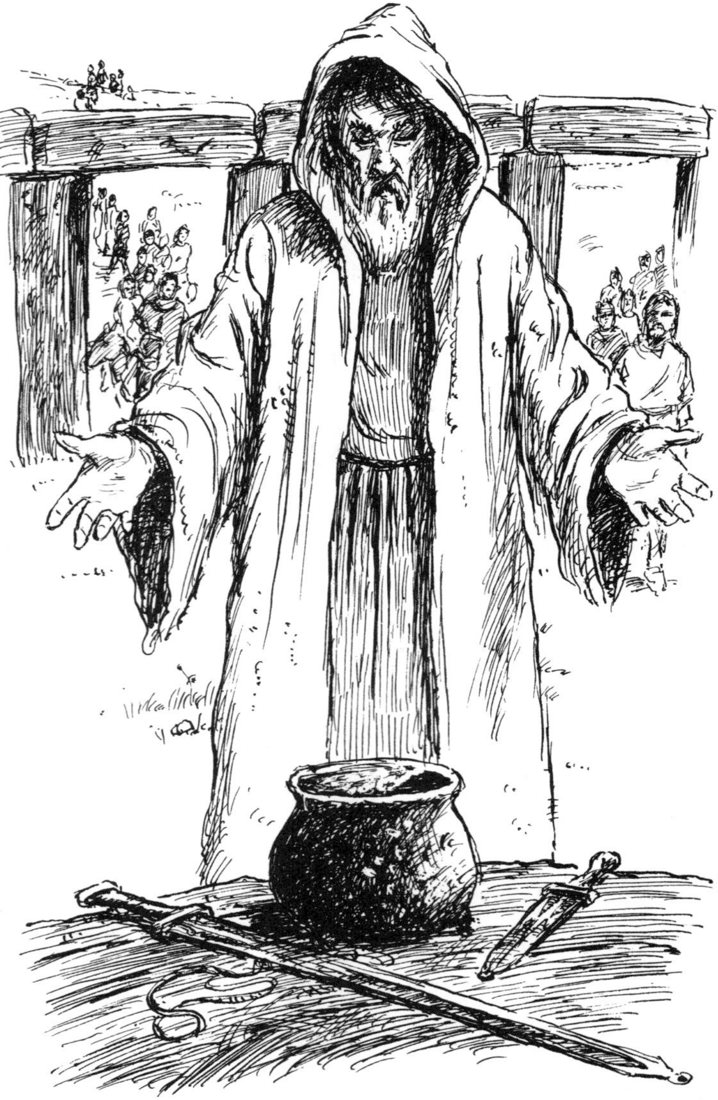

cauldron and the knife. Like the Crown Jewels in the Tower of London today, they were a sign: whoever owned them was the rightful Emperor of Britain.

As soon as Ambrosius had been buried, Myrddin summoned all the kings of Britain to meet in the great stone circle on Salisbury Plain. There, it would be decided once and for all who was to be the boss of bosses: the Emperor of Britain.

Just before noon on Midsummer's Day, standing in the stone circle, you could look across the great flat plain and see, coming from every direction along the ancient pathways, groups of men: the Kings of all Britain and their bodyguards.

Some were the kings of the greatest kingdoms – Powys, Gwynedd and Dyfed – wearing their richest robes. On horseback came King Marcus of Kernow, dressed in the patched remnants of a Roman general's armour. And there were others in the

organize an army from all the kingdoms of Britain to fight the invaders. A man named Ambrosius tried to form new legions. Some of the people even called him Emperor. But he was poisoned by a rival chief, jealous of his power.

The Saxons set up their own kingdoms in Kent and Sussex. British bards sang mournful songs about the Lost Lands, but with Ambrosius dead, no one seemed able to do much more than that.

Something had to be done. It was Myrddin's idea to hold the Emperor ceremony.

Myrddin claimed to be the last Druid. No one knew if that was true. (No one could remember what Druids were supposed to do, because it had been three hundred years since the Roman legions had massacred the last Druids on the Island of Anglesey.) But Myrddin had been Ambrosius' adviser. And Myrddin had the treasures of Britain: the sword, the

hundred years too early. And... I think I'd better tell you what really happened."

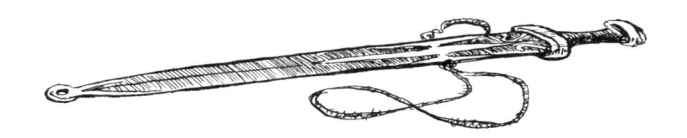

For over three hundred years, Britain had been part of the Roman Empire and many people in Britain only knew Roman ways. They had the Roman army, the legions, to protect them from their enemies – the wild Picts who lived in Scotland, and the Saxons who attacked the towns on the South Coast every summer and sailed away with whatever they could steal.

Then, within a couple of generations, it was all gone. The city of Rome itself was under attack, and the Roman Emperor said he could no longer afford to send troops to protect Britain.

With the Roman army gone, the Saxons launched a full-scale invasion.

Someone had to take command and

give him the number of National Rail Enquiries to make him go away. Tea?"

He poured two mugs and placed them on a small table. Also on the table was the ancient sword blade.

"I was going to tell you the story of Arthur and the sword, and how he became leader of Britain. But you probably know about it already from what your teacher told you."

Anthony nodded. "Miss Green said there was a magic sword in a stone, and all the knights tried to pull it out. But none of them could. Then Arthur pulled it out. And that showed he was the real king. But I missed the end, because it got a bit boring, and I was messing about, and she sent me to Mr Boardman."

Mr Rhys shook his head and sighed. "It's hard to know where to begin. To start with, Anthony, the sword wasn't in the stone, it was *on* the stone. And there weren't any knights, because it was five

Chapter Two

The next evening, Mr Rhys took Anthony through the side door in the saloon into a small room.

"This is the Keeper's room," he said. "It's where I hide from the really awful visitors. There was a chap here the other day who begged me for the phone number of the person who'd stuffed all the animals in the saloon. His budgie had just died and he wanted it stuffed. I tried to tell him that whoever the taxidermist was must have died a hundred years ago, but he wouldn't take no for an answer. In the end I had to

"Oh, that," said Mr Rhys, walking towards the bank of light switches. "That can wait until tomorrow."

rubbish. He didn't know what he had. He just hoarded things like a magpie. But some of the things he found may be priceless. Like this. It's a sword blade – very old.

It's made of a strange metal. I've never seen one like it, but I have heard of one, in stories and legends. It just might be from the time of Arthur – the real Arthur – maybe even older. It just might be –" He suddenly stopped. "Good Heavens! Look at the time!" He pointed to a huge grandfather clock in the corner. It's time to lock up, and get you home. I've got my bike downstairs, in the back kitchen. We can cycle together."

"But what about the sword, and the stuff in the glass?" asked Anthony, intrigued in spite of himself.

"I don't know anybody called Arthur," replied Anthony, thoroughly confused.

"No, not someone you know. I meant the Arthur from history."

"Oh, do you mean King Arthur?" asked Anthony.

Mr Rhys nodded.

"Miss Green at school told us some stories about him, and the Knights of the Round Table. But it wasn't in History, it was English. He wasn't a real king, he was just in stories and stuff like that. He was made up, Miss Green said."

"Hmmm," said Mr Rhys, frowning. "That's not quite true, Anthony. He paused. "I can assure you, Arthur was real, although he wasn't a king. He was a general, a fighter. And I'm afraid there were no Knights of the Round Table – at least, not in the sense you mean."

Mr Rhys picked up the long strip of metal. "The last owner of Pendine Hall collected all sort of things, most of it

"Phosphorus," said Mr Rhys. "Dangerous stuff if it gets near water." He put the smoking glass onto the floor. "Now, what do you know about Arthur, Anthony?"

very hard to follow what Mr Rhys was saying. He seemed to jump from one subject to another without any connection. Fairy-story treasure, chemistry, and the lump of old iron he was still clutching: none of it made sense.

"I'll show you," said Mr Rhys. He put down the lump of metal and walked briskly out of a small side door. When he came back, he was carrying a thick drinking glass half-filled with water.

"Watch carefully." Mr Rhys pulled a thick gardening glove out of his pocket and put it on. Then he opened the display case next to him, and with his gloved hand lifted out what looked to Anthony like the worn remnant of a stick of chalk.

Mr Rhys dropped the chalk end into the water. Immediately, it started to bubble furiously and sparks flew out from the chalk. The top of the glass was soon filled with dense, white smoke.

was covered by a vast white sheet.

Something long, thin and metal was resting on the edge of the table. "What is it?" asked Anthony.

"Would you believe long lost treasure?" asked Mr Rhys.

Anthony looked at him suspiciously.

"Yes," said Mr Rhys, "that does sound a bit childish, but..." He lifted up the long strip of discoloured metal. "It could be..."

"Could be what?" asked Anthony.

"Have you ever heard of the lost treasures of Britain?" asked Mr Rhys. "The sword, the sacrificial knife, the cauldron?"

Anthony shook his head. "Sounds made-up, like fairy-story stuff."

"Yes it does, doesn't it?" agreed Mr Rhys. "But have you ever seen what happens when you put phosphorous in water?"

"Sorry, what? "Anthony was finding it

panel on the far side of the room.

It was the biggest room Anthony had ever been in. It was much bigger than the school hall. He and Mr Rhys were alone in the room. The eyes which Anthony had seen were staring out from dozens of cases of stuffed animals which were crammed against the walls, piled one on one on top of another. Above the stuffed animals were paintings of men in long wigs, and ladies dressed in velvet gowns with lace collars. It was a room full of of dead things – dead birds and animals, and long-dead people – and they all looked horribly alive.

"It can be a bit creepy at first, but you'll get used to it," said Mr Rhys.

"I don't want to get used to it," thought Anthony. He tried to ignore the accusing stares of the motionless hares, owls and weasels.

"Anthony, come and look at this." Mr Rhys was in the centre of the room standing next to a snooker table which

you like history and stories about the past, Anthony?"

"No," said Anthony.

"Pity," said Mr Rhys. "This house is full of stories, if you know where to look."

At the top of the stairs was a set of brown-stained double doors. "This is the main saloon, the room that was supposed to be used for entertaining important guests," said Mr Rhys. "But the last owner kept his collections in it."

He flung open the doors, and led Anthony into the saloon. Anthony could sense that it was huge. He couldn't see much because the shuttered windows made the room dark and eerie.

As he walked, shining eyes seemed to follow him across the dark room. Anthony realized with shudder of fear that they weren't alone. An enormous crowd of people must be standing in the room, motionless, silent and watching.

Mr Rhys switched on the lights from a

go inside out of the cold and wet."

Mr Rhys opened the big door and led Anthony into a large, dingy lobby. The walls were the colour of stewed tea. Even through the thick soles of his trainers Anthony could feel the chill of the stone floor.

"We're trying to keep the house exactly as it was in when the last owner died," said Mr Rhys. "Come on, I'll show you around. I think you'll find it interesting."

"I doubt it," thought Anthony. Reluctantly, he followed Mr Rhys through the lobby and up a large, curving flight of stairs.

"I'm the Keeper," said Mr Rhys, over his shoulder. "That means I look after the collections in the house – the armour, the paintings, the books, the stuffed animals. I also help people who want to know about the past. I try to help them understand what it was really like to live one hundred, five hundred – even a 1,000 years ago. Do

TV and eat crisps!"

A man's voice came from behind him: "Anthony! Welcome to Pendine Hall!" It was Mr Rhys.

"I hope you haven't been waiting long. I was just checking the outbuildings. Let's

"I don't care what Darren Crockett does," said Mum firmly. "I've got to work late every night next week, and Mr Rhys has agreed to keep an eye on you. You're to go to Pendine Hall after school."

"Ohhhh, Mum!" wailed Anthony. "It's miles away and my bike's broken."

"That's OK," said Mum. "You can borrow mine!"

"Ohhhh, Mum...!"

Reluctantly, Anthony pushed off and let the ancient iron bulk of the bike carry him freewheeling down the winding gravel road towards Pendine Hall. He put on the brakes and slithered to a stop on the wet gravel drive in front of the house. Close up, the house with its pillars and broad steps looked larger and grander. It also looked shut.

Anthony gazed up at three rows of windows all shuttered, not a chink of light. "Great!" thought Anthony. "There's no one there. Now I can go home and watch

Anthony and worked at Pendine Hall, the old Manor House at the edge of the village where Anthony lived.

Pendine Hall had recently been turned into a museum. Anthony's teacher, Miss Green, had promised the class a trip to Pendine Hall in the Summer Term, when the end of year tests were over. Anthony was already planning ways to get out of going.

Anthony hated going to museums, old churches, libraries and art galleries – all the places Mum thought were really interesting and would do him good. Anthony didn't like Mr Rhys either, which was a pity because Mr Rhys was Anthony's new babysitter.

"I don't need a babysitter," Anthony had insisted. "I'm in year six now. I can look after myself. No one else in my class has a babysitter. Darren Crockett spends whole nights on his own, and he's a year younger than me."

Chapter One

Anthony cycled to the top of the rise and stopped. Ahead of him, the narrow, private road wound down a gentle slope. At the bottom of the slope, in a damp hollow, was Pendine Hall.

Despite the cold drizzle, Anthony was in no hurry to continue his journey. For one thing, his legs ached from the slog of pedalling his mum's ancient bicycle up the sloping drive. For another, he didn't want to spend a boring evening with Mr Rhys.

Mr Rhys lived in the house next door to

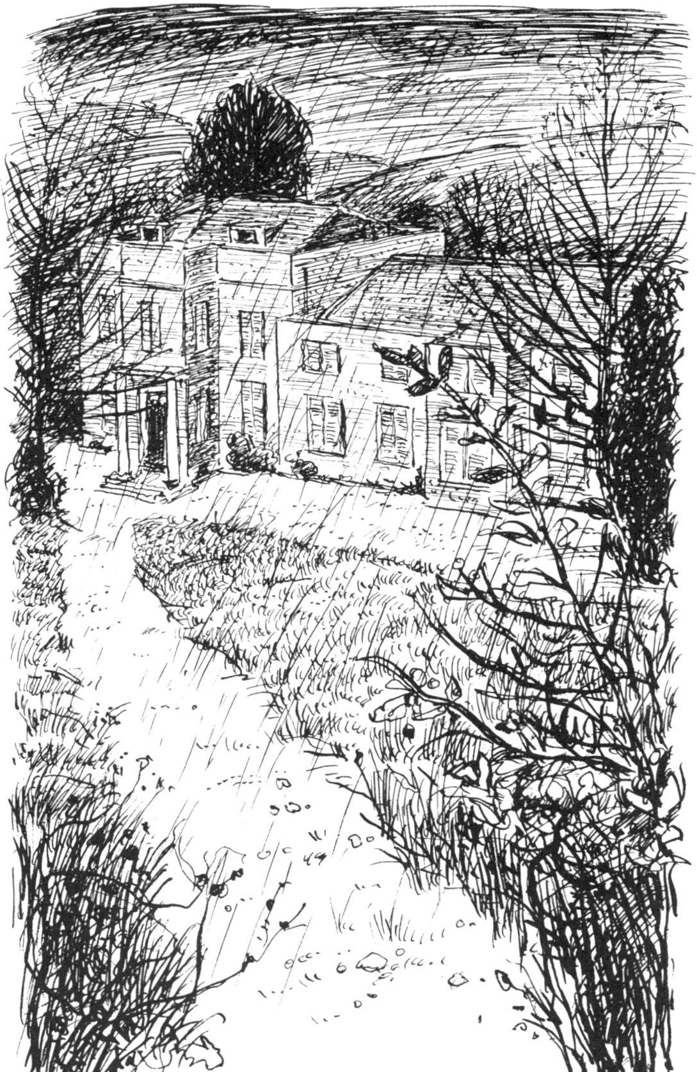

Contents

Chapter One	5
Chapter Two	18
Chapter Three	35
Chapter Four	50
Chapter Five	75
About the author	88

OXFORD
UNIVERSITY PRESS

Great Clarendon Street, Oxford OX2 6DP

Oxford University Press is a department of the University of Oxford.
It furthers the University's objective of excellence in research, scholarship,
and education by publishing worldwide in

Oxford New York

Athens Auckland Bangkok Bogotá Buenos Aires Cape Town
Chennai Dar es Salaam Delhi Florence Hong Kong Istanbul Karachi
Kolkata Kuala Lumpur Madrid Melbourne Mexico City Mumbai Nairobi
Paris São Paulo Shanghai Singapore Taipei Tokyo Toronto Warsaw

and associated companies in Berlin Ibadan

Oxford is a trade mark of Oxford University Press
in the UK and in certain other countries

© Oxford University Press 2001
Text © Mick Gowar 2001
The moral rights of the author have been asserted
Database right Oxford University Press (maker)
First published 2001

All rights reserved
No part of this publication may be reproduced,
stored in a retrieval system, or transmitted, in any form or by any means,
without the prior permission in writing of Oxford University Press,
or as expressly permitted by law, or under terms agreed with the appropriate
reprographics rights organisation. Enquiries concerning reproduction
outside the scope of the above should be sent to the Rights Department,
Oxford University Press, at the address above

You must not circulate this book in any other binding or cover
and you must impose this same condition on any acquirer

British Library Cataloguing in Publication Data
Data available

ISBN 0 19 915960 2

Printed in the UK by Ebenezer Baylis & Son Ltd

Available in packs
Year 5 / Primary 6 Pack of Six (one of each book)   ISBN 0 19 915963 7
Year 5 / Primary 6 Class Pack (six of each book)   ISBN 0 19 915964 5

Arthur
WARRIOR CHIEF

Illustrated by
Martin Salisbury

OXFORD
UNIVERSITY PRESS

RATE A DATE

MONICA MURPHY

Copyright © 2020 by Monica Murphy

All rights reserved.

No part of this book may be reproduced in any form or by any electronic or mechanical means, including information storage and retrieval systems, without written permission from the author, except for the use of brief quotations in a book review.

This book is a work of fiction. Names, characters, places, and incidents are used fictitiously. Any resemblance to actual persons, living or dead, events, or locales, is entirely coincidental.

Cover design: Hang Le
byhangle.com

Editor: Mackenzie Walton
Proofreader: Holly Malgieri

THE DATING SERIES

If you enjoy **RATE A DATE**, make sure you check out the other books in the series!

Out Now:

Save The Date
Fake Date
Holidate
Hate to Date You
Rate A Date

Coming Soon:

Wedding Date

DEDICATION

This book is for my son, Jack. Thank you for the title. And thank you for being you. Love you.

ONE
ELEANOR

"YOU NEED TO FIND YOURSELF A MAN."

I blink at my friend Kelsey, who's slowly weaving back and forth in her seat, trying to point at me, but her arm wavers so it's like she's pointing at everything she sees.

I think she might be drunk.

"*You* need to find yourself a man," I tell her, trying to hide the fact that I'm offended by keeping a neutral expression on my face.

But yes. I'm totally offended.

We're at a local bar on a Saturday night, drowning our sorrows in booze after our friend Caroline's bridal shower. Kelsey and I are the only single ones left from our friend group. All the rest of them went home to their boyfriends. Fiancés. Side pieces. Whatever you want to call them.

No, wait. None of our friends have side pieces. That's such a gross term, so I'm taking it back. I know I would never be a man's side piece. That implies I'm not even worthy of being his *main* piece, if you know what I mean.

Huh. Does that even make sense? I might be a little drunk too.

Milligan's Pub is one of our favorite places to hang out, considering its central location. I can walk to the bar from my salon. I'm a hairstylist at Inspirations Salon and Day Spa in downtown Carmel. I've been there for seven years. It's the first and only salon I've ever worked at, and it's one of the most popular in the area. My mom worked there before me and got me the job. But she's retired now, living in Florida with her husband, my stepdad. I see her twice a year if I'm lucky.

I really miss my mom.

"I think I found one," Kelsey says, pulling me back to the here and now.

I frown at her. "You found what?"

"A man. Okay fine, I've found a couple, and we've started chatting." Kelsey rolls her eyes and slaps her hand on the table, making our empty glasses rattle and me jump a little in my seat. "Keep up, lady! There's a new app that I've been trying out since last night, and I like it. A lot."

"A dating app?" I wrinkle my nose. That is not the way to find true love, if you ask me. Shouldn't you meet your true love in person? Or have one of those cute accidental meetings? Like *oops, you picked up my coffee order by mistake! Let's swap drinks—and phone numbers.*

Okay, look, I've had a few *I want to meet my true love in the Sweet Dreams Café* fantasies, okay? My friend Stella, who works there, would tell me I'm being ridiculous if she knew this fun little fact.

I can't help that I'm a total romantic.

"Yes, a dating app. Don't say it like it's a dirty word. You should give it a try. I bet you'd find someone. In fact, I know you would." Kelsey picks up her phone and starts tapping away. Her brows furrow in concentration. "How tall are you?"

"Um, five-four? Maybe five-five?" Why is she asking me this?

"Blonde hair. Hazel eyes, curvy." Kelsey's fingers are flying as she types. "Hairstylist to the stars."

"Not quite," I say.

"Close enough." She shrugs before she starts tapping the screen again. "So...you have a positive attitude, you're kind and thoughtful, and you're looking for a man who can commit and isn't afraid of making those big romantic gestures."

Alarm rises in me, making my entire body go stiff as I watch her. "Wait a minute. What are you doing?"

"Nothing." Her voice is deceptively innocent. She keeps her gaze fixed on the screen. I want to snatch that stupid phone out of her hands and see exactly what she's putting together, but I restrain myself. Barely.

But after approximately one minute of restraining myself, I can't take it anymore. "*Kelsey.*"

"*Eleanor.*" She's still typing, a little smile curling her lips. "Oh, this is gonna be so good. You'll thank me for this, I promise."

Unable to stand it any longer, I grab the phone from her hands.

"Hey!" Kelsey glares at me, reaching over the table to take her phone back, but I turn away from her, holding it up in the air. "Give it back!"

"No way." I keep my back to her as I study the screen. It's a dating profile on what must be that new app she's talking about: Rate A Date.

Huh.

The information is all about...me.

The profile pic is one of...me.

The user name is *qtstylist926*. September 26 is my birthday...

"Kelsey, this is a dating profile for *me*." I turn to face her, my mouth hanging open in shock. Holy crap, I need to delete this. Stat. Beyond stat. Like *yesterday* stat. "What in the world did you do?"

"I did exactly what you just said. Created a profile for you, so you can be on this new dating site," Kelsey explains, her eyes big, her gaze one of complete and utter innocence.

I'm not buying it. Not for one minute. In fact, I'm fuming mad.

Like, super angry.

Livid, even.

"Kelsey, I am *livid*."

Isn't that a great word? Livid? I never get a chance to use it, considering I'm not what I would call an angry person. I'm usually pretty positive.

"Why? Oh, come on," Kelsey whines. "You need to give it a chance."

I read over my info again, getting to the *what I'm looking for* section.

I've discovered that short-term relationships aren't my thing. I'm an old-fashioned woman looking for a serious relationship. Are you willing to commit? Not afraid of big romantic gestures? Like to read, watch movies and take long walks on the beach? Then I'm your girl. It helps if you're at least six-foot and physically fit, but still like to eat ice cream and pizza.

Kelsey's not wrong with this description, but also, she made me sound kind of ridiculous.

"How do I delete this?" I click on the little gear symbol in the top right corner, see the words *profile settings* and select it.

"No way." Kelsey snatches the phone out of my hands, smiling at me while I glare. "You're not deleting it."

"I don't want to be on that app," I tell her, stomping my foot. Considering how loud it currently is in this crowded bar, my stomping is completely ineffective.

"Come on, do it for me. Please?" Kelsey flashes me her puppy-dog eyes and bats her lashes. She's annoyingly attractive. Plump lips and dark eyes and beautiful silky brown hair. She came into the salon once asking for highlights and I convinced her not to do it. Her hair is gorgeous as is. Instead, I applied a special gloss treatment that made her hair even shinier than usual.

"I don't believe in dating sites," I say primly, resting my clutched hands on the table. "Delete it."

"Give it a month," she says, sticking out her lower lip in a mock pout. "They let you use the site for free for the first thirty days."

"No."

"I'll do it with you."

"You were already doing it, whether I was on the app or not."

She considers me for a moment, and I swear I can see her brain working, trying to come up with a convincing idea. "We could go on double dates together."

Hmm. That's not a bad idea. I say nothing, contemplating her offer.

"It's not a sleazy app, I swear. It's only been out for a couple of months, and everyone's raving about it," she explains.

"It's called Rate A Date, Kels. Meaning you *rate* your *dates*. That sounds like a disaster in the making."

Now, look. I'm not usually reluctant to put myself out there. I'm the romantic one of our friend group. I believe in true love. I know my soul mate is out there somewhere, just waiting for me. Someday, we will find each other, fall madly in love, and I'll end up sending smug texts to our friend group chat, telling them all I know love is real, accompanied by a photo with the most handsome man on the planet standing next to me, our arms around each other and a giant rock on my finger.

I *know* that will happen. I've said it out loud multiple times. I've written it down in my daily journal. It goes in my both my monthly plan list and my quarterly plans. If you write something down enough, put it out into the universe, eventually...

It comes true.

And that's #facts.

"I just don't want to do this alone. I'd rather have a friend on this app with me, but every single one of our friends is currently involved with someone else. Close to being married, just engaged or they've recently fallen madly in love," Kelsey explains. "With the exception of me and you."

"What about Amelia?" She's another fringe member of our friend group. She works at the jewelry store in the same shopping center where my hair salon's at, and we do lunch together on occasion. I love Amelia.

"She got back together with her boyfriend."

"Ew." I make a face. I may love Amelia, but I do *not* like her boyfriend. Those two have been off and on for years. It's frustrating. He treats her like garbage, they break up, she tells us all about the awful things he did or said to her, and then they end up back together.

None of us like him. We don't even like to say his name out loud. Like we might invoke evil spirits or something.

"It's just me and you, babe," Kelsey says, her voice softening. Encouraging even. "I'm sorry I created that profile for you without your consent, but you gotta admit, I've got you figured out."

I say nothing. But I'm not as irritated as I was feeling a few minutes ago.

"How about this—you can edit my profile. Then we're even." Kelsey smiles. "And then we'll be in this together, we'll go on a couple of dates, report back to each other, and when the month is up, we're done. Well, you're done. I might continue. What do you say?"

Of course, I'm skeptical. I shouldn't agree to this. It sounds like a bunch of trouble. What if we meet psychos? Stalkers who won't leave us alone and we'll have to call the cops and file a restraining order...

"It could be unsafe," I say.

"If you won't do it with me, I'm still going to do it, regardless." Kelsey shrugs.

Ooh, she knows I worry about everyone and everything. I can't stand the thought of her doing this all on her own. I need to be there, be her partner in dating, and make sure nothing terrible happens to her.

"I don't like that," I tell her.

"Too bad. I'm still going to do it. I might meet a serial killer, but I watch enough true crime shows so I'll be able to tell if something's wrong with them pretty quickly." Another casual shrug from my friend. "Besides, there are cameras everywhere. If I end up dead, they'll figure it out quick."

She knows exactly what she's doing to me.

"Oh my God, fine," I reluctantly say, and Kelsey squeals so loudly I rest my hands over my ears, only dropping them when I know she's gone quiet. "I'll keep my profile on the app and I'll even talk to guys for thirty days, but as soon as my month is up, I'm out."

"You'll have to go on at least one date," Kelsey points out. "Maybe two. Three if you want a good assessment of your dating pool."

"Don't try to make this sound like a science experiment. That won't work on me." I always sucked at science.

Kelsey waves a hand. "You know what I mean."

"I also want to rewrite your profile description," I tell her, making a gimme motion with my hand. "Let me see your phone."

"You promise you won't delete your profile?" She raises her brows.

Sighing, I roll my eyes. "Promise."

She taps at her phone and then hands it over. Her profile photo is almost a full-body shot of her in a provocative pose, and she's wearing a really cute red sundress—that shows cleavage.

"You're just going to get a bunch of dick pics with this profile pic."

"Maybe that's what I'm looking for." She keeps a straight face for about a second before we both start laughing.

"First things first, you need to get rid of that photo." I hit delete and then aim the phone at her. "Smile."

Before she can say anything, I snap a photo of her, then look at it.

"I bet I look terrible," she complains.

"Not too bad at all." I hand the phone back over and she contemplates it.

"I don't mind this." She returns her phone to me. "I took the photo of you at Caroline's shower earlier."

"I figured, since I'm wearing the same outfit."

"I had to capture the moment, Eleanor. You were laughing and having such a good time," Kelsey says, her voice soft.

"Gee, thanks." I *was* having fun at the shower. But it also made me a little sad. We're all changing so much. By the end of the year both Caroline and Candice will be married. Sarah is mostly likely the next to go, and I have a feeling Stella and her new boyfriend—who also happens to be Caroline's big brother—will move in together as soon as her new house is remodeled.

All happily coupled while I'm unhappily…

Single.

Maybe this dating app is just what I need to find the man of my dreams.

TWO
MITCH

"I'M SO OVER THIS."

We're at a nightclub in San Francisco, me and my friends. It's a Saturday night, the place is packed, the booze is flowing and the music is so damn loud, it makes my body throb.

And not in a good way.

"What did you say?" My friend and teammate Clayton frowns at me. There's a pretty girl with giant tits hanging all over him, trying to whisper in his ear, but he's not even paying her any mind.

This is typical. We're used to it.

"I said..." I lean in closer to him, my face practically in his. "I'm. So. Over. This."

Clayton leans back, his expression incredulous, the woman petting his head like he's a dog. "Oh, come on. Are you serious? Look where we're at. Look who *we are*. You're bound to find someone to, uh, spend a little time with."

He raises his brows and strokes his chin for emphasis.

Clay sounds like an egotistical asshole, but he's right. We're in the middle of the most popular nightclub downtown, and all the women in this place are circling our booth, looking for a way to get close to us.

I honestly don't care.

"Yeah. No." I shake my head. "Not interested."

Clayton's eyes nearly bug out of his head. "You're not interested? Really?" The woman with the tits whispers something to him and he nods. Smiles. Calls her baby, strokes her bare thigh, but I can't hear the rest.

The music just switched to another song, and I swear to God it got louder.

"What's your problem?" he yells at me once the woman slides out of our booth, heading to the bathroom, I presume. "You not feeling well?"

Clayton hasn't been on the grind as long as I have. You see, I'm a professional football player. And I play for the motherfuckin' Raiders. Defensive line. We're tough as hell, we don't take any shit, but we sucked. Got into the playoffs the first two seasons I was with the team before we started getting our asses kicked on the regular. It's awful. A real mood killer.

The women keep coming around, though, so that's cool.

Clayton is our new pretty boy quarterback. One season in and we've turned ourselves around. We even made the playoffs—first time we've done that in a few years.

I like Clayton. We've become friends. We're both single, and we both like to go out, have a few drinks, spend our time with beautiful women. It's easy when we're...us. Women always want a piece of us. We're big. Muscular. Rich. Some of us are better looking than others—Clay and his billboard face, for instance—but looks don't seem to matter to some of these women.

When I first started as a professional athlete, I was young, dumb and full of come. That's what my grandpa always said. Just out of college, horny as fuck and with all sorts of money filling my pockets, I was down for the one-night stand. The casual hookup. Most of the women I met were feeling my vibe. They knew what the score was. I was blown away that they threw themselves so easily at me—I'm not what they call classically handsome. But I can hold my own, I'm at my athletic prime, and I have a decent-sized dick and a skilled tongue, so yeah. I guess I was considered a catch.

I figured out pretty fast that so many of them were just looking to get their hooks in us. In me. They're just chasing the dream. And their dream is to find a successful professional athlete to keep them in extensions, Chanel bags and Range Rovers for the rest of their lives.

No thanks.

"Yo, Anderson. Answer me. You feeling okay or what?" Clayton yells, knocking me out of my thoughts.

I blink at him, noting the amused gleam in his eyes. This guy. He gets a kick out of everything. It's like he's high on life. "I'm tired of dealing with these women," I mutter, sounding completely put out.

Clay starts to laugh, shaking his head. "Dealing with these women? Are you serious right now? You can have free pussy whenever you want and you're *tired* of it?"

"I've been getting free pussy longer than you have," I remind him. "And yeah. I'm—bored. I can have this." I wave my hand around. At the club, at the flock of women standing nearby, watching us with hungry eyes. "But I want something real."

I press my palm against my chest, like some sort of sap, and Clay rolls his eyes. I'd probably do the same thing if he said that to me.

"This *is* real, bro. This is as real as it gets." Clay slaps the edge of the table. "There are women everywhere. And we can have any of them. They say the right things, we say the right things, and next thing we know, we're all snug as a bug in a rug, their hands in our hair and their tits in our face. Why would you ever get tired of that?"

He sounds utterly confused by my protests. And I suppose I can't blame him. Why would we ever tire of that? Most men think we're living the dream. For the last five years, I've felt exactly like that.

But I'm over it. I want something...

Different.

"I want a real relationship."

There. I said it. Out loud.

Miss Big Tits chooses that exact moment to return to our table, her lips freshly glossed, the neckline of her dress so low, I'm worried I might catch sight of a nipple. She settles right in next to Clayton, cozying up to his side, her hand resting on his thigh possessively, and I know without a doubt Clay is gonna get lucky tonight.

I'm not feeling even an ounce of jealousy.

"You won't find that here," Clay says after a moment, dropping his arm around the woman's slender shoulders and tugging her even closer to his side. "Though I think you already know that."

I do. This is not the place to search for a real relationship, no matter how bad some of these women might want that.

They're going about it the wrong way, if you ask me.

But hell. What *is* the right way?

I have no clue.

"I'm out of here," I tell Clay, scooting out of the booth and rising to my feet. I tower over the table, over Clay and his new lady friend, and she gazes up at me with wide, almost frightened eyes. I offer her up a slow smile and the tension eases out of her. Somewhat. "You two have a good night."

"We sure as hell will," Clay tells me with a wink, and the woman laughs.

If I had a hat, I'd tip it at his date like I'm some homegrown cowboy, but I don't. So I keep walking, making my way out of the crowded, hot-as-fuck nightclub as fast as possible. The lights flash in my eyes, keeping time with the beat of the music, and I don't miss the way some of the women watch me as I pass.

Like I'm a prime slab of meat and they can't wait to take a big, juicy bite.

Fuck this shit.

The moment I push through those double doors, I take a deep, cleansing breath. Though it doesn't smell the best out here, considering I'm smack dab in the middle of downtown San Francisco. Wrinkling my nose, I glance around, spotting the black Yukon sitting by the curb a couple of cars down, and I make my way toward it.

"Howard," I say when the passenger-side window rolls down, revealing our driver. He works for the team, even during the off-season, and somehow he's able to sit right in the front of the clubs, waiting for us every weekend when we go out. "Do you mind taking me home?"

"Sure thing. Hop in."

The window goes up and I climb into the backseat, grateful for the chilled bottle of water Howard hands me once I'm settled.

"Just you this evening?" he asks, his thick, black eyebrows lifting. Howard is also used to me bringing home a sweet little cookie on the regular. Not that I actually bring them *home*. That's always kind of dangerous.

Nope, I usually take them to a hotel where we have a standing account. We can just call up and boom, there's a room available for us. That way women don't know where we live.

Just how I prefer it.

"Just me," I say easily, right before I drain the water bottle in a couple of gulps. Alcohol and stifling nightclubs always leave me dehydrated.

Howard shakes his head as he slowly pulls out into the street, flicking the signal on as he moves into the left turn lane. "When you ever gonna settle down, son?" His gaze meets mine in the rearview window. Howard is old enough to be my father, and infinitely patient with all of us. We're all a bunch of stupid assholes, especially when we're drunk and riding around in his car, but he never says a word. Never rats us out.

Unless there's drugs involved. Then he has to say something.

I keep myself clean. Drugs are a no go. When we're in season, I prefer to lay off the alcohol too. That's a new thing. As I get older, it gets harder to recover from a night of drinking.

We're getting closer to camp and the rigorous training that comes with it, and that means my days of clubbing and getting drunk are about to come to an end.

I sort of don't mind.

"I don't know," I finally answer Howard, leaning back in my chair and staring out the window at the passing city streets. My heart actually pangs, and I have a sudden realization.

I'm lonely.

"You're not getting any younger," Howard says, and I can tell he's just giving me a hard time. I can hear the teasing tone in his voice, see the faint smile curling his lips. "You need to find some pretty little thing who worships you and eventually gives you a couple of pretty babies. Someone you actually want to spend time with, you know what I mean?"

"I do know what you mean," I tell him sincerely.

Babies would be nice. A pretty little thing who worships me would be awfully nice too. Though I don't want her to worship Mitchell Anderson, all-star defensive lineman for the Raiders.

I want her to like me for me. Good ol' boring Mitch. The guy who wouldn't mind kicking back on the couch on a Saturday night with his pretty little thing who worships him. Watch a movie on Netflix right before she sat on his face and he made her come with his tongue.

Hey. I'm definitely looking for a woman to love, but when it comes down to it, I'm still a fuckin' horn dog.

THREE
ELEANOR

SUNDAY BRUNCH CONSISTS of our usual crowd. Even though we were just together yesterday for Caroline's bridal shower, we still can't resist a champagne brunch on a beautiful weekend morning. The sun is shining, the birds are chirping, the tourists are quiet—they'll be worse later in the afternoon—and I can hear the ocean waves crash against the beach just down the street. We're sitting outside in the front patio of one of our favorite restaurants in downtown Carmel, most of us wearing sunglasses on or even a hat.

Meaning me. I'm the one in the hat. It's large and it's made out of straw and I probably look ridiculous, but I don't care. Besides, I ran out of dry shampoo and I keep forgetting to buy some, so it's a hat day.

It's also one of those rare bright sunny days, which doesn't happen too often in Carmel during the summer. Most people imagine the California beaches as sunshiny and hot, palm trees waving with the warm breeze and bronze-skinned women clad in tiny bikinis as they sun themselves on the sand. And while that does exist...it's not completely true. At least, not where we live. During the summer, it's cold most days, and the fog rarely lifts. The average temperature is sixty degrees, and at night it's downright chilly. We get our warm season in the fall. No fog, just sunny skies and temperatures in the seventies. It's downright blissful.

I am not feeling so blissful at the moment, though. And neither is my friend and partner in crime from last night.

"I am so hungover," Kelsey moans just before she takes a swig of her mimosa. I'm jealous of that mimosa. I arrived a little later than everyone else, so I'm still waiting for mine. "I need hash browns."

I make a face. "Yuck, why?" That sounds terrible to my hungover self.

"Grease absorbs the liquor remnants in your system, duh." Kelsey sends me a *duh* look as well, though I'm not offended. She's extra grouchy in the morning, which is normal. Even if she isn't hungover. We're used to it.

"You two went out drinking last night?" Caroline asks brightly.

I wince at her overly loud voice, reaching for the mimosa that's just been set in front of me by our server, thank God. "Maybe," I answer after I take a sip.

"There's no maybe about it," Stella says with a knowing smirk on her face. "We saw you two."

"Saw us how?" I ask warily, sending a death glare in Kelsey's direction.

Her face is one of pure innocence as she gazes at me.

"On Kelsey's Instagram stories," Stella answers, making me rest my hand against my chest. I've told my friends time and again I don't like it when they document our drunken moments. Talk about not putting your best foot forward. "You two look like you were having fun."

Okay. I'm trusting Stella's assessment. She's brutally

honest most of the time, so if I looked like a complete ass, she'd tell me.

But how did I not realize Kelsey was filming me last night, and posting on social media? Of course, this was the same woman who snapped photos of me at the shower without me knowing. Pretty good photos of me too.

Maybe last night's stories aren't so bad.

Deciding I need to see what Stella's talking about, I grab my phone and open Instagram, scrolling through the stories until I find Kelsey's. The first one is a video of her talking into the camera.

"We're the last of the single girls," Kelsey says in this hushed voice, like she doesn't want anyone to hear her. And you barely can, thanks to the noisy bar we were sitting in. "The sole survivors!"

The video switches to me getting mad at her over the Rate a Date app, which I didn't need the reminder, thank you very much. Next is a video of a bunch of guys sitting at the bar, singing "Happy Birthday" to their friend. They were loud and sloppy drunk, and Kelsey couldn't stop laughing at them.

Me? I wasn't interested.

The last story video is of us waiting on the sidewalk for our Uber, me standing there with my arms wrapped around myself to ward off the chill as I stare off into the distance, my breasts looking ready to pop out of my dress. I'm a curvy girl, it's hard to tame those babies, but jeez, I look like I'm about to explode with boobage, if you know what I mean.

"I hate everything about your story," I tell Kelsey once it's finished.

"Ah, come on, it was no big deal." Kelsey shrugs.

"You make us sound desperate." She keeps looking at

me like she doesn't understand what I'm saying. "Why did you film those guys at the bar?"

"They were having fun. I thought they were cute."

"You looked like a stalker."

"Quit being so uptight." She drains her mimosa.

"And mentioning that we were the last single girls." I point at her. "That's where you really made us sound desperate."

I hate that word. *Desperate*. *Pathetic* isn't good either. I don't want to look like either of those things, you know? Who does?

"I was only speaking the truth! We should be proud of our single heritage," Kelsey protests.

"I don't even think that's a thing." I catch our friend Sarah watching us bicker and decide to draw her into it. "Is that a thing? Single heritage?"

Sarah frowns. "I have no idea what you're talking about."

I'm about to launch into a full-blown argument with Kelsey when I get an unfamiliar notification sound—it's like nothing I've ever heard come from my phone before.

It sounded like a...wolf whistle?

Glancing down at my phone, I see it's a notification from...

Rate a Date.

Mand.96 just sent you a message!

Frowning, I tap the notification, opening the app and waiting as the mailbox loads. Mand.96. Is that the person's user name? What if this person is named... Mandy? That makes sense, what with the username. Did I state on my profile that I'm heterosexual? Because I am. Heterosexual. I mean, I did have that one moment when I was in beauty school and we all went out drinking right before we graduated. The night went on and on, and there was a lot of liquor consumed. At one point, I made out with that one girl, but does it really count? It was all in good fun.

She had soft lips and a shy tongue. Her name was Josie. She had pink hair.

Those were good times.

Oops, I'm distracted. Okay, so I open the message to see this person's profile pic is of a football.

That's it.

Frowning, I stare at the image for a while. It looks like the person actually took the photo themselves. It's not some canned stock photo you can find on the web—the angle is weird and the sun is too bright.

Maybe Mandy is really into sports. Though I hate that there's no actual photo of her face. This feels like a trick.

I read the message.

Hey, you live in my hometown. You're beautiful.

My heart does a little leap at the beautiful comment. That's a very serious compliment, though I'm guessing it's tossed around a lot more freely on a dating app. But still. I appreciate the kind words.

Unfortunately, there's no name signed, so I don't know if this person is an actual Mandy or...not.

Lifting my head, I watch Kelsey steadily drink from her new mimosa while she chats with Sarah. Caroline and Candice have their heads bent together, and from the tone of their conversation, I can tell they're comparing wedding notes, since they're both our upcoming brides. Stella is currently on her phone, and I think she's talking to one of her brothers because her voice gets louder and louder, and she sounds angrier and angrier.

No one is paying attention to me. Meaning I can go ahead and chat this Mand.94 person up.

You grew up in Monterey? That's amazing. What a coincidence!

I frown. Do I sound too excited? I mean, really, is it that much of a coincidence? With this app, I tried to keep my parameters to our local area, though Kelsey encouraged me to include the Bay Area just so we could widen our scope, as she said. The man of my dreams could live in San Francisco. Or San Jose. Walnut Creek? I've always found that area cute. Redwood City? Even cuter.

Okay again. I'm getting distracted.

I decide to start over on my message.

You grew up in Monterey? I don't know how you could ever leave. This is my favorite place in the entire world. What's your name?

There. That's perfect. I go ahead and hit send.

"Kels mentioned you two joined a new dating app," Sarah says conversationally.

"Oh. Yeah." I set my phone facedown on the table. "I don't know if it'll work, but I'm trying to keep an open mind."

"What do you mean, you don't know if it will work?" Sarah asks with a tiny frown. "Why wouldn't it?"

"I've never tried one before. I'm worried I won't meet someone...worthy on a dating app. I don't know how I feel about dating sites in general," I explain.

I don't use Tinder or Bumble or whatever the heck they're all called. A lot of my friends have done so in the past, though of course, all the ones who are now taken met their men the old fashioned way—in person. I'm hoping for that. I want that.

But most of the guys I meet or get set up with never work out. It's always a bad match.

Maybe I do need to try something different to make a better match.

"You do know one in four couples together right now originally met on a dating site," Sarah says.

I've heard this stat before. Plenty of times. "No kidding," I murmur, just as our server returns and starts taking our orders.

I check my phone to see I have another notification from Mand.94. And lucky me, I do. I open it.

Had to leave for college. And then my job. My name is Mitch. What's yours?

Oh. It's a guy. I'm actually relieved. And that makes sense, leaving for college and then his job. I wonder what he does?

What do you do? And my name is Eleanor. I'm a hairstylist in Carmel.

He responds almost immediately. Like, the-server-hasn't-made-it-to-me-yet-to-take-my-order fast. **Eleanor. I like that. It fits you.**

Hmm. He didn't answer my question. Is he an avoider? Most men are. They're classic avoiders. They'd rather do anything else than face a question, a problem, head-on. I've had my experience with a few, and they about drove me out of my mind.

Once the server finally makes his way to me, I order eggs benedict and another mimosa.

"I'm bringing out a pitcher for the table to share," the server tells me, and I let him know that will be fine with a smile on my face.

Of course they ordered a pitcher for the table. This is why they're my friends.

I shove my phone into my bag and forget all about Mitch the avoider as we chat and eat and drink too much champagne. Well, I try to limit myself thanks to what happened last night, and I notice Kelsey restrains herself also. We don't need to extend our hangovers, though I keep hairstylist hours and don't have to be back at work until Tuesday.

Once we're all pretty much finished eating and most of the plates have been cleared, Caroline rises to her feet and taps the side of her empty champagne glass with her spoon, silencing all of us.

"I have an important announcement to make," she starts as we all swivel our heads in her direction.

"You're pregnant," Stella interrupts, causing the majority of the table to gasp and murmur among themselves.

Caroline sends her very best friend a dirty look. "Come on, Stel. I've been sucking back champagne the entirety of brunch. No, I am *not* pregnant."

I think I see disappointment on some of our friends' faces. I know I'm a little disappointed. Babies are so cute.

"No, this is about my...bachelorette party," she says with a sly smile.

I sit up straighter. I am all about the fun, cheesy bachelorette party. Penis-shaped straws and gaudy bride to be sashes are my jam.

"I hope you didn't forget to put in your time-off requests at work, because this isn't just your regular ol' bachelorette party," Caroline says with a sly smile, her gaze shifting to Stella, who returns her smile. These two are conspiring together, I'm sure, since Stella is her maid of honor.

"What exactly are we doing?" asks Candice. She's the sweetest one of the group. Even sweeter than me, and I'm pretty damn syrupy-sweet when I want to be, which is all the time. Together we make all of our cynical friends want to run away from us.

It's actually pretty fun.

"Well." Caroline hesitates for a beat, drawing the moment out, and I actually shift around in my seat, anticipation making me start to sweat. That, and the sun beating down on my face, even with the hat. I angle my head, the brim of my hat blocking the sun somewhat.

"We're going to...Las Vegas!" More gasps and murmurs after Caroline's announcement as she throws her arms up and makes a whooping noise. We all start clapping. People at the other tables are watching us like we're on a wacky reality TV show. "We're staying in the penthouse suite at the Wilder Hotel and Casino. Alex has already arranged everything for us. It's going to be *amazing*."

"Please tell me it's not some elegant affair with snooty sandwiches and sparkling wine," Kelsey says, worry lacing her tone.

We all send her a look. Does she not know us at all?

"What?" Kelsey shrugs. "We all deserve to cut loose, especially Caroline."

"Who do you think we are, a bunch of old ladies? We're going to have cheap liquor and strippers, baby," Stella says, making all of us start laughing.

Well, except me. I just smile, worry filling me at the idea of strippers.

I suppose they're fine. It's an expected part of any bachelor/bachelorette party. I just hope they don't try to gyrate on my lap and thrust their bulging crotches in my face. That's kind of gross.

Okay, *I* find it really gross.

I love men. I really do, but oily strippers who are too tan and just the slightest bit sleazy really aren't my bag.

Like, at all.

"Don't worry about the strippers," Candice tells me later, as we're all starting to leave the restaurant. She's resting her hand on my forearm, the giant diamond on her finger glinting in the sunlight. I can't help but stare at it, completely mesmerized. "I'll stick with you the entire time, just in case. We're vulnerable alone yet a force together."

She makes it sound like we're going into battle with strippers. I almost start giggling, but I stop myself just in time. I think it's the champagne.

"Thank you," I say, my voice solemn, my expression serious. "I appreciate it."

"This is going to be so much fun!" Candice says, punctuating the last word with the faintest squeal. "I'm *so* going shopping."

"Where?" The last time I went to Vegas, we went into those giant souvenir stores, but I can only look at so many things that say *Whatever Happens in Vegas* or *I Heart Las Vegas* before my eyes start to cross.

"Oh, I don't know. Chanel maybe? Louis Vuitton. Gucci. They always have fun stuff in the Vegas shops," Candice says excitedly.

"Right," I say, my hopes for shopping with Candice dashed. I could accompany her, but I won't be able to afford anything. Those types of shops are just too pricey for my blood. I do well in my job. I make decent money. I live in my mom's old house, which she owns outright, and that saves me big money. I only have to pay the property tax and house insurance, and whatever repairs might be needed—which are manageable, but not cheap.

And while I work at what many consider an exclusive salon in a wealthy area, I still don't make the kind of money that would allow me to shop freely at any of those designer stores. I inherited my mother's Vuitton Speedy handbag, and I sort of hate it. It's just so bulky. But that's the only thing I've got with LVs all over it, so I'll take it.

There's lot of hugging and air kisses as we all make our departures, until it's just Caroline and me standing together on the sidewalk in front of the restaurant. I can't remember the last time I spoke to Caroline one on one since we're always in a big group making wedding plans, so I take advantage of my situation.

"Do you have afternoon plans?" I ask.

Caroline shakes her head. "No, none. I was so overwhelmed with the bridal shower, I made sure my calendar was empty for Sunday, save for our brunch."

"Perfect." I smile at her. "Should we go to Sweet Dreams and have an iced coffee?"

"Sure. Let's go."

We make our way up the street to Sweet Dreams Café and Bakery, the shop Stella's family owns. She's the head barista there, and she just told us she plans on becoming the manager after the first of the year. Her father is retiring and handing the reins over to her, which is a big move for her traditional Italian family.

The café is bustling, the line snaking out the front door, and Caroline and I settle into it, me mostly listening while Caroline rattles on about her various wedding plans. This is her day to shine, and I don't mind that she talks about it all the time. This is a major moment in her life, and she's making sure everything is going to happen just so.

By the time we've paid for our coffees and picked them up from the barista, we're able to find a small table outside in front of the café, right on the sidewalk. We're under the awning so the sun isn't beating down on us, but I still refuse to take off my hat.

"I love your hat," Caroline says, as if she'd burrowed into my brain and read my thoughts. "It's so chic."

"Thank you." I touch the brim, pleased that she called it chic. I figured I just looked silly. "I ran out of dry shampoo."

Caroline laughs. "Typical Eleanor, keeping it real."

I frown. "What do you mean?"

Caroline's laughter slowly dies. "Well, you know." She takes a sip of her coffee, and I wonder if she's searching for the right words to say. "You always have to explain yourself and your choices when someone gives you a compliment."

"Are you saying I can't take a compliment?" I ask.

"Oh, you can. It's just you always have to give us the truth. I've complimented you on your clothes many, many times, and you always let me know where you got the dress, or the shirt. Or the shoes," Caroline explains.

"I'm just trying to help you guys out," I say with a little shrug. I just want them to find the sale prices like I do. "I always seem to find great deals."

"I know. Remember those sandals from last summer you found for like ten bucks?" When I nod, Caroline sticks her foot out, pointing it at me. I glance down to see the very same sandals she's talking about. "I bought them in white."

Those were great shoes. I wore them so much last summer. "I got bleach on my black ones at work, and didn't realize it until it was too late. Completely ruined them."

RIP those cute cheap sandals. I still mourn the loss.

"Aw, I hate that. You should go back to Target and see if they still have them. If a shoe is really popular, they'll rerelease them each season," Caroline suggests.

We talk about shoes and clothes and what to wear to

Las Vegas, never returning to the subject that's lingering in my mind.

How I'm too honest. Too real. How I have a hard time taking a compliment. I never really thought about it before, but maybe I do have a problem with that. Sometimes I can become uncomfortable when someone compliments me. I always wonder if they're being sincere, you know? Like maybe they're after something from me, and they're only trying to butter me up.

Why do I think like that? Why do I act that way? It's something I've never really thought about before, but...

I can almost guarantee I'll be extra conscious of it now.

FOUR
ELEANOR

SITTING in bed alone on a Sunday night is one of my favorite things to do. My Sunday is really like my Saturday. Normally, I work on Saturdays. It's our busiest day at a hair salon. Weddings and parties and girls' night out or a hot date on the agenda brings plenty of clients in. Or there's the fact that a lot of our clients can only come in on Saturdays because they don't have to work.

But we always have Sunday and Monday off. The salon is flat-out closed. Not even the spa is open, which makes some of our clients angry, considering they want to get a massage after an extra-stressful Monday, for example. And hey, I get it. But Connie, the owner of the salon and spa, won't budge from her very firm schedule. She's a believer in the entire staff having two full days off.

And I appreciate that about her.

Anyway, I'm already in bed, yet it's only a little after nine at night. There's a glass of wine on my bedside table, along with a small plate with cheese, crackers and salami, plus a few chilled grapes. My own personal charcuterie board.

I suppose I should catch up on *Ozark*, since everyone's currently watching and going crazy about it on social media. I've been putting it off, because while I love the show, it's so freaking stressful I can barely stand watching it sometimes. (Spoiler alert) Like that toenail-ripping scene? My God, that gave me nightmares.

So yeah, I'm not watching Netflix or Hulu or any of those streaming channels tonight. I've got my phone in my hand, and I'm scrolling through my prospects on the Rate a Date app. The more I scroll, the frownier my face gets. Like, I am full-on frowning, but that's only because I'm so disappointed. This all just feels so…

Fake.

A lot of the guys' photos seem really staged, which I guess shouldn't be a surprise. I look at the men's profiles that were recommended to me, and while some of them are extremely attractive and they claim to have good jobs, I don't know how I feel about this—this entire situation.

Am I getting scammed? I'm as real as someone gets, according to Caroline. I'm going to put it all out there for the most part. Are these guys doing the same?

Doubtful.

I'm sure there are some nice guys on this dating site, app, whatever you want to call it. Not all of them can be con artists, right? There are still decent human beings out there. I know there are.

"Oh no." I whisper this under my breath, my fingers scrambling to tap on the inbox icon. I never did answer Mand.94, which makes me feel like total shit—like I'm one of those deceptive people on dating sites.

Not good. Not good at all.

I open my inbox to find I do have a message waiting for me from Mand.94 that's approximately nine hours old, so I open it immediately, feeling terrible that I left him hanging for so long.

This is me, the flighty girl who keeps it real and who might also have a slight touch of ADD. And realizing I totally ignored someone?

I can't help but feel guilty.

Opening the message, I grab a piece of cheese and nibble on it as I read what he said.

I forgot to answer your question.

A smile touches the corners of my lips. Good for him, realizing that he didn't answer me.

I work with athletes.

Another message.

I need a haircut.

Well, the polite thing would be to answer him, so I do.

Make an appointment and I'll cut your hair for you. Where do you live?

I send another message. **And are you like a physical therapist or something?**

Surprisingly enough, he responds almost immediately.

Yeah. Something like that. I'm moving to Las Vegas soon for my job. I live in San Ramon right now.

Oh. He's probably like, a party guy. Who wants to actually work and live in Las Vegas?

Well, lots of people, of course. Definitely not me. I love going there on occasion, and it'll be fun to go for Caroline's bachelorette party, but I don't think I ever want to *live* there.

Though I'm sort of jumping the gun, thinking about this guy and moving to Vegas for him. I don't even know what he looks like. Meaning I should ask for a photo, though that's risky. He might send me a dick pic, and then it's over before he really ever had a chance.

Deciding to go for it, I send him a message.

Why don't you have any photos of yourself on your profile?

He responds to my question fairly quickly, which is nice.

You want to see a pic of me?

Uh, yeah, is what I want to type. Instead I say:

If you don't mind.

Within seconds he sends me his answer and I stare at it, noticing the little paperclip by it. That means there's a photo attached. Anticipation courses through me and I wait for a few seconds. Then a few more. Questions roll through my mind.

What if he's hideous?

What if he's beyond gorgeous?

Both possibilities scare the crap out of me. I have to be attracted to him, right? But I also don't want him to be prettier than me. That'll give me a complex,

I have enough complexes already, thank you very much.

After about three minutes of me imagining all sorts of scenarios, I finally open my message and click on the tiny photo attached, my eyes widening when I take him in.

Oh, he's very...big. As in muscular. Muscles on muscles. He looks tall and broad and like he could mow someone down with ease. He's definitely very physical. I can see his defined muscles, all that smooth skin exposed, even though he's clad in a simple black T-shirt, the fabric clinging downright lovingly to his chest.

His biceps—they're impressive. The sculpted shoulders. They're impressive too. He has golden-brown hair that's a little too long and curls at the ends around his face, and friendly brown eyes that seem to smile when he smiles. And while I wouldn't call him model-gorgeous, he definitely has a pleasant face. An attractive face.

A message comes through right as I'm staring at his photo. **Send me a photo of you.**

I go to my profile to see, yep, there's the photo Kelsey took of me in my avatar.

You've already seen me.

I'd like to see you again. Like right now, he says.

Deciding I may as well go for it, I hold my phone out, tilt my head to the side, stretch my lips into a smile and take a selfie, then check the photo out.

Huh. Should I use a filter? Maybe I should use the dog filter. I always feel like I look super cute with it, the floppy ears and the long, pink tongue. It's silly and cute and hides what I think is my big nose. Or there's that other filter on Snapchat, the one that makes my skin look really smooth.

I don't even have makeup on, my hair is in a messy bun, and here I am contemplating sending him this selfie? Kelsey would tell me no way. She'd make me delete the photo, we'd end up having a "quick" makeup session, and though it would take about thirty minutes and approximately thirty tries with the camera, I'd finally have what Kelsey would consider a semi-decent selfie to send this guy. Mitch. With the friendly brown eyes and the big, muscular body. I bet he knows how to throw a girl around in bed and not wimp out. Not complain about his back once it's all said and done, like it's all your fault he hurt himself in the relatively simple act of sex.

Yeah, maybe that's happened to me before. So what?

Deciding to go for it, I take another photo. And another.

No filters. No doggy ears. No floppy, long tongue. When I'm semi-pleased with the results, I send the photo, trying my best to not overthink it.

I immediately take a giant gulp of my wine and then nibble on a piece of cheese. And another one. Pop a few grapes in my mouth. My gaze never leaves my phone screen and when he finally, finally responds, I nearly sag with relief.

I'm sticking to my first statement. You're absolutely beautiful.

Awww. I rest my hand against my chest, having a moment. My heart is fluttering. He's so sweet!

Are you in bed right now?

Frowning, I glance around, wondering what clued him in.

Oh. Right. My headboard behind me.

Sighing, I don't bother taking another photo to try to prove him wrong. I send him a text with an honest answer.

I am.

I wish I would've thought about taking the photo without my headboard behind me. What if Mr. Friendly Eyes turns our conversation sexual? I just opened the door for him. There's a statistic floating out there on Facebook or Twitter or whatever that says men think about sex approximately every other second. Is that true?

I should fact check it on Snopes. I'm about to open the Snopes website when I receive a response from Mitch.

It's pretty early, he responds.

Relief floods me. No sexual talk yet! This is a plus.

I'm tired. Busy weekend. My friend is getting married. We had her bridal shower

yesterday and a bunch of us had brunch together today.

Sounds like fun, he says.

It was.

I chew on my lip, wondering if I should tell him. Should I? Oh, why not.

We're going to Vegas for her bachelorette party in a couple of weeks.

He responds so quick, it's almost like he was waiting for me to say something.

No kidding? I'll be living in Vegas in a couple of weeks.

A smile curls my lips.

He sends another text. **Maybe, if we're still talking, we could meet up and hang out.**

I'm full-blown smiling now. He's being very presumptive. That's usually my thing.

Maybe, I say, wondering if my response sounds as flirtatious in his head as it does in mine.

And then I realize he doesn't know what I sound like, so that's a big ol' probably not.

We chat for a little while longer about little things. And big things, like our lives. He tells me how he grew up in Monterey, and where he went to school—not any of the schools I attended, which is kind of a bummer. He's a little older than me, so we have no real mutual friends, and besides, he left right out of high school. He went to Texas A&M University, which impresses me. Says he played a little football there, which impresses me more. That's a big college for football, right?

I like how he downplays his accomplishments. That means he's modest.

We text until it's almost eleven-thirty, and my eyelids start to get heavy. I tell him good night, he wishes me sweet dreams, and it's like I fall asleep before my head barely touches the pillow with a big ol' smile on my face.

I should spend my time chatting away with a nice man on a dating app before bed more often.

FIVE
ELEANOR

"I FOUND two guys who want to go on a double date with us."

This is how Kelsey greets me when I find her in the waiting area of the hair salon. No, *hi how are you* or *gee, Eleanor, do you think you can fit me in for a trim?*

Nope, nothing like that. Leave it to Kelsey to get right to business.

"What do you mean, you found two guys who want to double date with us?" I ask warily, lowering my voice when I spot one of our regular clients Mrs. Rothschild, sitting not three feet away.

Mrs. Rothschild is very rich. And very, very nosy. She loves to gossip. About anyone and everyone, even one of the hairstylists at her salon.

Realizing that, I tilt my head toward the back and give Kelsey a meaningful look. She leaps to her feet and follows me to my chair, plopping herself down in it and spinning around. "I think that lady was listening to our conversation," she says with wide eyes.

Does she not realize how loud she can be sometimes? I

know she can be discreet. She works for Alex Wilder, for God's sake. He deals in delicate information on a daily basis, what with working for his family's hotel business. This means Kelsey, his assistant, is privy to the same delicate information.

Yet with us, her friends, she loves to blurt out our business. It's never malicious. She just—says things. Boldly. Always.

"I know she was, considering how loud you were." I grab a brush and start running it through Kelsey's perfect, dark brown hair, a wistful sigh escaping me. I'm satisfied with my hair, but Kelsey's is just...beyond. Luxurious strands that are glossy and thick, with the perfect amount of curl at the ends. I don't even think she uses a curling iron on her hair. It's just naturally that amazing.

"Sorry." Kelsey shoots me a smile in the mirror, not looking that sorry at all. "But hey, these guys. They want to go out with us Friday night."

Of course I have no plans.

"How in the world did you find a date for each of us? I thought I was supposed to find my own date, and you find yours." I glance at the counter in front of my mirror, scanning the schedule Bonnie prints out for us and delivers at all of our stations in the morning. Yes, Connie is the owner, and Bonnie, her twin sister, is the receptionist.

Connie and Bonnie. They're both lovely people, though they fight a lot, always behind closed doors (*Think about the business!* Connie shouts at her sister every time). Pretty sure it annoys Bonnie that Connie has such a successful business and she's just the receptionist. Not that there's anything wrong with her job, and honestly she's not "just the receptionist," though that's how she feels, as she expresses her feelings to us on pretty much the daily. We would be nothing at this salon without her, and we all know it. She keeps it together. I just think Bonnie wants a bigger piece of the pie, and she believes her sister is pretty tightfisted. As in, Connie doesn't allow Bonnie to try to buy into the business, no matter how many times Bonnie has offered. But that's another story for another day.

"I have a client coming in five minutes," I tell Kelsey, which is a bit of a stretch because my client actually doesn't come in for another fifteen minutes.

But that's okay. I don't want Kelsey to keep lingering and try to convince me I should go on this double date with her.

"You'll go out with us Friday, right?" Kelsey leaps out of the chair, tossing her hair over her shoulder. She looks like she's in a shampoo commercial. "Come on, it'll be fun."

I'm skeptical of course. "I need more information. What are these guys' names? And how did you meet them?"

"I met Paul on Rate a Date," she says, which I get since this is where we're supposed to meet them. "And his best friend's name is Theodore."

I wince. "Theodore?" I have an immediate image of what this man with the name Theodore must look like, and it's...

Not good.

I am being very judgmental, and that is not good either.

But I am getting serious *Alvin and the Chipmunks* vibes right about now.

"Yeah." Kelsey smiles. "Paul is really cute. So is his friend. He showed me a photo of the two of them last night."

"A recent photo?" Sometimes photos on the internet are ten years old and twenty-five pounds less ago. Yeah. I might've done that a few times. I was a lot cuter at twenty than I am now at twenty-seven.

"Of course," Kelsey says. "I've been talking with Paul since Saturday night. He seems really into me. We even FaceTimed last night, and it was so much fun. He started talking about Theo, and how he just came out of a relationship, and when I told Paul about you, he thought you sounded just like Theo's type."

Huh. I'm not so sure about this. Red flags are popping up. As in…

"He's just out of a relationship? Like, how long of a relationship?"

"Uh, long term. But it's no big deal." Kelsey waves her hand.

I stare at her, unease slipping down my spine. "How long are you talking?"

"Ummm." Kelsey makes a little face. "Five years, give or take?"

"*Five years?*" The words explode out of my mouth like I have no control of them. I'm so loud, I make the little old lady getting her hair colored in the chair two booths over startle, tossing her wrinkled copy of *People* magazine to the ground. It lands with a loud plop, and the hairstylist—her name is Jen, she's super sweet—shoots me a confused look before grabbing the magazine for her client.

"It's no big deal. They were engaged, but she cheated on him. It was this big thing, but that was a while ago and all is well now." The fake smile pasted on Kelsey's beautiful face is a dead giveaway. She's glossing over some fairly important facts. Meaning this woman cheated on poor Theodore and he probably only found out about it a few months ago and he's still wallowing in his sadness.

This is a disaster waiting to happen. Theodore is most

likely in a deep depression, and for all I know, he could still be in love with his former fiancée.

"I don't know..." My voice drifts. "This doesn't sound like a good idea."

"You'll lift his spirits. You love lifting people's spirits."

"People I know and love," I remind her. "I don't know this guy."

At all. She doesn't really know his friend either.

"Aw, come on. You should give him a chance. Like I'm going to give Paul a chance." Kelsey takes a step forward and grabs my hand, giving it a gentle shake. "Give him a chance, El. Go out with us. It won't be so bad, I swear. It's just dinner."

I've heard that before. *It's just a coffee date.* Or, *it's only meeting up for drinks. What's the harm in a couple of drinks?*

Those situations always end up not good. Not good at all.

"What if I've already met someone?" I think of Mitch. We've been talking, mostly at night. It's Wednesday, so that means we've been chatting for four days. Three and half really, since we haven't really talked today, which is fine. I don't expect to hear from him every hour or anything over the top like that.

It's been...nice. Our chats. He's easy to talk to. I'm not interested in anyone else who claims we're a match on Rate a Date, and I'm getting lots of suggestions. I ignore the notifications, telling myself I'll check them out later. That's not how it's done on a dating app, I know Kelsey will tell me I'm going about this all wrong, but I sort of don't care.

So far, I'm only interested in Mitch.

But he lives in Vegas. Or he will soon—like mere-days soon. Why would I start a long distance relationship with a

RATE A DATE 43

guy I barely know? It's fun chatting with him, we seem to have things in common, but I need to keep my options open.

Not that the option Kelsey is currently presenting to me sounds particularly inspiring...

"You've met someone? On the app?" Kelsey asks excitedly. When I nod, she starts doing a little hopping dance, clapping her hands. Making a scene and reminding me of myself. "That's so great! What's his name? When are you seeing him? Have you already met him?"

"We've just chatted for a bit." I shrug, suddenly feeling bashful. Secretive. I can actually sense my cheeks heating, like I'm embarrassed. "He's very nice."

"Nice? Come on, you have to give me more than that."

"What more could you want? We've been talking, our conversation flows, and he seems really nice."

"Has he sent you a dick pic yet?" Kelsey asks, dare I say, hopefully.

"No, oh my God!" I send her a look, jerking my head in the direction of the poor frazzled lady who's glaring at us. I'm sure she's still mad at us for making her drop the magazine. Realization slowly dawns and I lower my voice. "Why...has Paul sent *you* a dick pic yet?"

"Maybe." Kelsey shrugs, but I can tell from the shit-eating grin on her face that yes, Paul has most definitely sent her a pic. Of his dick. "It's large."

"Uh huh." I know they pull tricks. It's all in the pose. And the grip. You can make that thing look like a monster with a few select angles and expert shadowing.

"Don't be such a doubter. Seriously, it's big. Eight inches." Kelsey holds her hands out, keeping at least a foot between them. Terrifying. "It's been a while since I've had a decent-sized penis."

I offer a weak smile over at the older woman who is now

blatantly glaring at us before I grab Kelsey's arm and steer her toward the front of the salon. "It's time for you to go."

Kelsey laughs, the jerk. "Don't like my dick talk?"

"More like the clients don't." I try to sound angry, but I can't help but laugh with her. Kelsey means no harm. She enjoys riling me up. She does the same sort of thing to Candice. I suppose we're both easy targets, especially me. I overact to everything, even when I know I shouldn't. Plus, I'm just awkward. I know it.

"So." Kelsey turns to face me right at the reception desk. "Are you going with me to dinner this Friday?"

Ugh, the pressure. "Fine," I say with a sigh. "But if it's a total nightmare from the get-go, I'm out. Don't try to convince me to stay through the entrée."

"You can't bail after the appetizer and the first round of drinks! Come on, be real." Kelsey mock pouts. "Stay through dinner."

"Whatever." I roll my eyes. "I'll do dinner, but that's it. No drinks afterward. No walks on the beach in the moonlight either."

"Ew, no. Definitely no walks on the beach. Only psychos want to take you out to the beach, where they'll attack you and leave your body for dead, hoping the surf takes you away before the morning comes," Kelsey says, with ever the vivid imagination.

"Someone's been watching too much true crime TV," I tell her as I escort her to the front door.

"See you Friday?" Kelsey smiles brightly.

"Yes." I nod, withholding the weary sigh that wants to escape. "Friday.

WE MEET at a French restaurant in Monterey, Bistro Moulin. I drive myself there, refusing to ride with Kelsey or heaven forbid, have Theodore pick me up. My own car means I can make my escape when necessary. It also means I'll control my alcohol intake, because I have to drive myself home.

The moment I enter the cozy restaurant, I see that it is quite romantic. The tables are mostly for two, and every single one of them is filled. Black iron chandeliers hang from the ceiling, the walls are painted a warm gold hue, and there's an entire wall of shelves filled with bottles of wine. Impressive. Too bad I can't get my drink on. Though the smells emanating from the kitchen are promising.

At least I'll get a delicious meal out of the date. Hopefully.

"Eleanor!" I turn to spot Kelsey standing beside a table where two men are already sitting. She waves me over and I smile at the hostess standing behind the podium.

"My friends are already here," I tell her.

She smiles, though it's vague, her gaze already shifting to the couple who just walked in behind me. "Enjoy your meal, mademoiselle."

I approach the table with trepidation, watching as Kelsey settles into the chair next to the man who can't stop staring at her. I mean, can you blame him? She's absolutely stunning, and tonight is no exception. Her hair is down and flowing. She's wearing a black romper that would make me look dumpy, yet she looks downright glamorous. She accented the simple outfit with gold jewelry. Gold hoop earrings, thin gold necklace, a stack of gold bracelets on her left wrist.

Ugh. She's beyond chic. While I look like me. Which means I don't like particularly chic.

Okay, wait. I take that back. I work at a hair salon, meaning we all like to keep on top of fashion trends and we're always trying to outdo each other, outfit wise. It's actually a lot of fun.

So yes, I'm wearing a long black cotton sundress I found on the clearance rack at Old Navy at the end of last summer, with a denim jacket over it. Black slides. I did the gold jewelry thing too, though not as prettily as Kelsey put herself together. A single gold bangle on my wrist, and large, thin gold hoops. I curled my hair before I left work, and it's extra bouncy. Touched up my makeup too, including slathering on gloss that has lip-plumping serum in it.

My lips are still tingling. It's a tad worrisome.

"So glad you made it." Kelsey stands once more, pulling me into a quick hug, her mouth right at my ear as she whispers, "Be gentle."

Oh God. I stiffen in her embrace and when she releases me, she keeps one hand on my shoulder, steering me so I'm facing the table.

Here we go.

"Paul, meet one of my best friends, Eleanor," Kelsey says.

Aw. I'm touched. One of her best friends? I sort of want to cry.

"Eleanor. It's so great to meet you. Kel speaks highly of you." Paul smiles at me and stands, offering me his hand. I take it, wincing at the extra strong grip. He's handsome, though a little...bland? Blond hair. Light blue eyes. Wearing a suit, like he just got off work. I mean, he's attractive, but not really my type.

"And this is Theodore," Kelsey says, her voice soft. Almost sad.

My gaze alights on the man who's my date this evening.

Oh, he has such a hangdog face. It's not an unattractive face, but he looks so dreadfully sad. Dark brown eyes that seep to droop at the corners. A full mouth that's turned downward. His hair is black, slicked back but not in a sleazy way. He's wearing a suit as well. His looks nicer than Paul's, as in he might make more money than Kelsey's date. Or he just has better taste. Good taste is a plus, right?

"Eleanor." Theodore breathes out my name, sounding surprised as his gaze roams over me before he meets my eyes. "Thank you for coming to dinner with me tonight. And please, call me Theo."

He sounds so grateful. Like he can't believe I agreed to a date with him. The poor, poor man.

"Thank you for inviting me, Theo," I say as I shake his hand. We all settle into our seats at the table and I notice with envy that Kelsey already has a giant glass of wine. "Was I late?"

"Oh no." Kelsey smiles. "You're right on time. Paul and I got her about a half hour ago and had a drink."

I'm glad she didn't make me do that with Theo, but maybe it would've eased things between us. I can feel the nervousness radiating from him. He's so amped up, I'm tempted to order him a double of whatever he's drinking and encourage him to down it like a shot.

I glance over at Theo to offer him a smile and catch him staring at me. Not in a creeper way, more like in a I can't believe you're here with me way. It's sweet, but kind of off putting.

The man was previously engaged, yet he acts like he's never been on a date in his life.

The restaurant we're at is very French, as in it's very authentic. I scan the menu, ordering a glass of wine when the server appears. Paul orders appetizers for the table, and all I can do is hope they aren't frog's legs or snails. Not gonna lie: that sounds kind of gross.

"They have such a fabulous wine list," Kelsey says after she takes a generous gulp from her glass. "I wish I could sample them all."

"I could probably make that happen," Paul says, sounding vaguely perverted and arrogant all at once, and Kelsey laughs.

Ew.

"I know the owner," Paul tells me, and clearly he's flexing. Bragging me are the worst. "He owes me a couple of favors."

He winks at me.

Double ew.

"What are you thinking of having?" I ask Theo, who's blinking rapidly as he reads the menu.

Something clicks in my brain. This guy reminds me of Ross from *Friends*. Yes, definitely the sad-sack Ross, pining for his Rachel.

Oh. Shit. Let's not forget Ross pined for his Rachel the entirety of the series. He tried to move on multiple times. He married another woman and said Rachel's name in the wedding vows.

Clearly, I am not this man's Rachel. I'm one of those other women he's trying to move on with.

"I think I'm going to have the filet mignon," Theo says, his gaze skittering my way for the briefest moment before he returns his attention to the menu. It's giant. If he held it in front of his face, I wouldn't be able to see him. "How about you?"

"I want the chicken," I tell him, shutting my menu. When I've gone to French restaurants, I always enjoy the roast chicken. Plus, it's not very expensive. My gaze drops to the sides section of the menu, realizing that when I order chicken, that's all I'm going to get. "Should I get the pomme frites or the whipped potatoes?"

"I'm having the brussels sprouts," Kelsey says. "Along with the steamed mussels. I can't do potatoes, El. Too many carbs."

That makes me want to order both the frites and the whipped potatoes. "How about I get the pomme frites and we'll share?"

Kelsey smiles. "Perfect."

"You like clams? I didn't know you went that way," Paul says Kelsey right before he cracks up. Classy. I wonder if he's already drunk.

Kelsey sends him an irritated look. "Don't be crass."

"What? I was just teasing." The innocent look on Paul's face is complete bullshit. "Though you do seem to be a little too abnormally into your friend Eleanor here."

The tension ratchets up between Paul and Kelsey, just like that. Huh. I thought they got along so well and he was sending her dick pics. Maybe there's already trouble in their dating app paradise.

Deciding to let them be, I turn my attention onto Theodore. "So Kelsey never told me what exactly you do."

"What I do? You mean for a living?" He grabs the white cloth napkin from his lap and dabs at his sweating forehead. "I handle investments at the Bank of Monterey."

"Oh, nice. So you could give me some investment advice? I've always wanted to dip my toe into the stock market. I just didn't know how to start," I tell him, which is all true. I have a savings account that is actually more than the five-dollar minimum they require we keep. I have a 401k account too, but I'd love some financial advice.

I never thought a banker would be what I consider a

sexy profession, but someone who knows how to manage your money and help it grow? Let's be real.

That is hella sexy.

"Sorry little lady, but he probably can't help you. Theo here only deals with million-dollar accounts," Paul interjects, like he was spying on our conversation. Not that he can help it—the table is very small.

But still.

Did he really just call me little lady?

"Don't listen to him." Theo laughs nervously, his attention only for me, and there's an apologetic glow in his sad eyes. "If you have questions, please don't hesitate to ask. I actually like talking about my job."

Well, he told me I could, so...

We start talking money and investments, and this keeps Theo going and going like the Energizer Bunny. He only breaks to place his dinner order, to request another bourbon on the rocks—such a grownup man drink—and when our dinner finally arrives.

He didn't bother eating the appetizer, and neither did I, we just kept talking. Pate is not my favorite thing. It looks like a block of weird meat and I'm not feeling it. Apparently, Theo isn't either.

But when our plates are placed before us with a flourish, I dig right in, Theo not even missing a beat as I fork up a bite of chicken that falls right off the bone.

Mmm, just as delicious as it looks.

"I'm rambling," Theo says once everyone at the table starts eating. His cheeks turn the faintest shade of pink, and it's rather sweet, how embarrassed he is. "Sorry, guys."

"Eat your steak, bro," Paul says, gesturing with his knife and fork toward Theo's plate. "That shit ain't cheap."

I meet Kelsey's gaze, her face forming a slight grimace at

Paul's complete lack of tact. I'm guessing she's disappointed in his behavior tonight, and all I can say is...

I'm so glad he's not my date.

Theo might not be my type of guy. As in, I don't really feel any chemistry or physical attraction toward him, but he's perfectly nice. Polite. Interesting, really, and I'm not just saying that. I like listening to him talk. I like that he's so passionate about his job, and that he makes investing sound interesting.

"Maybe you could come into the bank in the next few weeks and we can set you up an account," Theo suggests about halfway through the meal.

"Really? I would love to do that." My enthusiasm is one hundred percent real, but my excitement sinks when Paul rolls his eyes, dropping his knife onto his plate with a clatter.

"Are you for real right now? No one can be that excited about a bank appointment with Theo," Paul says drolly.

I glare at him, not caring that he's Kelsey's date. That she's watching me from across the table, her face full of embarrassment.

Yeah, I'd be embarrassed too if this guy was my date.

"Leave her alone," Theo says, his voice quiet, his expression fierce.

"What? You afraid I'm going to ruin your chances to take her home and fuck the pain away? Give me a break." Paul leans back in his chair, swigging from his glass. Something he's been doing all night long, and apparently the liquor has loosened his tongue. "Don't blow smoke up this chick's skirt. We all know you're still stuck on Jessica."

The table goes silent. Theo is completely still. I'm gaping at Paul, unable to come up with any words. Kelsey turns toward him. "Why in the world would you say something so rude like that to your best friend? While you're both on a first date?"

Paul glances around the table before he shrugs. "What? I'm just being truthful."

"You told me Eleanor would be perfect for Theo," Kelsey says, her voice like a hiss.

"I didn't realize she'd be such a wide-eyed innocent." I blink at him when our gazes meet, dumbfounded. "From the photo you showed me, I thought she'd be a good time for my miserable friend, if you know what I mean."

Without hesitation Kelsey rises to her feet, throwing her napkin on her mostly full plate. She grabs her purse, slipping it onto her shoulder. "Let's go, El."

"Wait a minute—" Paul reaches out to grab Kelsey's hand, but she snatches it back before he can make contact.

"Don't touch me." Now her voice is like ice, and Paul shrinks away.

I glance over at Theo. "I'm so sorry," I say softly as I dip down to grab my bag off the floor. "You're a nice man. Thank you for the financial advice."

We're out the door in seconds, neither of us saying a word until we walk around to the side of the building and my friend comes to a complete stop.

"Fuck!" Kelsey yells the word as loud as she can, causing a bunch of seagulls sitting on top of a house across the street to fly away, their wings flapping noisily. "Paul is such an asshole!"

I say nothing. I don't need to. She's right. Her date was a complete asshole.

"Theo was nice," I say after a few seconds.

Kelsey sends me a look. "Come on. He was pitiful."

"A little pitiful, yet nice. I actually learned a few things from him tonight."

"What? How to not be pitiful?" Kelsey huffs out a sigh. "I'm sorry. I'm being mean. Like Paul. Ugh." She kicks the side of the building, then cries out in pain.

"That was—not smart," I tell her, trying to be kind. Kelsey hops around on one foot, shaking out the injured one before she slips her foot out of the shoe completely and checks the damage. It looks okay to me, but I'm not the one with a throbbing toe.

"He tricked me. I thought he was nice. Fun. Interesting," Kelsey says miserably, her head hanging down as she stares at the sidewalk and her still exposed foot. "He made me laugh when we started messaging each other, and he asked me so many questions. Like he was really into me, you know? He's attractive. Has a good job. He assured me that you and Theo would get along, that Theo was completely over his ex-fiancée. I thought it would be a good match for me, and for you."

A breeze washes over us, bringing with it the salty scent of the ocean. The sun is dropping, the temperature is cooling, and I shiver, even though I'm wearing the denim jacket. "Theo is a good guy. I have zero interest in him beyond being his friend, and I would guess he feels the same way about me."

"Are you mad at me for setting this up?" Kelsey lifts her head, her turbulent gaze meeting mine.

"No way." I shake my head, the breeze whipping my hair in front of my face. I brush it away irritably. "I feel bad that Paul tricked you, though."

"He's an asshole," Kelsey says bitterly, repeating herself. But come on, it's warranted. "Why are all men such assholes?"

I decide to give her my honest take on it. "They're too dazzled by your pretty face and will do whatever it takes to get with you. No, I'm being serious," I say when she shoots me a skeptical glance. "Like I said, they will do whatever it takes to get with you, including masking their true personality."

"Sometimes I wish someone could like me for just...me. I wonder if I can get on that one reality show." She mutters the last part under her breath.

Frowning, I ask, "What show?"

"That *Love is Blind* show. Where they sit in pods by themselves and they can't see who they're with. They just have to talk. Get to know each other through words. They end up falling in love with personalities, and souls, not looks. Not your face or body. Looks are just the bonus," Kelsey explains.

"Life is not like a reality dating TV show," I tell her, wishing that wasn't the case. Honestly? I'd rather be on *The Bachelorette*. All the attention would be focused on me, and I'm the one who gets to choose from a bunch of gorgeous men. Doesn't that sound awesome?

Of course, I'd have a hard time choosing, and I wouldn't want to hurt anyone's feelings, so maybe that wouldn't be the right way to go.

Not so sure meeting up with men we meet on a dating app is the right way to go either.

SIX
MITCH

MOVING SUCKS. I've never liked it, and I've done it a lot over the years. When I was a kid, my mom was moving us all the time, from one apartment to another, but always keeping it in the same school district for me and my little brother. She's done a lot of careless shit over the years, but at least she did that.

Once she and Dad divorced, though, she turned us all into vagabonds, chasing one dream after another. One man after another too.

Until I was about ten and my brother was eight, and we ended up moving in with grandma and grandpa in Monterey. Mom disappeared for a few years. Dad never really came around anymore. I still haven't heard from that motherfucker, and I've been in the NFL for a few years now, my face splashed on TV screens across the country.

He was never really a part of my life, so I can't miss someone I don't really know, right?

My grandparents meant stability for my brother and me, and I never knew how much I craved it, how much I needed it, until I had to move for college. I was homesick for at least the first two months, until I finally found my groove. I was doing okay at school, I had friends, I felt like I had purpose on the team. In life. The college years were good. Felt like one big party, though I did manage to graduate with a business degree.

When I was drafted into the NFL with the Buccaneers and had to move halfway across the country, from Texas to Florida—that sucked balls. I lasted in Florida for all of one season before I was traded to the Raiders, thank Jesus. Back to Cali I went, having to move clear across the country in a short amount of time. I hired a moving company, but it was still a disaster. Some items were broken. They lost my dresser. I suppose it was no big deal, I got it at IKEA. Moving means you have to readjust—to a new place, a new town, a new team.

Being the new guy can work in your favor, or they can treat you like absolute crap and you're doomed from the start. Luckily enough with my current team, we bonded. We're good. I have friends. I respect the coaches, and they seem to respect me back. I like being a part of the Raiders.

Now the entire team is moving to Las Vegas, and while I'm excited as shit to play in the new stadium that's fancy as fuck, it's still an adjustment. Packing up all my stuff yet again after being in the Bay Area for only a couple of years is hitting me kind of hard. I'm having all sorts of flashbacks to the times my brother and I moved with Mom.

It wasn't just the constant moving that got to us. It was having to deal with yet another one of her new boyfriends. They were all assholes. Every single one of them. Mom has incredibly bad taste in men. She still does.

What sucks more? Over the last few years, I found myself turning into one of those callous assholes. Going through women, one after the other. Not taking into consideration their feelings, what they might want from a relationship, what they might want from *me*. I knew what I wanted, and for a long time, that's all that mattered.

Easy sex. A hot, quick fuck. That's all. Seeing the same woman more than three times? Huge mistake. Three times in the sack and a woman wanted more. More, more, more.

I had nothing to give. I was empty. Hit it and forget it, that was my mantra for a long time.

Not anymore. I've seen the light, so they say. My grandma would tell me it's about time, and I suppose she's right. I'm a man on a mission, trying to find a woman who I might be interested in the long term. Someone who doesn't immediately know who I am either. That's why I went on the Rate A Date app. To connect with someone on a real level, not because of who I am and all the baggage that comes with me.

I just didn't expect it to happen so fast. I tell myself I'm probably rushing things, but I think I've already found her, though I barely know her.

Eleanor.

Sweet, funny Eleanor. She of the bright blonde hair and nice rack. Yes, I sound like a jackass who's only looking at the physical attributes of a woman, but I can't help it. I have to find her attractive, am I right? The spark is necessary in order for us to continue.

At least, the spark is necessary for me, and I feel it just looking at her photo, though there's so much more to her than her beauty. She piques my interest.

When we have our nightly chats, I'm always left wanting to know more about her. She has a good sense of humor and laughs a lot, and I appreciate that. She listens to me intently when I talk, and always offers up her opinion on things. I like that about her too. She doesn't seem timid or bashful, and she's not fake either. I can tell.

I have a good sense about those things.

If she does talk about herself, she delivers the information in small bits. Like clues. Like the bread crumbs good ol' Hansel and Gretel dropped as they made their way through the woods. I'm following behind Eleanor, picking up all those clues and breadcrumbs, yet I'm still hungry. She makes me feel greedy in all ways.

That's something that's never really happened to me before. I haven't been bored once during our conversations, and that tends to happen pretty easily for me. And when I'm bored, I end up doing things I shouldn't.

Like taking the chat from normal conversation to sexting, only because I'm looking to spice things up a little bit. When they know who they're dealing with, some women are a little too readily agreeable.

This makes me sound like an egotistical jerk, but it's true. Certain women want to be with famous men. Star fuckers are what we call them. It doesn't matter what you look like. They don't care about your personality. If you're famous? Yeah, let's do it. They're down.

When I've shifted it to sexting before, we always get off. I get titty shots, bootie shots and maybe even catch a glimpse of some pink parts. I send her a dick pic, we type some dirty shit to each other, and boom, masturbation heaven,

I'm not tempted whatsoever to send Eleanor a dick pic, or switch the conversation to dirty talk. She actually interests me. I look forward to our evening chats. Tonight, though, I want to try something a little different.

Video chatting. FaceTime. Whatever you want to call it,

I want to actually see her. Hear her voice. Watch her laugh, examine her facial expressions, try to figure her out. With the move happening next week, I'm feeling a little melancholy.

I'm hoping seeing Eleanor will cheer me up.

She texts me around nine o'clock, her usual time to jump online. We didn't chat last night, and it was a Friday, so I had a feeling she might've had a date. Not that I'm jealous or anything, but I'm definitely curious.

Eleanor: **Hey! Are you around?**

Me: **Sure am. How are you? I missed chatting with you last night.**

Look at me, cutting right to the chase and letting her know how I feel. Pretty sure I'm turning into an adult.

Eleanor: **Oh. Yeah. I had plans last night.**

Me: **A date?**

She goes silent for at least a minute, and I wonder if she's trying to come up with the right thing to say.

Eleanor: **A blind double date actually. My friend is on Rate a Date too, and she set me up on a date with this guy who's friends with the man she's been talking to.**

Jealousy streaks through me, hot and quick. I tamp the feeling back.

Me: **How did it go?**

Eleanor: **It was…oh God, it was so awful. But not necessarily for me. More for my friend.**

Jealousy is now raining down upon me, making me tense. Am I wasting my time here? Is she about to tell me she's not interested after all? That she's met the love of her life and while yeah, it's been great, I live too far and we're done?

Shit, my imagination is getting the best of me. I decide to ask her what I need to know.

Me: **Are you friend zoning me?**

Eleanor: **Wait, what? NO! There's so much I need to tell you about this date and how much of a disaster it was, but I'd be typing all night. There's too much to say.**

Ah, this is almost too easy for me to make my suggestion.

Me: **We should FaceTime then.**

She goes quiet again. I might've sent her into a panic. I've noticed it's pretty easy to do that.

Eleanor: **Right now?**

Me: **No, two weeks from now.**

More silence.

Me: **Yes of course right now. You got an iPhone?**

Eleanor: **Yes.**

Me: **Give me your number.**

Within a minute of her sending her number to me, I'm calling her via FaceTime. It rings so many times, I'm afraid she's not going to answer but at the last minute, there she is.

In the flesh, via my phone screen.

I can't help but smile.

"Hey."

"Hey." She waves. Laughs. Her cheeks turn pink. Her blonde hair is piled on top of her head in this cute sloppy bun, and she's wearing giant silver hoops that are very, very thin. The white V-neck T-shirt she's wearing is oversized, meaning it keeps slipping off her shoulder, offering me a glimpse of her pale pink bra strap.

Oh, and her generous cleavage is flashing me from the deep V of her neckline too.

My dick twitches and I mentally tell it to calm down. I'm horny as fuck because I haven't had sex with a woman in weeks. Maybe a month? Oooh, maybe longer.

"So tell me what happened," I say, and when she frowns, I continue, "With your date last night."

She sighs. "Okay. This is going to take a while, so excuse me if I ramble."

"Go for it." I like her voice. It's sweet and light and cute.

"My friend met a guy on the app and she really liked him. He has a friend he wanted to set me up with, so Kelsey —that's my friend—asked if I wanted to go on a double date with them. I was kind of reluctant because I don't know this guy, right? Plus, I've been talking to you."

"Right." I like that she thought of me. It means she might do that. A lot.

Kind of like I think about her. A lot.

"Anyway, turns out the guy she was talking to was a bit of a jerk. I think he was drinking too much and was trying to show off. And the man they set me up with, he just got out of a long-term relationship. He was engaged to her, and I'm pretty sure it was a messy ending. Kelsey got mad at her date after he insulted me and we walked out together," Eleanor explains.

"Sounds complicated." I'm not even sure exactly what happened, but I'm glad it was a flop.

"Here's the thing. Theodore, the guy they set me up with? He's very nice. And he's an investment manager at one of the local banks here. He was full of good financial advice. I think I'm going to make an appointment to meet with him. He gave me his business card," she says.

"Ah, so you do like him."

"Not like that! He was very nice. I could see us being friends, but that's it." She leans in closer, giving me an even better shot of her shadowy cleavage, and I let my gaze linger there. Those tits are definitely more than a handful. "It's so nice to see your face!"

Wariness hits me and I realize I didn't even think about her recognizing me. I've never once mentioned what I actually do. She thinks I work in fitness, which is the vaguest answer ever. And maybe that's why I'm enjoying these moments with Eleanor. She doesn't care if I'm a professional football player or not. She just likes me for...

Me.

"It's nice to see your face too," I tell her, my voice soft. I clear my throat, not wanting to sound too much like a sap. "Did you work today?"

She nods. "It was so busy. One client after the other. My feet are killing me."

"If I were there with you, I'd give you a foot massage."

"That sounds like heaven," she says with a little sigh.

That sigh goes straight to my dick.

Down, boy.

"When do you move again?" she asks.

"Mid next week," I answer as I pick up the phone, flip the camera and do a sweep of my living room. "As you can see, I'm not even close to being packed up."

There are empty boxes scattered around, not a one of them full of anything.

"You don't have much furniture. No pictures on the wall. No knickknacks on your bookshelves," she points out.

"I'm not home much. And those aren't bookshelves." I do a slow scan over the shelves that flank either side of the big-screen TV that hangs on the wall. "Those are video game shelves."

She laughs. "You do own a lot of video games."

"And those are the old ones. I'm downloading most of the newer games now," I explain.

I go on about my favorite video games and she listens and nods, asking questions at the right spots. Like she's actually interested. She tells me about a few of her clients today. How she did hair for a bridal party and the bride was so demanding.

"Are you doing your friend's hair when she gets married?" I ask.

"I am, but she won't be a total diva. Caroline isn't like that," she says.

"And you're still coming to Vegas for her bachelorette weekend, right?" I keep my voice even, as if my question is no big deal.

But it's a huge deal. If she comes to Vegas, I want to see her. In person. I want to smell her. Touch her. I am totally thinking ahead here, and rushing the game, but just talking to her like this has me feeling antsy. Eager.

Ready to see her.

"I am! Next weekend." She smiles prettily. "You'll be living in Vegas by then."

"Yeah, I will." Next weekend. The timing couldn't be better. Almost like our meeting is meant to be.

"Did you still maybe want to...meet up?" she asks hopefully.

"Yeah. I'd love to," I say without hesitation.

"Good." She smiles, and I swear her eyes are glowing. Her cheeks are pink, and she's just radiating light. Is that because she's pleased with the thought of us meeting in person? Or is she sitting under a really flattering lamp right now? "Maybe I can introduce you to my friends."

Wariness settles back in. I'd love to meet her friends, but...

What if one of them recognizes me? She's bound to be friends with at least one football fan. And considering they live in the Monterey area, which is pretty close to Oakland, most everyone in that vicinity is either a Niner fan or a Raider fan.

"First I just want to see you," I tell her, my voice heavy with flirtation. "Take you to dinner. Maybe to a show."

"Ugh, no show. Just take me to some fancy dinner. Like Gordon Ramsey's place," she suggests.

Really? The kitchen nightmare himself? "You want to go to his restaurant?"

"Yes! I've always wanted to try the beef wellington," she says. "I used to watch that show with my mom when I was younger. I loved it."

"Do you like to cook?"

She wrinkles her nose, and it's kind of adorable. "I'm not the best, though I'm always willing to work on it. I've been told I don't have enough patience."

"I can't cook for shit," I say. "And I have no idea what beef wellington is."

"Oh, it looks delicious. We'll have to try it." She wiggles a little bit, her tits bouncing, and I appreciate the view more than she'll ever know. "I'm so excited that we'll actually get to meet."

"Me too," I tell her.

"I have to warn you, though." She pauses, her teeth sinking into her lower lip. I bet she doesn't mean for that face to be sexy, but damn it is.

"Warn me about what?"

"I'm really awkward in person." My doubtful look makes her forge on. "No, I'm serious! I'm so awkward with guys, it's kind of embarrassing. I say the weirdest stuff. I act weird. Give me a glass of wine or two and I turn super awkward."

"I can handle awkward," I say with ease.

"I don't know." The skeptical look she sends me is obvious. "I'm a bit of a mess."

"You're a cute mess," I tell her, and she starts blushing again.

"You're not so bad yourself," she says, her gaze meeting mine through the camera. "You're very...muscular."

"I work out a lot." I turn to the side and show off my right bicep like a bragging bastard. I even flex it. "My body is a temple."

"It's a pretty sexy temple," she says. The moment the words leave her mouth, she's covering it with her hand. "Ooops. I didn't mean to say that out loud."

Her voice is muffled from her hand and I can't help but laugh.

"I don't mind. I like your honesty." She's a breath of fresh air.

"Honesty, awkwardness, whatever you want to call it," she says after she drops her hand from her face.

"Am I your usual type?"

"Um, I don't really have a type, I don't think?" There she goes again, wrinkling her nose. It's a cute look for her. She tugs on the neckline of her shirt, pulling it over her exposed shoulder, but it just slides right back down again. "I like them tall."

"I'm six-one."

"I like a man with a sense of humor."

"I'll make you laugh your ass off."

"I don't want them skinnier than me."

"I am definitely not skinnier than you," I reassure her.

"Good, because I'm kind of a—curvy girl."

"I like my hands to be full of curves when I touch a woman," I say.

She giggles. "You're going to embarrass me."

"What? It's true. I appreciate a woman's curves."

"Glad to hear it, because I have plenty of them."

I lean in a little closer to the screen. "I can't wait to explore them."

"Are you dropping some sexual innuendo right now?"

"I sure as shit hope so," I answer.

Eleanor laughs. "I like you."

A warm sensation wraps around my heart, giving it a squeeze. That same warm feeling is also wrapping around my dick. "I like you too. A lot."

Fuck holding back. Fuck playing it cool. I'm excited to meet this woman in the flesh.

Can't wait to get my hands on her flesh too.

SEVEN

ELEANOR

"I'VE MET SOMEONE," I announce.

It's Monday, it's my day off, and I'm at lunch with Kelsey and Sarah in downtown Carmel, at a restaurant in the same complex where my salon and Sarah's work are located. It's Sarah's day off too, though Kelsey had to work, since she's Alex's assistant. Alex, as in Caroline's fiancé.

Yes, we're all interconnected somehow.

Kelsey had to come into Carmel to drop off some paperwork to Caroline for Alex, so when she texted us asking if we wanted to meet up and have lunch, both Sarah and I jumped on it. We're all about lunch. And brunch. We eat out a lot. Drink a lot of wine too.

No wonder I have curves. I try my best to curb my caloric intake, but sometimes, especially with this group of friends, it's difficult.

But back to the juicy stuff.

At my sudden declaration, Sarah's eyes go wide and she settles back in her chair. "What do you mean, you've met someone?"

"Is it that same guy you've been talking to on the app?" Kelsey asks.

Sarah looks from me to Kelsey in confusion. "What app? What are you talking about?"

"Yes, it's the same guy," I tell Kelsey before turning to Sarah. "Kelsey and I are on that new Rate a Date app. Trying to find ourselves some decent men."

Sarah makes a face. "Please tell me it's not some sleazy hookup place."

"Well, the first guy I went out with from that app turned out to be a complete jackass," Kelsey mutters.

I'm a little offended Sarah thinks we're on some *sleazy hookup place*. I mean, come on. Doesn't she think we have better judgment than that? Or is she just lumping all dating apps into the sleazy category?

"The date Kelsey set me up on is now my new financial guru," I say, pointing at Kelsey. When they both stare at me in silence, I explain further. "I have an appointment with Theo this Wednesday. We're going to talk sound investments and which ones I should tackle first."

"God, that guy was boring," Kelsey mutters.

I give her a hard stare. "I'll have you know Theo is very sweet."

"So not my type," she says.

No surprise. I think she must be drawn to jerks.

"Good thing you two weren't matched up then, huh?" I tease her.

"Tell me about this Rate A Date app," Sarah says, looking vaguely suspicious.

"It's all on the up and up, like every other dating app out there," Kelsey reassures her. "Besides, you can't judge us for using one. Your fiancé is the same guy who came into

Bliss on a regular basis and bought lingerie for his many mistresses."

Sarah's cheeks turn pink and she lifts her chin, looking like a haughty princess. "I'll have you know he bought most of that lingerie with me in mind the whole time."

"I rest my case," Kelsey says, glancing over at me. "That's vaguely sleazy."

"It is not," Sarah protests.

"I always thought it was kind of romantic," I offer, and Sarah jumps on it.

"It was definitely romantic. And—unique," she adds.

"That's one way to describe it," Kelsey says, laughing as she dodges away from Sarah's finger. She looked ready to poke Kelsey right in the side. "Let's stop focusing on Sarah's fiancé's weird lingerie fetish and focus on Eleanor's new man."

"Tell us everything you know," Sarah practically demands.

I launch into a description of Mitch. How he's so easy to talk to and he makes me laugh. How he was extra flirtatious the first time we FaceTimed and even made a few sexual comments, which didn't bother me in the least. In fact, I responded to them to the best of my ability, though I was a tad awkward.

"Of course," Sarah says when I tell them that.

I describe him as tall and broad and very muscular, like muscles on muscles, and that's when they both demand to see a photo of him. Lucky me, I'm able to whip one out pretty fast.

"He's cute," Sarah says as she examines my phone screen closely. She frowns before lifting her head, her gaze meeting mine. "I feel like I recognize him, but from where? Like maybe I know him or something."

"He grew up around here. Well, in Monterey."

"Really? What's his last name?" Sarah hands my phone to Kelsey, who examines Mitch's image thoroughly.

"Um..." My voice drifts, and I feel super dumb right now. "I don't know."

"Eleanor. You don't know his last name? Come on, girl, you gotta stay on top of that stuff. How else can we Google him for you?" Kelsey says as she hands my phone back to me. "What does he do for a living?"

"Well, he says he works in fitness." That is a really vague response. I don't know what he means by that, and sitting here now, in the light of day with my two friends looking at me like I've lost my marbles, I'm feeling kind of lame for buying into that explanation.

"Fitness? That's all he told you? That could mean anything. He could be a physical therapist. He could own a gym. Or he could be a gym rat who does nothing but work out all day," Kelsey says. "Oh! He could work the front desk at a gym part time and only making minimum wage. The possibilities are endless."

"I swear I've seen him before," Sarah says, tapping her chin as she appears lost in thought. "He's super familiar."

"He's older than you. I doubt you went to school together," I say, shoving my phone in my bag. I have failed in the dating app department by not getting the important facts straight. Like finding out Mitch's actual occupation and you know, his full name. "And you're both right. I need to find out his last name. I also need to ask him more questions about his job."

"Yes to both. When they're secretive, there's usually a reason," Kelsey says with a sigh. "Like maybe he's a serial killer or something."

My entire friend group is fascinated with serial killers. I

don't know how many times one of them has used that term lately. "Are there really serial killers around anymore? It's too easy to get caught nowadays. There are cameras everywhere."

"Isn't that the truth," Sarah says with a little laugh. "Pretty sure Caroline called Jared a potential serial killer. Or was it Stella?"

We laugh. We order lunch when our server appears. We discuss Caroline's wedding and how we all have a fitting next week for our bridesmaid gowns. The last fitting before the big day, and how we all need to lay off the carbs and alcohol if we want to look good in our dress. Kelsey's kind of quiet, and I wonder if it's because she's not actually in the wedding, which is a bummer, but she's the newest addition to our friend group besides Candice, so I get why neither of them are in the wedding.

"Are you okay?" I ask Kelsey when there's a lull in the conversation.

She sends me a look that clearly says *no, I'm not*, before she starts talking. "Look, I don't mean to swing the conversation back so it's all about me, but seriously, guys. I'm done with men. They all suck. I finally had to block Paul on all social media and my phone. He wouldn't stop trying to call me, text me, the works. All the apologies and the 'oh, baby, I didn't mean to make such an ass of myself' only goes so far, you know?"

"I'm so sorry," I say, reaching out to rest my hand over my friend's. "That's terrible."

"*He's* terrible," Kelsey says irritably. "I'm glad you at least got to make a friend out of the deal."

It's true. Theo and I had a wonderful phone conversation yesterday afternoon, and he spilled every little detail about his relationship with the wretched Jessica. They were high school sweethearts. They'd been together for over ten years before he finally convinced her they should get married. And two weeks before the big day, he caught her naked in their bed, having sex with one of his groomsmen.

That groomsman happened to be Theo's cousin. Ouch.

Needless to say, the wedding was cancelled, the breakup was messy, and Jessica is still with Theo's cousin. As a matter of fact, they just announced their engagement.

Double ouch.

"Theo is *so* nice," I tell Kelsey. "Maybe he's the one you should've gone out with."

"No way. He is so not my type." Kelsey waves a hand, dismissing my suggestion.

"Yeah, same," I say sadly. "He's not quite over Jessica anyway, so it's not like he's even ready for a relationship yet. He was very upset by how Paul treated you, though. He wanted me to apologize to you on his behalf."

Kelsey rests her hand against her chest. "Aw. That really is super sweet."

We talk a little more about Friday night's disastrous double date, only because it's fun to rehash the details. Sarah is completely enthralled with our story, and by the time we're reaching the end, she can't stop laughing.

"Was this Paul guy really that big of a douche?" she asks for about the tenth time. "It feels like you're making this stuff up."

Kelsey and I both nod vigorously. "Yes," we say in sync before we dissolve into laughter.

Yeah, it still doesn't seem real to me either, but I lived it, so...

"Let's swing back to your new guy," Sarah says at one point, long after our meals have arrived and we're halfway through with them. "I want more details."

"Here's something I didn't mention." I set my fork down. I ordered a salad and an iced tea. Trying to take the carbs down a couple of notches. "He's moving to Las Vegas for his job, and he wants to meet up with me while we're there."

They both gape at me for a too-long moment.

"What? Do you think it's too soon?" I ask.

"Oh, Eleanor." Kelsey shakes her head. "Are you sure it's a good idea to meet him in Vegas?"

"Why wouldn't it be?"

The worried look on Sarah's pretty face is undeniable. "What if he's like...a stripper? I mean, why else would he move to Vegas for his career?" She throws up air quotes around the last word.

"He's not a stripper," I say assuredly.

The doubt creeps in the moment the words escape me. God, what if he *is* a stripper? It would make a lot of sense. His job is in "fitness". He's super muscular—I bet he could slather his body in oil, roll those hips on a stage somewhere in the middle of Sin City and women would throw their money and their bodies at him, no questions asked.

Maybe that's why he's so vague about what he does for a living. Yes! Because he's a stripper. Maybe he got into the Magic Mike Revue! Or whatever they call it.

The more I think about it, the more I can see him giving me serious Channing Tatum vibes. And that is not a bad thing, trust me.

"What if he's part of the Vegas mob?" Kelsey asks, her gaze shooting from me to Sarah, her expression deadly serious. "Those guys are scary."

"Do they actually exist? I've seen the mob mentioned in a few movies but..." I let my voice drift because come on. The *mob?*

"He's pretty secretive. He didn't tell you much about himself," Kelsey points out. "And that worries me."

"You shouldn't meet him," Sarah chimes in, concern filling her dark eyes. "Or if you do, you should take a couple of us with you."

"Right, bring my friends on a date? I don't think so," I tell them, just before all of us break into laughter.

Though, really, I'm not feeling very humorous at the moment.

Their advice sticks with me as I drive home. I suppose they're right. Maybe I shouldn't meet Mitch. What if he *is* a psycho killer? Though I doubt that's the case. He's nice. He makes me smile. Just thinking about him right now is making me smile.

I force my lips into a straight line, trying to be serious. I need to know his last name. I need to know what he does for a living. I need to know all the facts before I just...meet him.

Determination filling me, I press my foot against the gas pedal, the car lurching forward as I go a few miles over the speed limit. I'm anxious to get home, get myself looking extra on fire and then I'm FaceTiming Mitch later tonight. And I plan on getting all the answers I need out of him.

Whether he likes it or not.

EIGHT

MITCH

I GOT the text from Eleanor around six.

Want to FaceTime tonight?

I leave her hanging for about an hour, only because I'm trying my damnedest to get my shit packed for the big move. I don't really own a lot of stuff, so I figured I could do it myself. That it would be easy.

Big mistake. It's been a huge pain in my ass.

The moving company is coming tomorrow and once everything's packed up and ready to go, I'm turning in my apartment keys before I head for Vegas in my SUV. It's over an eight-hour drive, it's going to be a long, miserable day, and I'm staying at a hotel the first night versus my new apartment, only so I'll have a bed to collapse in when I get there.

But come Wednesday, I'll be picking up the keys to my new place. The moving truck is scheduled to arrive at my new place nine a.m. They'll unload all the boxes and furniture, and then it'll be done. I'll just need to unpack.

Yet again.

By Friday night, I should be meeting Eleanor.

Frowning, I realize I forgot all about Eleanor. I need to text her back.

Sorry, I've been packing all day. Yeah, I'd like to FaceTime. Let me take a shower first.

She responds within minutes. **Text me when you're ready!**

Smiling, I plug my phone into my charger and head for the bathroom. I like that Eleanor is always cheerful. She doesn't ask a lot of annoying questions, and I appreciate that. Sometimes I feel bad that I'm keeping certain parts of my life a secret, but I don't want to admit to her that I'm a pro football player. Not yet. I know once I tell her, she'll immediately Google me and find out my net worth.

Or worse, she'll see photos of me with my hands all over some sexy woman's body. Because I know those photos are out there, of me and my friends at a club with women hanging all over us. All over me. I did that shit in college too. At one point, when I was young and stupid, that was the image I was going for. Party boy, drunk ass, man whore. Those descriptors were the sum of my personality.

Hell, right up to about six months ago, I was still working that image like nobody's business.

But not anymore. Nope. I'm trying out this one-woman man thing, and so far, I'm digging it.

I take a shower and consider jerking off before our call. That tends to ease the tension that always seems to consume me when I chat with Eleanor. This not having sex for an extended period of time thing is tough. I feel like every little thing she does sets me off and gets me hard. Her laughter gives me a boner, for Christ's sake. I can't imagine what it'll be like when we actually meet in person.

I'll probably spontaneously combust.

The hot water feels good on my aching muscles and I pour extra body wash into the palm of my hand before I wrap my fingers around the base of my hard dick. Closing my eyes, I envision Eleanor. Her sweet face. Sunny blonde hair. Curvy body. I try to imagine her naked. I've never really caught sight of her full length, so I'm not sure how tall she is, or how great—or not great—her ass might be, but I have a feeling she's perfectly proportioned.

Meaning with her more than ample chest, I'm pretty confident she must have a luscious ass too.

Pressing my forehead against the slick tile, I start to stroke. I think of her plump lips and her even plumper tits, and a groan escapes me. My imagination runs wild. Dim lighting. Rumpled white sheets. Eleanor's naked body stretched across the bed, her blue eyes sparkling as she smiles up at me. I settle in above her, my cock in front of her mouth, and she parts those glossy lips willingly, a sexy moan escaping her when I nudge just the head in. That mouth clamps down around my dick, milking me in this slow, rhythmic suction, her lids lifting, her eyes sparkling as she releases my cock, her tongue sneaking out for a lick and holy shit—

I'm coming, a guttural groan escaping me as I squeeze my fingers tight around the base of my shaft, milking all the come out. My knees are weak and I brace my hand against the shower wall, blinking my eyes open as the warm water rains down upon my head, blurring my vision.

Damn. That was fuckin' good. I start to laugh as I rinse off my body.

If it's that spectacular in my imagination, wait until we actually get together.

"HI!" Eleanor's cheerful voice blasts out as she bounces around, her phone falling to the side from wherever she's got it propped up, giving me a prime view of her ample chest. "Oh no! Hold on." She reaches for it, and now the phone is on the floor and I wait impatiently for her to set it against whatever she uses when we have these conversations.

"Having problems?" I'm teasing her, and I hope she can tell.

She laughs, righting the phone so I can once again see her pretty face. And she looks extra pretty tonight. "I'm a little clumsy, yeah. Sorry about that."

"No problem." I'm sitting at my kitchen table, my voice echoing since I've taken everything off the walls—not that I had a lot of things hung up anyway—and most everything is packed away. "How was your Monday?"

"It was good! It's my day off so I got to sleep in." I remember how I imagined her in bed, tangled up in a white sheet. "I did laundry. Had lunch with friends." She pauses, biting her lower lip and damn it, my dick twitches. See? Depriving myself is turning me into a needy bastard. "What about you?"

"I'm pretty much done packing. I leave for Las Vegas tomorrow," I tell her, scrubbing a hand over my face. "That's going to be a long drive."

She wrinkles her nose, and damn, she looks adorable. "How long will it take?"

"A little over eight hours? Eight and a half maybe?" I exhale loudly, already anticipating the endless drive and not looking forward to it. "I'll need lots of caffeine and some good songs to sing along with to get me through."

"Oh! Do you have a good singing voice?" She looks so hopeful. Too bad I'm gonna dash her hopes.

"Nope. I sound terrible most of the time. At least, that's what people tell me. In my own head, I think I sound just like the professionals," I answer.

"Speaking of professional…" Her voice drifts and my heart drops. Has she found out what I do? Did she somehow discover my true identity and she's ready to call me out for it? I deserve whatever beat down she wants to give me. "My friends and I were talking during lunch and I realized…I don't really know what you do."

"What I do?" I frown at her, playing it off.

Doing a shit job of it.

"For work. You mentioned fitness, but that's kind of a vague answer." Her determined gaze meets mine, and I'm mesmerized for a hot second as her face fills the screen. Her blonde hair tumbles past her shoulders in pretty waves. Her skin is clear, downright glowing, and her cheeks have this peachy tint to them. And her lips…her lips have that same peachy color, but deeper.

I'm starting to sweat.

"Yeah, I deal with—athletes." That's not a lie.

"Okay." She nods, her brows lowering. She has really great eyebrows. They're darker than her hair color and they have this perfect arch to them—I've never noticed a woman's brows before, but staring at Eleanor's right now, I can't help but appreciate them. "So you're like what? A trainer?"

"Sure." I nod enthusiastically. That's one way to put it. "Yes. I train athletes."

"Are you like a teacher or something? A gym coach?"

"Not quite," I hedge. The more I lie, the deeper in the hole I'm gonna get.

"Oh, I know! You train professional athletes, don't you?" She's the one nodding enthusiastically now. "That's why you don't want to reveal too much, am I right? You're trying to protect your clients?"

"Um, sort of?" This is getting complicated, when it doesn't need to be. And I feel like a complete shit for not telling her the truth.

But my entire plan in meeting Eleanor is to see if she can fall for me without the trappings of being a professional football player. No matter how much I want to confess and get it off my chest, telling her the truth could fuck everything up.

"Which sport?" she asks.

A big, ragged sigh escapes me and I hang my head for a moment, closing my eyes. Eleanor has gone quiet and I can practically feel her worry and confusion radiating toward me through the phone screen. "I have a little confession," I say softly.

"What is it? Oh my God, are you all right?"

Lifting my head, I meet her gaze. See all the concern swirling in her blue eyes, and in that moment, I silently freak out. I can't tell her. Not yet. I don't know her that well. And I can't tell her over FaceTime. This is something major, something you should share when you're in the same room together.

I can tell her later. For now, I'll keep my secret. If we make it, if we turn into an actual, real relationship, I'll come clean. And she'll understand.

I know she will.

"I've signed an NDA." She's still frowning, so I explain. "A non-disclosure agreement. I can't talk about my clients."

"Ohhh." She nods, all the concern vanishing from her eyes. "I get it. You're protecting their identity."

"It's more that they protect themselves so I can't go blab to a tabloid or TMZ or whatever," I explain. I know guys on the team who have employees sign NDAs, and I guess I can't blame them.

I've always felt like I have no secrets to hide. Everything I am is out there on the Internet. It'll take just a couple of clicks to find it all. And honestly, I'm pretty low key. I don't go around cheating on girlfriends or getting women pregnant. I don't do drugs or drink too much, or get into fights. I like women. I like to party. I like to spend money.

Is that against the law?

No.

"Can I admit something to you?"

I blink Eleanor back into focus. "Sure."

"I was talking about you to my friends today at lunch, and they were thinking that maybe you're a..." Her voice drifts and she covers her mouth with her fingers, stifling a giggle.

"They think I'm a what?" I ask.

She's still giggling. Actually, it's turned into full-blown laughter now. "They thought you were a probably a stripper."

I can't help but start laughing as well. "I would be the worst stripper ever."

Her laughter dies and a sexy glow lights up her eyes. "You look like you have the body for it."

Well damn. There goes my dick again, twitching like crazy. "I can't dance."

"It doesn't take much dancing skill," she teases. "You know how to roll your hips?"

I could sure as hell show you how I roll my hips—as I'm driving my cock deep inside your body.

No way can I say that to her. I'm not that much of a dick. Instead I just smile mysteriously and stroke my chin like I see all those fuckboy assholes do on that damn Tik Tok. Yes, I have a Tik Tok account, don't judge me.

"I might know how to do that," I tell her.

Her cheeks turn pink. Damn, she's cute. "So you're not a stripper working the Magic Mike show?"

"Uh, no." I start laughing again. "Are you disappointed?"

"Not at all. I started worrying that if you were a stripper, how could I measure up? Though I already feel that way, what with all your muscles." She points somewhere in the vicinity of where my shoulders are. "I bet you eat healthy."

"Most of the time." Being a lineman, I also need to bulk up. I eat healthy. Get my daily dosage of fruits and vegetables. I have to eat plenty of protein. But I also can devour an entire large pizza if I'm feeling like it. And I don't hold it against myself when I do. During football season, I burn off all those calories anyway.

"I don't," she says with a wistful sigh. "I drink too much wine and eat too much pasta. My friend's brothers own an Italian restaurant in downtown Carmel, and we go there a lot."

"Tuscany?" I ask.

Her eyes go wide. "You've been there?"

"A couple of times." I still own a small house in Monterey. A small house that costs over a million dollars, because real estate in that area is pricey as hell. I've considered selling it especially now that I'm leaving the state, but for now, I'm holding onto it. I might rent it out or something.

We'll see.

"I can't believe that! We could've been in Tuscany at

the same time and not even known!" She looks truly blown away by the coincidence.

"True," I say with a nod. "But I would've noticed you, so I'm guessing we've never crossed paths."

There go her cheeks again. Nice and pink. I wonder if her nipples are that pink. Or, you know, the pretty pink parts between her legs. "You're just saying that."

"Not really," I tell her truthfully. "You're gorgeous."

"Mitch." She draws my name out, like she's all embarrassed. "You really think so?"

"Oh, I know so." I lean back, taking her in. "I can't wait to meet you in person this weekend."

"Wait a minute. You're not some secret serial killer, are you?" She asks this with such seriousness, I start to laugh all over again.

"Even if I was, do you think I'd tell you?" I grin, unable to contain it. "I'd keep it a secret, right?"

"True." She smiles. Laughs a little. "It's just…my friends don't want me to meet you by myself. They want to come with me."

"Swear to God, I'm not a serial killer, Eleanor," I say solemnly, holding my hand up and making the peace sign. "Scout's honor."

"That's not what you do when you say scout's honor," she says quickly. Little Miss Smartypants. "You do your fingers like this." She holds up her hand, the first three fingers up and pressed close together.

"How do you know that? Were you a secret Boy Scout? Have a brother who was one?"

"I, um, dated a guy who was an Eagle Scout." Her expression turns sheepish. "He was really into the Boy Scouts."

"Was that in high school?"

"Uh. No. College."

I'm frowning. "College?"

"Well, he got his Eagle Scout status his senior year, but was still involved with the scouts through college. And—beyond." She presses her hand against her forehead and briefly closes her eyes. "Fine, I went out with him after he graduated college. I never really went to college. I went to beauty school." She drops her hand, sending me a meaningful look.

"So you went out with a guy who was still excited about being an Eagle Scout...and he was a grown man." I start to laugh. "Sounds fun."

"I've not had the greatest luck when it comes to dating guys," she admits.

"Oh yeah?" I'm rubbing my chin again, contemplating her. Wondering what the hell is wrong with all the men in her life that they don't know how to treat her.

And then I realize how lucky I am that they all blew it so now I have my chance.

"Yeah. I'm just—I don't pick well. And I always get really awkward around guys." She rolls her eyes. "I can say really dumb things. Or I just act all nervous and weird. I start to ramble."

"Like now?"

"Yes." She laughs. "Like now. I'm rambling. I'm totally rambling and you don't look bored, so I take that as a good sign."

"I think the rambling thing is cute. I like your awkwardness."

"Wait until you see it in person."

"I can't wait to see you in person," I tell her with a sly smile, making her blush. "I can't wait to give you a hug. See what you smell like."

"Mitch." Her cheeks look on fire.

"What? I'm serious. You wear perfume?"

"Of course."

"Use scented shampoo?"

"Duh. I'm a hairstylist."

"Then I can't wait to see how all those scents mix and create the essence of you." Oooh, that was a good one. I didn't even mean to say that. It just spilled out of my mouth.

"Aw, you're being so sweet." She sends me a heated glance. "Kind of sexy."

"You think me talking about how you smell is sexy?"

"Honestly, Mitch? I think everything about you is sexy," she says with a little sigh, right before she claps her hand over her mouth. "I probably shouldn't have said that." Her voice is muffled behind her palm.

"I love that you said that," I say, warming up to this conversation big time. "I think you're pretty fucking sexy too, Eleanor." Hesitating, I wonder if I should tell her what I did in the shower.

Maybe not.

"Have you ever sexted with someone before?" she asks, sounding genuinely curious.

"I guess." I shrug, not really wanting to answer her. Makes me feel like a slimy shit to admit that yes, I have. Lots of times. "Sort of. I've made plenty of booty call messages. DTF, stuff like that."

She frowns. "DTF?"

"Down to fuck."

"Oh." Her eyes are wide. Her mouth is formed in this perfect O. "Oh."

"Back when I wasn't big on relationships," I add. "But I've changed."

"You have?"

"Yeah. I'm looking for a special girl."

"Really?"

"I want a long-term relationship."

"It's too bad you're moving," she says, sounding sad.

I don't want to focus on that right now. I don't even know if this girl is the one. She has great potential. But we need to meet in person first. Test it out.

"We'll see each other this weekend," I remind her.

"I know!" Her face brightens. "And I'm excited."

"So am I, Eleanor."

So am I.

NINE
ELEANOR

WE HOP on a short flight to Los Angeles on a little plane, which sort of freaks me out. I'm not a big flyer, so I get nervous when I do. Small planes are scary.

But the flight from Los Angeles to Las Vegas is on a huge plane. It's a Friday afternoon and everyone aboard is ready for a fun weekend in Vegas. I know me and my friends are.

The bonus? I get to meet Mitch.

Sexy, hunky, handsome Mitch. The man who makes me laugh. Who sends me heated looks via FaceTime. The man who tells me I'm sexy, and I've never had a guy say that to me before.

Funny? Yes.

Goofy? Yep.

Awkward as hell? Definitely.

But sexy? Nope, that's a first.

Once we land, we get an Uber SUV and head for Wilder Las Vegas. The hotel was recently renovated, and Caroline shows us the photos Alex took when he was last here. Our jaws drop, especially when we see photos of the suite we're all sharing.

This is going to be a bachelorette weekend we're never going to forget.

"Hold on, you guys." Caroline turns to face all of us, an expectant expression on her flushed face. We're standing in the wide hall that leads to the penthouse suite at the Wilder hotel, and we're all crowded around her in front of the door, eager to get in.

At least, *I'm* eager to get in. First, I need to pee. And once that's handled, I can't wait to check this place out. Pick out my room. Unpack my stuff, hang my clothes in the closet. Eventually take a shower. Get ready.

Go meet Mitch.

Yeah. I mentioned to only a select few of the group that I'm meeting Mitch here this weekend. Caroline might be mad. This is supposed to be her weekend, and it is. I know it is. I am here to support her every minute of this weekend. But is she going to miss me for a few hours while they're all out having fun?

Doubtful.

"Come on, open the damn door," Stella yells at Caroline, making her laugh.

"Just—I want to say something first before we go inside. Thank you for taking the time off from your jobs, or being away from your boyfriends, and coming with me this weekend. We are going to have so much fun, and I just know this trip is going to be unforgettable." Caroline beams at us, and I swear she's getting teary eyed.

Which makes me want to get teary eyed too. In fact, I touch the corner of my eye and find it's wet. Yep, I'm crying.

And I still really need to pee.

"You're going to make me cry," Candice—my soul sister—says.

"No crying allowed," Stella says sternly, shooting me a look. Like she knows I'm guilty. I bet she saw the sparkle in my eyes, stupid tears. "This is a bachelorette weekend. It's about wickedness and debauchery, not tears."

Caroline's laugh is watery. But she still doesn't open that damn door.

"Jesus, Caroline, what are you waiting for?" Sarah pipes up. "Let us in!"

"God, fine. Don't let me revel in my moment." She turns and waves the card key in front of the reader, and the door opens—actually, it's two doors. The moment we walk inside, my jaw drops. The suite is two stories, and the ceiling soars above us, exposing the second level on one side. The other side of the cavernous room is floor-to-ceiling windows, revealing the city before us. It's late afternoon, the sun glinting off the windows of the other hotels and casinos, and I'd stop and check out the view but...

I rush around looking for a bathroom instead.

Once I've handled my business and washed my hands, I go out to admire the suite with everyone else. Downstairs there is a massive living room with buttery-soft leather couches and faux fur throw pillows. A massive big screen TV hangs on the wall, and the rug beneath my feet is plush and soft. There's a pool table covered in purple felt, and while I'm not a big pool player—okay, fine, I've never played pool in my life—I kind of want to give it a try.

"Oh my gosh, the fridge is fully stocked!" Candice holds the subzero refrigerator door open wide, showing us all the goodies inside. Sodas, water, fruits and cheeses are inside, along with a variety of vegetable dips and hummus. There's a bar at the end of the room, rows and rows of liquor on display.

On the table by the window, there's a giant flower arrangement consisting of mostly roses, with a card sticking out of it.

Caroline goes to the arrangement and bends her head, breathing deep. "They smell so good," she says as she tears into the card and reads it. A little smile curls her lips as she turns to face us. "They're from Alex."

"Of course," Stella says. "What's the note say?"

Caroline's cheeks turn crimson. "Just hoping we have a good time, blah blah blah."

"Uh huh." Stella strides over to Caroline and tries to snatch the card out of Caroline's fingers, but her grip is too tight. "It must be good if you won't let me see it."

"It's an—intimate message." Caroline shoves the card in her pants' pocket. "But never mind! Let's all go pick out our rooms!"

We all ended up the curved staircase to the second floor, where all the bedrooms are. Caroline gets the master suite, of course. It's huge. So is the bed. And the master bathroom is to die for, with a circular tub smack dab in the middle of the floor.

Stella nudges Caroline's side as we all admire it. "Too bad Alex isn't here with you," she says with a snicker.

Caroline smirks. "We'll have to come back sometime. Just the two of us."

I'm a little envious at the prospect. I try to imagine me and Mitch in that bathtub. I bet he'd look good surrounded by swirling hot water and frothy bubbles. I bet he'd whisper all the dirty things he wants to do to me if we were in that tub together.

I go hot just thinking about it.

Sarah and Candice are sharing a room. Stella asks Kelsey to share her room. So that leaves me...all alone.

"No one wants to share with me?" I ask sadly, feeling left out.

"Um, you're the one with plans to meet your mystery man this weekend," Kelsey points out. "You might need that bedroom all to yourself, if you get what I'm saying."

They all start talking when Kelsey makes that comment, and I briefly admit that I have other plans that don't involve them.

Of course, they all have plenty to say about it. Lots of questioning ensues, and I sort of wish Kelsey had never mentioned it.

But I'm also glad to have it all off my chest and out in the open.

"This works out perfectly," Stella says, an encouraging smile on her face. "So if you do bring him back to the hotel, you get your bedroom all to yourself."

Now it's my turn to blush. I imagined Mitch and I in the tub, but I truly wasn't planning on bringing him back to the suite. Though now that I think about it…

"That's not a bad idea," I say.

Kelsey laughs and holds up her hand. I slap my palm against hers. "Thank me later when you're all blissed out from the orgasms your Magic Mitch gives you."

"He's not going to give me any orgasms," I say as I enter my bedroom for the weekend. Kelsey follows me inside. "I barely know him."

"By the end of the weekend, I predict you'll know him very, very well."

Sending her an annoyed look, I go to the door and close it most of the way before I turn on her. "Listen, I don't plan on having sex with him this weekend, so don't say that around the other girls."

"You don't plan on it? Why not? Are you out of your mind? Didn't you say this guy is ultra flirty?" Kelsey asks.

"Well, yeah."

"And he has a nice body?"

I think of all his muscles. Those broad, broad shoulders. "Definitely."

"A panty-melting voice?" Kelsey lifts her brows.

"I never said that."

"Well, I get the sense that he just might." Kelsey watches me as I set my small suitcase on the luggage stand and zip it open. "You gotta jump on that, El. When was the last time you got laid?"

I stand in front of my suitcase, counting back the days. The weeks.

Oh crap. The *months*.

"It's been—a while," I hedge.

"How long is a while?"

"How long has it been since you had sex?"

"Hmm." Kelsey taps her finger against her pursed lips. Can I mention how gorgeous she looks after just getting off a plane? We're all a little frazzled and I know I plan on freshening up before we go to dinner, but Kelsey looks amazing. I sort of hate her.

Okay fine, I don't hate her. But what's that like, looking perfect all the time? I don't have a clue.

"A month," she finally says. "It's been a month."

"With who?"

"No one important."

"You have to tell me."

"He's some rando I met at a bar."

"Kelsey! What in the world? You should never do that!"

"I know him, don't worry. We used to work together at Wilder."

"Oh, that's interesting," I say. "Tell me his name."

She doesn't appear fazed by my questioning at all. "No way. You'll make a big deal out of nothing. We were just looking to scratch each other's itch, that's it."

I wish I could view sex as casually as Kelsey. Stella is the same way. Me? I get all weirdly emotional when it comes to getting naked in front of a guy. Like it's this giant, momentous thing. Which it is, am I right?

Not according to Kelsey. Or Stella. Well, Stella has changed her tune now that she's with Carter. Oh, they are disgustingly in love. I never thought I'd see Stella act that way, but the way she looks at him...it's straight out of a romance novel.

Once Kelsey leaves my room, I grab my phone and start texting Mitch. I told him when I'd landed and he asked that I text him when I arrived at the hotel. I take a photo of my view out the window along with a short message.

I'm here!

I'm hanging up the dresses I brought with me when my text notification sounds.

Glad you made it safely. Did you still want to meet up?

Butterflies flutter in my stomach as I stare at my phone screen. I want to meet up. Very, very badly. We're supposed to go out to dinner together tonight at the restaurant here in the hotel, but after I think I'm going to ditch my friends.

That sounds shitty, right? Like I'm a bad friend who doesn't want to hang out with the bachelorette party. But they're all encouraging me to do this. Every single one of them, even Caroline. I think they want to meet Mitch too, which I don't have a problem with.

But I want to meet him first. Spend time with him

alone, get to know him in person before I bring him around my friends.

I definitely want to meet up, I tell him. **We're going to dinner together tonight, so maybe after we're done you can come here to the hotel?**

He responds quickly. **Sure. Text me later when you think you'll be done with dinner.**

Our reservation is at 7:30, I tell him.

Great. Text me when you're ready. Can't wait to see you.

I press my lips together, trying to hold back the smile that wants to break free. I can't wait to see him either. I honestly can't believe I'm doing this. Meeting a man I don't really know in Las Vegas—Sin City—for the weekend. I sort of know him, I guess.

Not really.

He's a complete stranger. I have no idea what I could be getting myself into here. And while it's exciting to think about, it's also kind of...

Scary. I can't lie.

Seeing Mitch, spending time with him this weekend, means I *will* get to know him. I'm pretty sure I'll be able to tell if he's my kind of guy or not within the first ten minutes of being with him. Maybe sooner. We either connect or we don't, right? Isn't that how all of this works?

What's pitiful is I'm questioning myself on how this works, like I don't know. I sort of don't know.

But maybe. Just maybe...

I'll figure this dating thing out.

"DO YOU WANT ANOTHER DRINK?" Sarah turns away from the server to face me with an expectant expression on her face.

"Sure," I say with a nod, smiling up at the handsome waiter who's gathering up our empty glasses. "I'll take another one of these." I wave my hand at the half-full drink still sitting in front of me.

Once he's gone, I grab my glass and take another sip, making a face as the alcohol slides down my throat, warming my stomach. Whoever is at the bar tonight is making these cocktails extra strong, not that I'm complaining too much. I need liquid courage for my meeting with Mitch later tonight.

We're almost done with dinner, and I'm starting to get nervous. We went to the most upscale restaurant at the hotel, where Alex had made a reservation for us. We sat at a round table smack dab in the center of the room, our every taken care of by the attentive waitstaff. It's like Alex pulled out all the stops for his future wife's bachelorette weekend, and I know she's feeling special. Heck, *I'm* feeling special, and it's not even my weekend.

The food was delicious—and it was on the house. All of us talked and laughed, sharing stories about Caroline, focusing all of our attention on her. She basked in it, and the fun stuff isn't even happening until tomorrow night, when the actual bachelorette party is scheduled to go down.

I can't wait.

"Hey, I have a question," Caroline says after the server dropped off our fresh drinks. "What's going on with you tonight, Eleanor?"

I rest my hand against my chest, going for shocked. "What do you mean?"

"I hear you're meeting your new 'friend'." Caroline smiles.

"Magic Mitch," Kelsey adds, making them laugh.

Well, I don't laugh. I glare at her, though my glare feels more comical than anything else. Giving into the giggles, I reach for my new drink and take a sip from the tiny straw. "Don't call him that."

"Why exactly are you calling him that?" Candice asks.

Kelsey tells her the entire story about thinking Mitch might be a stripper and how I confessed to her that I got Channing Tatum vibes from him. That's when Kelsey came up with his new nickname. I sort of hate it.

But then again, I sort of secretly love it too.

"He promised he's not a stripper," I say once the laughter dies.

"That's unfortunate," Candice says, her gaze meeting mine. I'm sure I'm giving her a look because she throws her hands up. "What's the big deal? This is just some Vegas fling. So what if he's a stripper."

"Would you have a fling with a stripper?" I ask her. Really, I'm asking the entire table.

They all appear uncomfortable by my question, which is exactly my point.

"That's what I thought," I say as they remain quiet. "He's *not* a stripper. He's an athletic trainer for professional athletes."

"Really? Like, what athletes?" Stella asks.

"He's not allowed to say. They made him sign an NDA."

"Uh huh," says Sarah.

I ignore her doubtful tone. "I believe him."

"Are you sure you want to meet this guy on your own?"

This is from Caroline, who looks genuinely concerned. "Maybe you should take one of us with you."

I appreciate that they worry and only want the best for me. But I'm a big girl, and I'm meeting him in a very public place. I'll be fine.

"He's coming to the hotel to meet me later tonight." I reach toward the floor and grab my purse, pulling my phone out of it. I need to text him and let him know I'm almost finished. "I'm not leaving the premises."

"Maybe we should all go with you when you meet this guy for the first time," Candice says. "What time is your planned rendezvous?"

I check the time on my phone. It's almost ten. So late. I send him a quick text. **Dinner went longer than I expected. Do you want to meet in say an hour?**

I want to give him enough time to get ready and get here. I have no idea where he lives, or how long it'll take him to drive here.

My phone dings and I read the message from Mitch. **I can be there in probably twenty minutes.**

Oh. Well. I guess we'll see each other sooner than I thought. He sounds eager.

I kind of like it.

Nerves make me feel a little giddy. Well, nerves and a healthy dose of alcohol.

Text me when you're in the lobby, I tell him.

"He's meeting me in twenty minutes," I tell them as I set my phone on the table. "He's headed over now."

"We should go with you," Candice says yet again.

"No way. I'll be fine," I reassure them. The last thing I want is my friends trying to intimidate Mitch. That's not the first impression I want to make.

"We can all hide and watch," Stella suggests, her eyes sparkling. "Spy on them in the lobby."

"Absolutely not." My voice is firm, and I scan the table, sending every single one of them a stern look. "Please don't do that. Let me meet this guy in peace."

"Where are you going?" Caroline asks.

"We're staying here. Maybe we'll go grab a drink. Or gamble." Doubtful, unless he wants to. I'm not big on gambling. I'd rather buy a cute outfit than blow a hundred bucks on roulette or whatever.

"Or maybe she'll bring him back to the suite. She does have a room all to herself," Kelsey reminds them, making them all snicker.

Jerks.

"I am *not* bringing him back to the suite," I say haughtily, lifting my chin. "We're not going to mess around like that. Not on the first date."

I say it with such conviction, I've convinced myself it's true. No way will I bring him back to the room tonight.

No freaking way.

TEN
MITCH

I'M NERVOUS, and I rarely feel that way. Especially about a woman. I'm usually fairly confident, but this woman's got me on pins and needles, and I'm worried she might not like me. She's not just some random hookup to me. This is a woman I want to invest time in. A woman I want to spend time with.

Going on a dating app probably wasn't the smartest thing to do in order to find someone serious, but at least Eleanor doesn't know who I really am. And that's my biggest problem. Women who realize I play professional ball always want a piece of me. They don't even care who I actually am or what I might like. I can't take them seriously, not when they're looking at me like I'm an unlimited bank account and they want to go on a shopping spree.

This has been my life since I started with the NFL. Hell, this was my life in college. I've never had a steady girlfriend. What was the point? I didn't need one. There were guys I knew, guys I still know, who play with me or on other teams, and they've been with the same woman since high school.

Since *high school*. Can you imagine?

I can't. That's a long-ass time. My parents have been married for over thirty years, and I can't wrap my head around that. I can barely stand myself. How am I supposed to be with a woman for that long?

It sounds impossible.

Tonight, I'm meeting a woman I'm considering having a relationship with—for the first time. And while I don't know Eleanor that well, I have high fuckin' hopes. I have a feeling we're going to have chemistry, though I'm not sure if Eleanor is even going to let me kiss her. I'd like to kiss her and test this out. She hasn't given me prude vibes, but who knows?

The fact that I feel patient, that I'm cool with not getting any action from her, has to say something about my maturity level.

Yep. I am a new man.

I arrive at Wilder Las Vegas in exactly twenty minutes, which is some sort of miracle because traffic is shit on a Friday night, and I'm not one-hundred percent familiar with the area yet. I pull into the entrance and steer my truck toward valet parking, because I'm not dealing with that monstrous parking garage tonight.

When the valet kid approaches me, his eyes go wide the moment he sees my face. "Are you Mitch Anderson? With the Raiders?"

I toss him my keys. "The one and only."

His gaze goes to my gleaming black truck. It's nothing too flashy, but it did set me back a cool eighty grand. "I'll take care of your vehicle, sir." He reaches into his pocket and tears off a ticket with a long number printed in red on the top. "Don't lose this."

"Don't lose that either." I point at my truck and smile, and I swear he looks like he's about to piss his pants.

"Um, do you mind..." Nerves make his voice that slightest bit shaky.

When he says nothing else, I decide to help him along. "You want to take a photo?"

The kid nods. I'd put him in his late teens. Maybe even his very early twenties. He looks very young, like he's playing dress-up in the white jacket and black bow tie all the valet employees are wearing.

"Sure," I say easily. Never do I want to be a complete asshole who turns down a fan. No one else is even paying us much attention, so I don't mind taking a photo with him at all. It's the least I can do.

The kid digs into the pocket of his black pants, producing his phone. He calls one of the other valets over and hands his phone to him before he comes to stand beside me. "Sorry," he apologizes as we both turn and face his friend, who doesn't seem fazed by me in the least. Must not be a football fan.

"Don't apologize. It's no problem." I smile and the other guy takes a bunch of photos in a burst before he hands his photo back to the kid.

"Thank you. I'm glad you guys have moved here. I definitely plan on going to a few of your games this season," he says, full of wide-eyed wonder.

"Thanks for the support." I was only going to give the valet twenty bucks, but this kid deserves more. I slap two twenties in his palm. "See ya later."

Pausing in front of the hotel entrance, I pull my phone out of my jeans and send Eleanor a quick text. **Just arrived. Where are you?**

I enter through the revolving door and come to a stop, absorbing the glittery opulence of the Wilder Hotel lobby. These place is chic as fuck, and those are words I would've never figured I'd think, but it's true. No stale cigarette smoke or the clanging sound of slot machines coming from the casino in this lobby. Hell no. All I see is low lighting and elegant furniture. Jazz music plays, though it's not too loud. The air smells like a motherfuckin' flower garden on a perfect spring day, and the men and women who are standing behind the sleek counter helping guests are all really attractive.

I'm impressed.

My phone buzzes and I check to find a message from Eleanor.

I'm coming to the lobby right now! OMG I can't believe this is finally happening!

I can't help but smile at the enthusiasm in her text. I hope she's pleased when she actually sees me. I'm not drop-dead handsome like Clay, our pretty boy QB, but I'm not a troll. More than anything, I hope she doesn't recognize me.

Shit. Glancing about the room, I check the crowd around me, but no one's paying me any attention. The light is so dim in here, they might not recognize me anyway.

Not that I'm an attention whore or anything, but I've welcomed fans' attention in the past. Tonight, I want no one to realize who I am. I want to avoid the celebrity recognition at all costs.

Shoving my hands in my pockets, I pace around, scanning the room every other second. I'm agitated. Anxious. Full of adrenaline. All the A words. I run a hand through my hair, hoping it looks good. Discreetly sniff near my armpits, making sure the sudden sweat that's come upon me isn't making me stink. I took a long, hot shower before I left the apartment. I might've even jerked off—news flash, I did jerk off.

So what the hell is wrong with me? Why am I feeling this way over a woman I barely know?

Swear to God, I feel her before I actually see her. The air in the room shifts, and the hairs on the back of my neck stand on end. Slowly I turn, just in time to see a blonde dynamo making her way toward me, a giant smile on her face.

Seeing that smile in person hits me like a ton of bricks. Damn, she's beautiful. She's wearing a cream-colored dress with sprigs of pink flowers scattered all over it. It has this square neckline that shows off her tits in the most perfect way possible. And the skirt is short, giving me a view of long, tanned legs.

"Mitch," she calls, appearing as if she's about to break into a run. But she glances down at her high-heeled sandals and reconsiders her options, I suppose.

No running. I can't blame her.

"Eleanor," I say when she stops directly in front of me, tilting her head back. "You look—gorgeous."

Her cheeks turn pink and she leans a little to the right. "Thank you. I bought this dress special. Special for the bachelorette weekend."

"I like it." My gaze can't help but settle on her ample cleavage. "A lot."

"Are you talking to my boobs?" she asks, amusement tingeing her voice.

I lift my gaze to hers, hoping she's not pissed. But no. The pleasant expression on her face tells me she's not. "Sorry. They're just..."

"So on display? I know. I thought maybe I shouldn't

wear it, but then I told myself, nah. Who cares if your tits fall out?" She starts laughing.

I laugh too. Who is this woman? I like her.

I like her a lot.

"We should hug," she says once her laughter dies, and before I can say anything, she practically stands on top of my shoes and wraps herself around me. My arms go automatically around her waist, and I realize she fits perfectly against me. The scent of her shampoo reaches my nostrils and I breathe deep, savoring the fruity smell. "You are *extremely* tall."

"That's how my mom and dad made me," I tease.

"And you smell really good." She reluctantly pulls away, tilting her head back so her gaze meets mine. I haven't released my hold on her waist, and her skin is so warm. Everything about her is inviting. As in, she's giving me really positive vibes. "Want to get a drink?"

I raise my brows. "How many have you had?"

She shrugs, and the sleeve of her dress threatens to fall off. "A few."

Releasing my hold on her, I grab her sleeve and push it back into place, my fingers tingling from where they made contact with her smooth skin. "You're not drunk, are you?"

"Noooo. Maybe a little buzzed, but I'm not sloppy drunk." She takes my hand and starts leading me out of the massive lobby. "Let's go find a bar."

I follow after her, letting her take me. I see more than a few people do a doubletake as I pass by them, and I silently send up a prayer that no one will recognize me or approach us.

I'll have some explaining to do if that happens, and I don't want that. Not yet.

Not tonight.

The corridor Eleanor is taking me down is wide, with lots of shops and restaurants. The shops are closed, though the restaurants are still open and full of people. She comes to a stop in front of a bar, a pink neon sign above it saying *Wild* in cursive.

She turns to smile up at me. "Is this okay? Maybe we can find a table inside and talk."

"Sounds good to me," I say easily.

We somehow find a small table tucked into the far side of the bar, where it's so dark I can barely see her. The only light we have is from a votive candle in the center of the tiny, round table we're sitting at. My knees knock against hers as we settle in and she laughs, resting her hand briefly on my thigh.

Her touch goes straight to my dick—no surprise.

"You're too big for the table," she says with a little laugh.

I'd like to show her how I'm too big, but I don't want to push too hard, too fast. But damn. Just being near her is making my body light up like a Christmas tree. I stare at her lips. They're still that peachy color I remember from our FaceTime call, only they're shinier. Like she's got some gloss on.

I want to lick it off her.

Taking a deep breath, I shove all dirty thoughts to the darkest corner of my mind and try to focus on what she's saying.

"...and the dinner was *so* delicious. I can't even believe the man my friend is marrying owns this hotel," she says, waving her hand around.

"Wait a minute," I say, and she stops talking, her wide-eyed gaze meeting mine. "Your friend is marrying the dude who owns this *entire* hotel?"

"Yes! Isn't it crazy? Well, his family owns the hotel

chain, not just him. His name is Alex Wilder, and he's going to take over the entire corporation someday. He's like the vice president or something." She glances around the bar, her face full of wonder before her gaze returns to mine. "Can you imagine owning something as big as this? Multiple times over?"

"No, I can't." I think of the owners of NFL franchises. What's that like, being able to own an actual sports team? That's some mad money right there.

"Sometimes I wonder what it's like to be filthy rich." There's so much longing in her voice, I can't help but lean toward her, wanting to hear more. "I'm not complaining. I do well for myself. I make decent money being a hairstylist. But I will never know what it's like to be a millionaire."

I do. I know what that's like. I'm a millionaire many times over. I'm not the highest paid linebacker in the NFL, but I've been at it for a while, and while I know I'm looking at my career ending here in the next season or two, I am set up very comfortably, thanks to the giant contract I signed after my first season with the Raiders.

I'm a lucky bastard and I know it.

"Money isn't everything," I tell her, and it's easy for me to say that. I have more than I could ever spend in my lifetime. Well, I could run right through it if I was a complete idiot who bought expensive cars and giant mansions for my friends and family. But I haven't done that. I don't plan on doing it either.

I paid of my parents' mortgage, but that's really it. Oh, and everyone in my family makes out pretty nicely for their birthdays and at Christmas.

"True, but it would be nice to never have to worry about it, you know?" She smiles at me and I stare at her in return, dumbfounded by her beauty. "I bet you meet a lot of guys like that, what with your job."

My job? Wait a minute...

Oh right. I'm a trainer.

"Yeah," I say, glancing around the room, wishing for a cocktail waitress to appear. I need a drink. Desperately. "We don't really discuss money when we're together though."

"Of course not! You're too busy working on their fitness." She smiles and reaches for me, settling her warm hand on my arm. "Wow. Your bicep is, like, rock hard."

She presses her fingers into my skin, essentially feeling me up. If she keeps touching me like that, there will be something else that's rock hard too.

I really, really need to get my sexual appetite under control. Nothing like that is gonna happen tonight. In my dreams will we get naked and get busy.

"I work out a lot," I tell her, trying to think of other things. Like my grandma. Like math. Or cauliflower—I hate that shit. Or our defensive coach, who's an ugly son of a bitch and yells a lot for no good reason.

Anything to get my mind out of the gutter.

"I bet you do," she murmurs. She's petting me now. Her fingers are trailing down my arm, touching my bare skin, and a jolt runs through me, making me achingly aware of her closeness. "Like every day, huh?"

"Especially during—" I clamp my lips shut.

I was going to say during football season.

"Hello! Can I get you two something to drink?"

Eleanor drops her hand from my arm, and I immediately miss her touch. We both turn to find a tall, thin brunette standing in front of our table, a friendly smile on her face. Our server is a knockout. She's wearing a lot of makeup, though. And the top she's wearing is so low-cut, her tits are ready to spill out. I discreetly check her out, but don't feel anything.

I glance over at Eleanor, and feel...

Everything.

Damn, I am in big, *big* trouble with this girl.

"Ooh, hold on. Let me look at your drink specials." Eleanor grabs the tiny menu propped on our table and starts scanning it, squinting so much, she moves the menu closer to the candle so she can see. "Do you know what you want, Mitch?"

Realization dawns in the server's eyes and she points at me. "Aren't you..."

I shake my head once, my expression like stone as I meet her gaze. I'm doing my best to communicate with just my eyes, and I have no idea if it's working. Thankfully, Eleanor is still looking over the menu and doesn't notice. "I'll take whatever beer you've got on tap."

The server frowns. "Do you have a preference?"

"Surprise me," I say nonchalantly.

"Okay." She sends me a look that says *whatever, weirdo* before turning her attention to Eleanor. "What about you, hon?"

"I'll have the blue hawaiian." She smiles up at the server before she turns her attention to me. "I love blue alcoholic drinks. They're always so delicious."

"I'm not one for frilly blue drinks," I tell her.

"Most guys aren't." She smiles. "They're not macho enough."

"Are you calling me macho?"

"You're very, very manly," she says with the utmost sincerity.

Damn, this girl is cute. "And you're very, very...girly."

She raises her brows. "Is that a compliment?"

"Of course," I practically scoff.

Eleanor laughs. "I'm teasing you. Isn't it a little surreal, that we're sitting here together? Only a few days ago we FaceTimed."

"If we lived in the same city, we'd have already met," I point out.

"You think so?"

"Oh, I know so." It's my turn to touch her, and I do, settling my big hand over hers. I skim my thumb over her knuckles, my gaze never leaving hers. "I'm glad your friend is having her bachelorette party this weekend."

"Me too," she breathes, her expression borderline dazed, like I'm putting her under a trance.

I can relate.

The server makes her appearance, depositing a giant mug of beer in front of me and a tall glass of electric blue liquid in front of Eleanor. "Anything else, guys?"

"We're good," I tell the server with a tight smile.

"Oooh, this looks delicious." Eleanor scoots the drink closer to her and dips her head, wrapping her plump lips around the straw. My imagination runs fucking wild, thinking of all the things she could do with those lips wrapped around a particular body part of mine.

As discreetly as possible, I readjust my junk, praying I don't sport a boner for the rest of the evening in this bar.

"It's so good," she says once she's had a few swallows. I check the glass to find a quarter of it already gone.

"Great." I clear my throat and take a sip of my beer. "Mine's good too."

"I've never been a big beer drinker." She wrinkles her nose. "I prefer vodka."

I laugh. "I'm not a picky drinker. Well, I used to drink

just about anything I got my hands on, especially when I was in college."

"Where did you go to college again?" she asks before she takes another sip.

"Texas A & M." I hesitate for a moment before I decide to tell her the truth. "I played football there."

"Really? What position?"

"Defensive lineman." Another hesitation. "I got a football scholarship when I was in high school."

"Wow, that's amazing. You must've been really good," she says.

"I was all right," I say with a casual shrug.

I was amazing. I broke all the high school records in my position. We went to state three times out of four during my high school career. We won two, including during my senior year. That's what got me the scholarship. Helped that my parents rode my ass about school and I got decent grades. I wanted to make something of myself, and my parents encouraged me every step of the way.

"I can only imagine you out on the field, mowing everyone down." She starts to laugh. "I'm sure you were really intimidating."

I have a bit of a reputation out on the field. I growl. I curse. I come for them with an intensity that scares the shit out of some players on opposing teams. I want them scared. It means I'm doing my job.

We talk some more about football. About her job and how much she loves it. About Las Vegas and how she hasn't been here in a while. About her friends, and when the wedding is. She gets a little melancholy, and I don't know if it's because of the alcohol—she stuck to only one drink, but it's a big one—or the fact that her friend is getting married.

Women get weird sometimes when their friends get

married and they're still single. I remember my sister acting this way. But now she's hitched with a toddler and another one on the way, soooo...

Eleanor starts raving about the suite they're staying in, and of course, I'm intrigued.

"It's so freaking amazing," she says, her glass empty by now, the ice cubes still faintly coated with bright blue. "The suite is two stories, can you believe it? It's like a freaking house! It has four bedrooms—or was it five?" She frowns, counting all the rooms on her fingers.

"Two stories, huh? Sounds impressive." I've never stayed at a fancy suite in a Las Vegas hotel. What's the point? You're rarely in the room anyway, and even if you are, it's used for only a few things.

Two of them being sleeping and fucking.

"It is *so* impressive," she says with a vigorous nod. "Plus there's this giant pool table. And the view is like...oh my God." She rests her hand against her chest, her gaze meeting mine. "You want to see it?"

Well damn. I didn't expect that invitation tonight. "Yeah. Sure." I keep my voice cool. Nonchalant. Like no big deal.

But deep down inside, excitement fills me. Hopefully none of her friends are currently in the suite. It'll just be me and Eleanor.

Alone.

ELEVEN
ELEANOR

WE RIDE up in the elevator standing next to each other in silence. There's soft music playing from invisible speakers and the walls are mirrored. Even the ceiling. All I can see is myself and Mitch, and I stare unabashedly at his face, which is currently averted, his gaze aimed downward.

It's a good face. Strong boned. Sharp cheekbones. A few scars here and there, and I can only assume they're from past football injuries. Granite-hard jaw and chin counterbalanced by that sensuous mouth. Light brown hair that's a little shaggy. Golden-brown eyes that are friendly and always sparkling when he watches me

And he watches me a lot. As if he likes what he sees. As if he finds me amusing. And not in a bad way. In a good way.

I feel beautiful under his steady gaze. Interesting. Not awkward at all, and I've been awkward AF tonight with Mitch, as per usual. I shouldn't have had those drinks at dinner. And I definitely didn't need that blue hawaiian at the bar. Whatever they put in there, it sure packed a punch.

Feeling a little woozy, I curl my arm around Mitch's to

anchor myself, smiling up at him when he glances down at me. Did I mention how tall he is? I'm no shrimp, but he *towers* over me. He makes me feel small and delicate, when I am so not. I'm a sturdy girl. I always have been, and when I blossomed at the age of eleven, there was no stopping it. I had the biggest boobs in the sixth grade. Probably straight through middle school, which I hated at the time. I was so self-conscious.

Eventually, I embraced myself. I have hips and thighs and boobs. There is no mistaking that I'm a woman.

Standing next to Mitch makes me feel like a delicate little flower.

We finally come to a stop at the top floor, and when the doors slide open, we exit the elevator together, our arms still entwined. I lead him to the penthouse suite's massive double doors, coming to a stop so I can dig the keycard out of my tiny bar-hopping purse. My mom gave it to me a few years ago for Christmas, specifically calling it a bar-hopping purse, and at first, I'd been offended. Like what, she thought I was going out to bars and drinking too much every weekend?

Within a couple of uses, I appreciated the purse. It's black and tiny and goes with everything. It's big enough for my phone, a few bucks and my ID and credit card, plus a lipstick. Oh, and when needed, a keycard.

I take said keycard and wave it in front of the super-fancy technological lockscreen, and hear the lock spring open. With a flourish I throw open both doors, smiling over my shoulder at Mitch. "Here we go!"

We enter the giant suite, our footsteps echoing against the marble floor. It's empty, I can tell, and I'm relieved. I don't want to deal with my friends.

Not yet.

I can feel the cool breeze from the air conditioning blowing throughout the room, and I shiver. The curtains are pulled back—why, I don't know—revealing the massive floor-to-ceiling windows and the glittering city stretched out before us.

"What a view," Mitch says as he approaches the window, stopping right in the center and resting his hands on his hips as he stares out at the cityscape. "Impressive."

"Isn't it beautiful?" I walk over to where he's standing, stopping right next to him.

He glances over at me, appreciation warming his eyes. "Yeah. Sure is."

Oh. I think he might be talking about me.

This guy. I've been feeling nervous all night. Expectant. Hyperaware of everything about him. His scent. His presence. His warmth. His size. I wonder what he tastes like. I wonder what he looks like naked. I wonder what sounds he makes when he's having sex. I wonder about his dick size.

Yes. I just totally went there. I bet he's big. Look at him!

Pushing my sex on the brain thoughts, I take him for a short tour around the suite, though I keep it strictly downstairs. Checking out bedrooms might lead to other things, and I don't want him to think I'm that type of girl on the first date. Even though I'm dying to be that type of girl right now.

Yep. Dying to.

We end up in the kitchen, and he grabs a bottle of cold water out of the fridge. I do the same. We admire the artwork on the walls and I eye the couch, wondering if we should settle in. Naughty things could happen there too, and I'm tempted to make the suggestion. My friends aren't here yet. We could indulge in a naughty thing or two.

Kissing. That's all I'm thinking of. Kissing and

wandering hands. Maybe hands could slip beneath clothes. Maybe long, thick fingers could slip beneath my panties too...

Focus! No sex! Not yet!

I hate the nagging voice in my head. Really I do.

We find ourselves standing in front of the pool table, and I watch dazedly as Mitch runs his big hand across the vibrant purple felt that covers the table, almost as if he's caressing it.

I wonder what it would feel like, to have his big hands caressing me.

"You play pool?" he asks, his deep, rumbling voice washing over me.

"Never."

"I haven't played since college." He shrugs. "Don't have enough time anymore."

"It looks boring," I admit. "Though this table is pretty."

"Looks pretty sturdy." Mitch reaches out and grips the edge of the sleek wooden edge of the table.

He could be talking to me. Like I thought earlier, I'm a sturdy girl.

"Think it could handle our weight?" I ask.

His head jerks in my direction, his eyes wide as he stares at me for a few seconds too long. As if he's trying to figure me out. "What do you mean?" he asks slowly.

"I mean, if we were both to crawl on top of that table, could it handle our weight?" I wave a hand at it, surprised by what I'm suggesting.

But yep. I'm not backing down. I put it out there. Let's see what he does with it.

He considers me for a moment, his hand going to his jaw and giving it a slow stroke. I wish I could touch him like that.

"Let's try it out and see." Without warning, he reaches for me and hauls me into his arms. A shriek escapes me when I'm lifted into the air, and I clasp the back of his neck, holding onto him for dear life, afraid he might drop me.

Men don't just haul me around. This sort of thing doesn't happen to me.

But no. I'm going nowhere. This man has a firm grip on me, and he settles my butt onto the edge of the pool table, though he's still standing directly in front of me. And I've got my arms wrapped around his neck. Our chests are nestled close. My legs are spread, the skirt of my dress hiking up my thighs and he's standing right in between them.

We are very, very close. And I just know...

Very, very naughty things are about to happen.

"Are you drunk?" he asks, his gaze meeting mine.

I stare up at him and slowly shake my head. "Maybe just a little."

"I usually don't take advantage of drunk women," he murmurs, his head dipping closer.

I plunge my fingers into his silky soft hair, urging him closer. "I don't take advantage of drunk men either."

He chuckles, and the sound vibrates smack between my legs. "I am far from drunk, Eleanor."

I like hearing his rough, deep voice say my name. I like everything about this man.

"I'm not that drunk," I say. "I know exactly what I'm doing."

He raises his brows. "Do you now?"

"Yeah, I do. You should join me on this table," I whisper.

This low growling noise sounds from deep in his chest and then his mouth is on mine, stealing my breath. The kiss starts out simple. Just a press of lips on lips. But I tug on his hair and shift my body closer to his, and he opens his mouth. Parts my lips with his tongue.

And then somehow, we're devouring each other.

Thank God no one is here to see us, because I am making an absolute fool of myself for this man. I just want more. More kissing. More tongue. More big hands. More growling. I like the growling. It's actually really sexy.

Who knew?

I'm pulling him with me, our mouths connected, my hands in his hair, tugging him down with me. His arms are around my waist, I can tell when his body hits the edge of the pool table, and then the next thing I know, I'm sprawled on top of the table and he's on top of me.

On top of the table.

I start to laugh. I can't help it.

Mitch silences me with his lips, and all my laughter is forgotten.

At some point after some lengthy kissing, he rises up on his knees, staring down at me. There was only a couple of lamps lit within the living room, so it's fairly dim in here, and the lights from the city outside catch in his hair, his eyes, making them glow. "What were you laughing at earlier?"

"Oh. Well, we're both on this table," I say, reaching for him, my fingers going for his tucked-in, button-down shirt. I start pulling it out of his jeans, desperate to touch actual skin. "And we haven't broke it."

"It's high quality," he says, batting my hands away so he can undo the buttons on his shirt himself.

I watch in breathless anticipation as he undoes every single button before the fabric parts. And holy fucking moly, what he reveals is just like, say whaaaat?

Is he even real?

Like, I feel inferior when I see all the muscle there. The shoulders and the pecs and the washboard abs and the flat stomach, and *oh!* That trail of golden brown hair leading from just below his navel and disappearing into his pants. I want to see where that path leads. I want to follow down the yellow brick road with my tongue.

I start to giggle. It's obvious I am still a little drunk.

"I'm going to develop a complex," he says.

"I giggle when I'm nervous. Remember how I told you I get super awkward around guys?" When he nods, I point at my chest with my thumb. "This is me. Being awkward. Laughing while you're trying to kiss me."

"Let's see if you'll still be laughing after I'm through with you," he says, like I dared him.

I watch in breathless anticipation as he leans over me, his mouth hovering above mine, our gazes locked. I've gone completely still, the giggling is long gone, and I wait for him to kiss me.

I'm dying for him to kiss me.

At the last second, he swerves, his mouth landing on my throat. His lips are hot. Damp. Feather soft. I go completely limp beneath him, my lids fluttering closed as he blazes a trail down my neck. Along my exposed collarbone. Across the tops of my breasts.

Thank God, I wore this dress with its low-cut, square neckline. Such a good choice for tonight.

"You're not laughing now," he murmurs against my skin, making me shiver. "You want me to stop?"

"God no," I say immediately, making him laugh instead.

"Your skin is so soft," he says just as he rests his hand beneath my right breast, giving it the gentlest squeeze. "I shouldn't do this."

"Oh yes," I tell him fiercely. "You should."

"Your friends could walk into the suite at any minute," he reminds me.

"I sort of don't care." Oh my God, I really don't. I mean, here I am on top of a pool table in the middle of the suite we're sharing, with a man I barely know, and I swear to God, I just want him to...

Do me on this table. They happen to walk in during the middle of it? I might ask him to stop.

Or I might not.

Mitch tugs on the front of my dress, sending the neckline lower, and my breasts pop out even more. "You got a bra on under here?"

I shake my head, my hair spread out across the bright purple felt. I must look a sight. "The bodice was too tight, so it kept the girls pretty much contained." I probably shouldn't have said that. "Didn't think I needed one."

And trust me, folks, that never happens.

"I guess it's my lucky night." His hand shifts upward, pushing my right breast up, his fingers curling beneath the abundant flesh. My boobs are my favorite feature, yet they are also the bane of my existence. They're just so big. Sometimes, I think they're too big.

I watch as his fingers work the neckline of my dress and my breast all at once, his gaze determined, his ministrations patient. He has good hands. They're large, with long fingers, and I can't wait to feel them all over my naked body.

Yep, I'm rushing right to the good stuff in my mind, when I should slow down. I need to focus on the here and now.

All that hard work eventually pays off. My nipple pops out just above the fabric. It's already hard, and when his warm breath wafts across my skin, it tightens. Aches. I twist and turn, like I'm about to come out of my skin. I place my hands on the back of his head when he dips down and wraps his lips around my nipple.

I buck beneath him, a whimper sounding low in my throat. His lips pull and suck, his tongue lashing out, and I swear to God, if he keeps this up, I could probably come. Just from him sucking on my nipple.

Oh, this man is talented.

"You want to take this to your bedroom?" he asks at one point, his lips moving against my sensitive flesh and making me squirm.

I shake my head, my gaze meeting his. "I want to stay right here."

Does he realize how much this is turning me on, being on this pool table, knowing my friends could possibly show up at any moment?

Who knew I could feel this way? Certainly not me.

With purposeful intent, his eyes never leaving mine, he reaches beneath my skirt, his fingers trailing the inside of my thighs, stopping right in between my legs, his knuckles brushing against the front of my panties. My lips part, but no sound comes out.

No breath either.

I'm frozen. Waiting. I can feel the muscles in my thighs trembling, and I tilt my head down, my gaze zeroing in on his thick forearm, his wrist and hand hidden because they're underneath my skirt. He's watching me, I can feel his hot gaze on my face, but I want to see what he does next.

With infinite slowness, he traces the edge of my lacy underwear with a single finger.

"Oh God." The words come out choked. Barely formed.

I immediately want more.

He hesitates. I see it in his eyes. In the way he moves.

Carefully, he removes his hand from under my skirt and rises back onto his knees, hovering above me. Watching me. My heart is beating so wildly, I'm afraid it might break free and leap out of my chest.

"You sure you want this?" He squints at me. Licks his lips. Runs his fingers through his hair. Oh, he appears conflicted. Like he wants to jump me yet run far, far away from me, all at once.

"Do *you* want this?" I ask as I bend my legs at the knee and plant my feet onto the table. My skirt is still bunched around my thighs, he can't see my panties, but I don't think I should worry about that.

He was, after all, just touching them.

"Fuck yes," he says raggedly, rubbing at the back of his neck. "But we just met. You're a good girl. I can tell. You're sweet and you're funny, and you think you're awkward, but you're not. You're sexy as fuck. But we're in your friend's suite, and we're on top of a goddamn pool table, and that's just kind of..."

"Bad?" I ask, my eyebrows raised.

"Raunchy," he corrects.

There's a word I don't hear much. I can confirm with the utmost sincerity that I have never really done a raunchy thing in my life.

Well, I think I'm about to change that.

"What do you want to do to me, Mitch?" I ask, my voice pitched low. Downright sultry.

His expression darkens. "Make you come," he answers without hesitation.

"How?" I reach for the hem of my skirt and gather as much fabric as I can in my hand, pulling it up. I lift my butt a little, and now my skirt is around my waist. He can take a nice, long look at my lacy, cream-colored thong.

His eyes appear ready to bug out of his head as he stares at my lower extremities. "With my fingers." His gaze shifts to mine briefly before they return to the spot between my legs. "Or my mouth."

Um, my panties are now officially soaked. "Then do it." I don't know where this comes from, but I slide my hand down, across the front of my panties. "With your fingers." I cup myself, and oh *wow,* that feels good. "And your mouth."

There is no hesitation from him whatsoever. Mitch gets right down to business, resting his big hands on the inside of my thighs for a moment, assessing me with his hooded gaze. I want to squirm. Beg. Where is this coming from? It has to be the blue hawaiian drink. Maybe it was full of some sort of magic sex serum.

Or is it just the explosive chemistry between me and this man? I can feel it now, crackling and popping between us. His hands on my skin feel like heaven. The way he's looking at me, as if he wants to devour me whole, is making everything inside my body feel loose and warm.

"I can smell you," he whispers harshly just before he dives in and presses a kiss on the inside of my knee. "I bet your panties are wet." He kisses my left thigh. "I bet I'd barely have to touch you and you'd come." He kisses my right thigh, his face dangerously close to where I want him.

"Touch me and find out," I whisper just before I become momentarily stunned by my blatant invitation.

I have never said anything like that before in my life.

He goes completely still and glances up, toward the doorway. My heart stops. Is someone here? Is the door opening?

Oh God, are all of my friends about to barge in here and catch us?

But no. The door doesn't open. No one else appears. It's just me. And him.

On the pool table.

"I might need to be quick," he says as he returns to his task. "Before your friends show up."

"It, um, takes me a while usually." When he frowns in confusion, I explain. "To...you know."

Well, that really isn't an explanation.

"To 'you know' what?" He leans in and presses his mouth just above the waistband of my underwear, on my lower belly. A jolt slams through me at first contact, and I press my lips together so I don't scream.

I am not a screamer, people. Not at all.

"Orgasm. Climax. Whatever you want to call it." The awkward, embarrassed Eleanor I know comes back out with those words, and I drape my arm over my eyes so I don't have to look at him.

He shifts his position, and the next thing I know, he's removing my arm from my face, his warm gaze meeting mine. "Challenge accepted."

Now I'm the one frowning. "What?"

"Game fucking on, Eleanor. I bet I can make you come in less than five minutes."

"Oh, that's never happened to me before in my li—"

He cuts off my protest with his lips, kissing me senseless. His hungry mouth consumes mine, his tongue doing this sensual stroke thing that immediately makes me want to lose my mind. I wrap my arms around him, holding him close, drowning in his taste, and somehow, his hand ends up back on my panties again, settling directly between my thighs. He presses his palm against me with just enough pressure that I gasp into his mouth.

"Like that?" he asks, his voice brimming with confidence.

I don't bother answering. He knows I like it.

Mitch continues kissing me. Touching me. For at least thirty seconds he keeps it fairly clean. Hand over the panties, not under them. Mouth firmly glued to mine. I am a squirming, uncontrollable mess, but somehow he calms me. Captivates me.

Lulls me into this sex-induced trance.

He slips his fingers beneath my panties, holding them there for an excruciatingly long moment, cupping me. My lips go still and my body becomes tense. All I can concentrate on is his fingers right there. Touching me.

I hardly know him. We only just met in person tonight. Yet here I am letting him finger me on top of a pool table.

Who am I?

"So wet," he murmurs against my lips as he starts to stroke. And he's not wrong. I am so wet, I can hear his fingers move through my slick folds.

I strain toward his fingers, a hiss escaping when he slips one inside me. Then another. His movements are restricted thanks to my panties, and with impatience he tugs them down. Past my hips, leaving them winding around my thighs when he resumes touching me.

I'm held prisoner by my thong. I can't spread my legs wide enough, and he's working magic between my thighs, stroking me deep, his mouth still on mine. I pull away from him, a frustrated noise escaping me as I reach for my panties and try to take them off.

He gets the hint quickly and helps me, tossing them over his shoulder as if he doesn't have a care in the world. For some reason, this gesture cracks me up, and I start laughing.

Hysterically.

Mitch grins, scooting away from me, repositioning his large body. I don't know how we're making this work, but we are. And the next thing I know, he's lodged his face in front of my spread legs, his gaze on mine as he settles his mouth right on my pink parts.

Oh. I arch my back, head tilting, eyes closing. He licks and sucks, teases and torments. I remember what he said, how he could make me come in less than five minutes, and I know without a doubt that if he keeps this up…

He's right.

But I don't want it to end in less than five minutes. His talented mouth is sending me straight into bliss. My legs are shaking. My belly is clenching. My clit is throbbing and I squeeze my eyes shut, my breaths becoming shorter. Shorter. Shorter…

God, he spreads my folds open and feasts on my clit with lips and tongue and teeth. I am shamelessly rubbing myself against his face, needing the friction, desperate for blessed release. I am right there. Hovering on the precipice, dangling on the edge, a keening cry starting in the back of my throat right before it all comes crashing down.

And then I'm coming. I'm shouting. Screaming. Panting like an animal, my entire body pulsating from my orgasm. He lets me ride it out, his mouth gentling, though it's still there, and I'm still thrusting against his face like I have no control over myself.

My entire body is quaking when he pulls away, his fingers sliding over my thighs as if he's trying to calm me down. But that doesn't work. His touch feels so good. Too good. And just like that, I want him again.

"That was some show you put on for me," he says, his voice this sexy drawl as he wipes at his lower face. Wiping away all my juices because you know, I was grinding my vagina against his chin only moments ago.

"You won," I say, my voice raspy. I think I hurt my throat when I shouted. "You did it. You made me come in less than five minutes."

"Worth every second too. I wouldn't figure you for a screamer." He hops off the pool table, making it look easy. For such a large man, he's good on his feet. Must be the athlete in him.

"You're right. I'm not normally a screamer," I tell him, sitting up a little too quickly. My head spins, and I sit there for a moment, running my hand over my hair, trying to gather my bearings.

"You okay?" He reaches for my hand, intertwining my fingers with his own. It's a romantic gesture, and I'm touched. I'm also reeling from the orgasm he just gave me, so the combination is heady stuff.

"I'm great," I murmur, and that is one hundred percent the truth. "Can you help me off the table?"

Like a complete gentleman, he assists me off the pool table, tugging my skirt down along the way. I realize I still have my shoes on and I start giggling, unable to help myself, and he sends me a look.

"You're going to give a man a complex with how you're always laughing during sex," he says, though I can tell by the gleam in his warm brown eyes that he's teasing me.

"Trust me, I'm not laughing at you." I wave a hand around the giant, beautiful suite. "This entire moment is surreal."

"Yeah." He pulls me in close and kisses me. I can taste myself on his lips, and I'm not squicked out. Not at all. In fact, I'd like to take this to my bedroom. "I enjoyed every second of it, though."

I sneak my hands beneath his still-open shirt and rest them on his hot, bare skin. Oh man, he's got muscles for days. My mouth is literally watering at the thought of me exploring every single inch of his bare body with my lips and tongue. "I did too," I confess.

Should I invite him to stay? I should. Nope, no second-guessing myself, I'm just doing it.

"Want to stay the night?"

He lifts a brow. "You sure?"

I nod. Remain quiet. Ever so hopeful.

"Show me your room," he says before he leans in for a soft kiss.

We start to head for the stairwell when he pulls away from me, running back over to the pool table. He bends down and swipes something off the ground, and I wait for him at the base of the stairs, curious. As he approaches, I see his fingers are curled into a fist, and when he's standing right next to me, he opens his hand, showing me my crumpled up thong.

"Wouldn't want to leave this evidence behind," he says, his smile full of mischief. "Your friends would have you all figured out."

That would've been so embarrassing. "Thank you for remembering." I hold out my hand. "I can take them."

"I want to keep them." He shoves my panties into the front pocket of his jeans. "Thanks."

What a perv, I think as we head up the stairs, me leading the way. He slaps my butt, making it sting, making me tingle, and I glance at him from over my shoulder, that dark smile on his face doing things to me.

Maybe I'm a perv too.

TWELVE
MITCH

I WAKE up completely disoriented and to the sound of muffled conversation happening outside of this room. A room. I'm in a bed.

Is it my bedroom?

Cracking an eye open, I realize I can't see shit because it's so dark thanks to those heavy-duty shades on the window. I immediately close it again, thinking. Remembering.

Definitely not my room. I'm not at my apartment. I'm with Eleanor the sex goddess in her friend's fancy hotel suite after I spent the night. Something I normally don't do. Oh, I've always been about one-night stands, but I never sleep in the chick's bed all night long. Hell no.

No way.

But here I am, in one of the most comfortable beds I've ever slept in, a blonde, naked cutie snuggled up right next to me, her ass smack against my stirring dick, my arm draped around her waist as if I'm desperate to keep her close.

I don't sleep snuggled up close to women either. I need my space. I'm a big dude. I don't like feeling restricted in bed. I sprawl across my California king every night just because I can.

More conversation is happening and I figure it's coming from downstairs. Those women—Eleanor's friends—are kind of noisy. I have no clue what time it is, but I'm sure it's too early for them to make this much racket. It's a Saturday morning in Las Vegas, for God's sake. Have a little consideration.

As I lie in bed and drift off back to sleep, memories hit me, all of them outstanding. Me eating Eleanor out on the pool table until she came with a shout, her fingers in my hair, tugging on it a little too hard. That was one for the books.

Us going upstairs to her bedroom. We got naked. She demanded I sit on the edge of the mattress, and next thing I knew, she was on her knees in front of me, giving me the best blow job I've had since I don't know when. She was all about the visual too. Putting on a real show for me. Plenty of eye contact, and at one point pouty, peachy lips pursed at the tip of my erection. Licking my shaft like a Popsicle with her pretty pink tongue. At one point, she nestled my cock in between her abundant breasts, rubbing it up and down, and holy shit, I about shot off like a rocket.

But I restrained myself. I let her work me over, I let her have her fun. Right before I got down to business and gathered her hair in my fist, fucking her mouth with my cock until I was the one coming with a shout.

It was hot as fuck. She took it like a champ. She was laughing yet again when we were done, and then we both crawled into bed and collapsed into exhausted sleep, wrapped all around each other.

So no penetration yet. Just all the other fun stuff first.

Maybe that's the key. Leave them hanging.

Leave me wanting more.

I drift in and out of sleep for I don't know how long, only to be completely awoken by my pretty blonde bundle of fun rubbing her ass cheeks against my growing cock. I don't know how long I slept again, but the loud conversation downstairs is gone. It's blissfully quiet, save for the little puffs of breath I hear coming from Eleanor as she wiggles her ass on my junk.

"God, you are so big," she whispers.

I rest a hand on her hip, and she goes still. "You weren't complaining last night."

"Neither were you," she tosses back.

True.

Unable to resist her soft, supple skin, I start to stroke. Along her hip. Her waist. Back down, my fingers teasing the outer edge of her thigh. She starts squirming like she does, her cheeks jiggling against my dick, and it would be so easy for me to slip inside her. Fill her up. Pump deep and make us both come.

"You keep that up and I'll start fucking you right here, right now," I whisper close to her ear just before I bite it.

Another shiver moves through her. "Maybe we should wait."

I go still. So does she. Is she having second thoughts? Is the morning light helping her realize that maybe this wasn't such a good idea after all?

What am I thinking? There's no morning light. It's still pretty damn dark in here.

"I mean, we barely know each other," she continues, and I can hear it. All the worry in her sweet voice.

"We know each other a lot better than we did before last night," I tell her, nuzzling the back of her neck with my nose. I curl my arm around her front, resting my hand on her breast. Her nipple is hard and I tease the little nub with my fingers, making her gasp. Making her bite back a moan. "But I get it. Let's take it slow."

There she goes, laughing again. "Right. Take it slow."

"Is that what you want?"

"Anticipation is a delicious thing," she answers.

"You are a delicious thing." I deliver a smacking kiss on her neck before I reluctantly roll away from her and climb out of bed. "I'll be right back."

I saunter into the connected bathroom, hoping she can see well enough in the dark to take a gander at my naked self. My cock is waving at half-staff and when I handle my business, it's a struggle. Peeing with a hard-on is not comfortable.

I flush the toilet and wash my hands. Take a good, long look at myself in the mirror. My hair is a mess and my face is covered in scruff. I wouldn't mind brushing my teeth, and when I spot the travel-sized tube of Crest sitting on the counter, I go for it. I put a dollop on my index finger and work it around my teeth, running the water over my finger and swishing around in my mouth before I spit it all out. I grab a clean glass and rinse my mouth, then shut off the water.

There. Fresh as a motherfuckin' daisy.

Exiting the bathroom, I come to a stop when I find Eleanor sitting up in bed, the bedside table lamp on and offering me a view of her spectacular breasts. The sheet is bunched around her waist, and damn if she doesn't look like a goddess. She's on her phone, her brows scrunched together and her lips pursed.

She is really so freaking pretty, even with the smudges of last night's mascara beneath her eyes.

"You wouldn't believe the messages my friends have

been sending me." She keeps her gaze glued to the phone as she starts typing. "They say you're my booty call."

I shrug before resting my hands on my hips. "If the shoe fits."

"I'm glad you're so easygoing about this. I'm never going to hear the end of it from them," she says, sinking her teeth into her lower lip as she keeps typing. I hear all the swooshing noises as the texts are sent and received, and I know she's having a full-on conversation with her friends. And I also know that her friends are the true reason why she's here this weekend but...

Come on. Pay attention to me right now. Your friends can wait.

"And it's so late! It's almost noon." She glances up, doing a doubletake when she realizes I'm standing before her completely naked. Her gaze drops to my crotch, and my erection grows right in front of her.

He's always been a sucker for attention.

"You want to go grab some lunch?" she asks weakly, her gaze still zeroed in on my johnson.

"Yeah, I'm down," I tell her as I start to approach the bed.

Her eyes go wide before they lift back up to mine. "I want you to know, what happened last night wasn't normal."

"What do you mean?"

"That BJ I gave you. I was really..."

"Fucking great?" I suggest.

Her cheeks turn pink. "Over the top."

I go to the other side of the bed and crawl onto the mattress, stopping right next to her. "I liked it."

"I'm sure you did." She's still blushing. In fact, she's keeping her face averted.

"Did you like it?" I ask her.

With her back angled toward me, she nods.

I crawl even closer, my face hovering just above her right shoulder, my mouth at her ear. "I wouldn't mind a repeat performance. Later."

She hesitates before saying, "It was—raunchy, how I acted."

"I like you raunchy."

She turns to look at me, her eyes big and full of concern. "Really? I mean, I was sort of a tramp last night. Do people still say that word? Well, I was. I let you go down on me on the pool table, Mitch." More blushing. This girl is going to turn as red as a tomato if she keeps it up. "And then I licked your dick like it was my favorite dessert."

"Pretty hot evening, if you ask me." I lean in and kiss her, and she rears back, surprise written all over her face.

"You taste like mint." She frowns. "Do you wake up like that?"

Why do I find this woman so amusing? "I brushed my teeth with my finger and the toothpaste I saw in there."

She immediately covers her mouth with her hand. "I'm sure my breath is awful."

"There is nothing awful about you." I pry her hand away from her face and kiss her lightly. "Don't give yourself a complex."

"I'm just..." She leans her forehead against mine and closes her eyes, inhaling slowly. "Not used to this sort of thing."

"Waking up with a stud?" I'm teasing, and she laughs, which is what I was aiming for.

"Definitely not used to that. But I'm also not used to meeting someone and letting loose so quickly with him."

She opens her eyes, her gaze locking onto mine. "You make me forget all about my inhibitions."

"Isn't that great? I fucking love it." I pull away from her and grab hold of her waist, my fingers tickling. She tries to get away from me, but there's no use. I am everywhere. "You never mentioned you were ticklish."

"You never asked." She bats my hands away, her giggling taking over, as per usual. "Stop."

I don't stop. It's fun, torturing her. Plus she's giving me a bird's-eye view of her jiggling tits, and every time those legs of hers move, I swear I catch a glimpse of her pussy.

This naked tickling thing is a stellar idea.

When she's finally giggled herself into exhaustion and I've looked my fill, I stop tickling her and start kissing her neck instead. I let my mouth wander all over her body, squeezing her breasts together before I suck one nipple into my mouth, then the other. I lick the underside of one perfectly plump tit, then draw a damp path along her trembling stomach, around her bellybutton.

"Are you really going to do this again?" she asks, her voice hopeful.

"Why? You don't want me to?" I pull away and the look of pure frustration on her pretty face is a sight to see.

"I want you to." She doesn't even hesitate. "Please."

Ah, that prim little *please* is what sets me over the edge.

I decide to make it extra dirty.

She offers up weak protests at first. If she said no, I'd stop, but she's not saying no. After a while, she starts encouraging me. I'm sticking fingers into spots I can just deal she normally doesn't deal with, but I sort of don't care. I want to make her come. Multiple times. I like how loud she is. And squirmy. The woman never stops moving. And once I start going down on her, she rubs that pretty pussy all over my mouth, shamelessly seeking her orgasm and not caring in the least what she looks or sounds like.

It's the hottest thing I've ever seen.

Once I've made her come twice and she's a trembling, incoherent mess, I guide her into the shower, then decide to join her. We soap each other up and she gives me a hand job with the slick body wash. It foams up pretty nicely, and it smells good too.

After she finishes me off and I've come all over her hand, I press her against the cool marble tile and finger her into yet another climax. When we're done, we towel each other off, my cock in a perpetual hardened state, and at one point, she drops the towel on top of it, laughing when it just hangs there.

I'm so glad I can entertain her.

After we get dressed—me in my clothes from last night, sans my boxer briefs—and she's slicking her wet hair into a bun on top of her head, we turn to face each other.

It feels like a moment of truth.

"I'd love to grab lunch with you, but afterwards, I have to go meet up with my friends." She winces, like she knows she's letting me down.

I realize quick she *is* letting me down. And I am let down. I am sad at the thought of her leaving.

"I totally understand," I reassure her, because I don't want to be a greedy boyfriend.

Wait a minute.

Boyfriend?

Scratch that.

"Good." She appears relieved. She is adorable. "Maybe we could see each other later tonight? After the bachelorette party?"

"Won't that probably go long into the evening?"

Though what do I know? I have zero experience when it comes to bachelorette parties.

"I'm sure at some point I can get away from them." There's a devious gleam in her eyes, and I like what I see. "You won't mind if I tell them about you, right?"

"Naw." I shake my head. Pull her into my arms and deliver a kiss to her shiny peach-colored lips. "You going to give them a play by play of last night and this morning?"

"I'll gloss over the finer points," she says, laughter filling her voice. "Now let go of me before we start doing something we might regret."

"I will never regret any of the things I want to do to you," I tell her with the utmost sincerity.

And I mean every word I say.

THIRTEEN
ELEANOR

MY ENTIRE BODY aches in the best possible way, especially between my thighs. My muscles protest as my friends and I walk all over the indoor shopping area that's connected to the Wilder Hotel, passing by all the designer stores.

Gucci. Louis Vuitton. Dior. Chanel. Burberry. They are all here, and they are all full of customers. Vegas has really got it figured out. If you're not gambling, you're spending big money at a show. Or at a top-rated restaurant.

Or at all of these designer shops.

Candice is dragging us into them, though most everyone is willing and eager to buy something. I'm just going along for the ride, watching my friends *ooh* and *aah* over purses and bags and wallets and sunglasses. On the flight over I considered the possibility that I might buy myself something "cheap" from one of these stores. Cheap being a minimum of four hundred dollars, which isn't cheap at all for my budget, but I wanted to splurge. Treat myself, you know?

Forget it. I don't need any of those treats. I got all sorts of treats last night and this morning, thanks to Mitch.

My entire body goes hot just from thinking about last night. And this morning. The shower. Lunchtime. The man has no shame. He is wicked. But there's something so endearingly sweet about him too. Like...he cares. About my pleasure, which is huge. What a bonus!

I've had decent sex in my life. I've also had awkward sex.

What do you expect? This is me we're talking about.

But anyway, I've never had sex with a man who's so concerned about my orgasm. It's not like he's asking questions or anything like that. He's just—always making sure I'm getting mine.

I like that. I like that a lot.

Good Lord, the man knows exactly what he's doing with his hands and mouth. And the things he says. Oh, and the size of his dick. Holy shit. It's huge. I still can't believe I had that thing in my mouth.

I wonder what it will feel like, to have actual sex with him.

"Eleanor, are you even listening to what we're saying?"

I blink myself back into consciousness to find every single one of my friends standing around me in a circle. We've ended up in the middle of the Vuitton store and Candice has a giant bag slung over her shoulder, the salesperson standing just behind her and looking anxious.

"What did you say?" I blink them into focus. I was seriously zoned out just now.

They all appear either slightly irritated with or worried about me. Candice turns her attention back to the salesperson, which was probably the right move. Sarah and Caroline wander off in search of who knows what, but I'm sure it's expensive. Only Kelsey and Stella remain with me.

"I know what's wrong with her," Stella says, her voice deadly serious as she crosses her arms.

"What is it?" Kelsey asks, her gaze skittering in my direction before she returns her attention to Stella.

"She's been dickmitized."

"What?" Kelsey practically shrieks, and I step in closer to them, shushing them both.

"I have not," I tell Stella, knowing exactly what she's talking about.

Dickmitized. Where does my friend come up with this stuff?

"What does she mean?" Kelsey asks, apparently clueless.

Maybe I understand Stella's latest terminology because I currently have dick on the brain? Who knows.

"This Mitch guy's big dick energy is sucking all the life out of her. It's all she can think about. Instead of hypnotized, Eleanor's been dickmitized," Stella explains.

"That is the most ridiculous thing I've ever heard," I grumble.

Ridiculous because she's on to something here.

Not that I'll tell her that.

"It was that good, huh," Kelsey says, sounding all down and out. "I am so jealous."

Glancing around the posh, elegant store, I realize I can't talk about Mitch and his dick and all the dirty things we did together in here. Someone might hear us.

And judge me.

Not that I care since I'll never see these people again, but come on. We can't talk about big dick energy in a Louis Vuitton store, right?

Instead, I hook my arms through my friends' and lead them out of the store so we can chat with a little more privacy.

After my lunch with Mitch, I texted the group chat, asking where they were, and I went in search of them in the shopping area of the hotel since that's what they told me. Since I joined them, I've kept pretty quiet, not talking much about what happened last night—and this morning. Oh, and at lunch, but they all saw the smug look on my face when I first showed up. They knew we had a good time.

Understatement of the year, but okay.

Once we're outside of the store, I launch into a quick story about what happened last night with Mitch. I don't mention the pool table, but I do let them know we did everything but have actual sex, and that it was really, *really* good.

I realize halfway through my story that *good* is not a good enough word. So instead I use the word...

"It was extraordinary."

Both women's eyebrows shoot straight up.

During lunch, he started to get this look in his eyes. Right there, in the middle of the restaurant. We were sitting close to each other, and he reached over, settling his large hand on my thigh. Shifting his hand beneath my skirt. Toying with the front of my panties before he slipped his long fingers beneath the thin fabric to find me soaking wet for him.

We ran off into the bathroom and locked the door, and I let him finger me into yet another orgasm right there against the sink.

When I finish my sink story, they're both staring at me with wide eyes.

"Carter and I have never experimented in public before," Stella says once she finds her tongue.

"I highly recommend it. Ten out of ten for me," I tell her, my voice serious.

"Everyone is having sex except me," Kelsey whines, and I can tell she's over it. "This is bullshit."

"You could've had sex with that one guy," Stella says, and I know she's referring to Paul.

Kelsey wrinkles her nose. "Ew. No. He was disgusting."

I make a sympathetic noise. He really was awful.

"I'm happy for you," Stella says. "You are literally glowing right now, and I know it's thanks to that Mitch guy. I can't wait to meet him."

Panic hits me. I don't want any of my friends to meet him. Not yet. I want to keep him to myself, as if he's my little secret. Well, he's a big secret. In every single way, because he's so large. Get it?

Okay, I'm awkward in my own head. I need to stop.

Anyway, I want to keep him to myself for the weekend because my friends will reveal the truth about me. And the truth is this:

I am boring. Awkward, as I have previously mentioned numerous times. I get embarrassed easily. I don't date a lot. I have a bad picker, my friends have told me this for a while now. I'm always drawn to losers, and not a one of them has ever truly appreciated or valued me for me.

Until now. Until Mitch. I don't know him that well, and maybe I shouldn't trust my picker just yet because it's been off most of my life, but this guy. He feels...

Different.

In the best possible way.

"He's also really nice," I add, but the skeptical looks

Stella and Kelsey send my direction tell me they don't really believe me. "What? It's true. We get along so easily."

"Clearly," Stella says, making Kelsey snort.

"Sexual chemistry is important," I remind them, lifting my chin and trying to remain dignified. "And we have it." I hesitate before I decide to tell them the truth. "I've never had that with someone before. Not like this."

"Carter and I have serious sexual chemistry going on," Stella says, a wistful look on her face. She's told us enough about Carter to know that she's definitely speaking the truth.

"I hate being a jealous person, but right now, I'm a jealous person," Kelsey says, a glum expression on her pretty face. "Our entire friend group are in these amazing relationships and I'm out here all by myself."

Stella starts singing the song "All By Myself," and she's so terribly off-key, we can't help but laugh at her.

"I'm not in a relationship," I reassure Kelsey once we've settled down. I glance toward the store to see Caroline and Sarah are walking toward us. "With my luck, it's probably going to end up being a memorable one-weekend stand. That's it."

Not bad luck, though. My moments with Mitch are definitely ones I never want to forget, that's for sure.

"Whatever it ends up being, at least you found someone who makes you look like that." Kelsey waves a hand toward my face.

I frown. "Look like what?"

"Like you're radiating sunshine and rainbows," Kelsey says morosely.

Her comment stays with me the rest of the afternoon, and I can't stop smiling. I'm usually the sun-shiniest one of the bunch, but I'm feeling extra Rainbow Brite right now.

And it's all thanks to Mitch.

WE DECORATE the suite for over an hour while Caroline's in her room upstairs, getting her hair and makeup done thanks to the hairstylist and makeup artist Alex hired as a surprise for her. Once we're finished, they do our hair and makeup as well, which is amazing.

I'm always the hairstylist on call for my friends. I do everyone's hair, because hello. That's what I do. And I never mind. It's my one way to give back.

But it's so nice to sit in the chair and be tended to by someone else. I request a simple blow out with loose curls, and he delivers. The makeup artist gives me winged eyeliner and perfectly poppin' highlight.

Getting ready takes way longer than anticipated, so we have to bump out our dinner reservation. Before we leave the suite, we show Caroline the decorations and games we set up, which has her squealing and crying and hugging every single one of us.

All the decorations are completely inappropriate, which was Stella's idea, of course. I wanted to go the more romantic route, but Stella wouldn't hear of it. Neither would the rest of them.

Typical.

I bought shiny pink letter mylar balloons that spell out "Wifey for Lifey" and hung them on a string in the kitchen while Stella and Sarah hung the "Same Penis Forever" banner in the living room. The i in penis is shaped exactly like a penis, just FYI.

Sarah brought penis-themed games for us to play later tonight (pecker ring toss, for one). I found a pinata in the shape of a giant solitaire diamond ring that I filled with candy, plus I hung pink and black balloons everywhere. Kelsey brought the sashes. A white one for Caroline that says *Bride To Be*, a maid of honor one for Stella and the rest of us are wearing bridesmaid sashes, even Kelsey and Candice, who aren't officially bridesmaids, but for the weekend, it's all good.

We're going to look ridiculous, but we don't care.

We're just about to walk out the door when room service arrives with a bottle of Veuve Clicquot champagne, compliments of Alex Wilder, of course. Stella opens the bottle and pours us each a glass of bubbly.

"To Caroline." Stella raises her glass and we all follow suit. "We're so happy for you, and so grateful we can celebrate you in style this weekend. You're marrying a great guy but never forget—his is the last penis you will ever have." She lifts her glass even higher. "Cheers!"

We all laugh and clink glasses, and I'm hit with an overwhelming sensation of love and happiness as I stand among my friends, drinking expensive champagne and feeling the bubbles tickle as they slide down my throat. I even start to get teary-eyed, and I do my best to discreetly wipe at my face as I turn away from the group.

"Are you actually crying?" Caroline asks me, sounding horrified.

Candice makes a tsking noise and rushes toward me, wrapping me up in her arms. "If you don't stop, I'm going to start crying too."

A watery laugh escapes me as I cling to my friend. "I'm just so happy, you guys. I can't believe we're here, staying in this fabulous suite and drinking expensive champagne while we celebrate Caroline's upcoming wedding."

"All thanks to Alex," Caroline says as she joins me and Candice. So we're all three wrapped around each other.

"I'm feeling left out," Stella says as she walks over to our trio. Sarah and Kelsey follow after her, and then we're all wrapped around each other in a six-person group hug.

"Enough with the sappiness," Stella says after about thirty seconds of hugging. "I want more champagne. And I'm hungry. Let's get this party started!"

Caroline grabs Stella's arm, stopping her from draining her glass. "Tell me we're not going to a strip club."

Stella's expression is solemn. "We're not going to a strip club," she repeats.

"Are you just saying that?" Caroline's expression is full of doubt.

"Yes. I'm just saying that," Stella says just before she drinks the last of her champagne. "Now let's go!"

I know for a fact Stella arranged for a couple of strippers to show up at our suite. Not sure what time that's going to happen, but it is definitely happening.

It's definitely going to be an interesting night.

Grabbing my bar purse, I pull my phone out to see I have a text from Mitch. **Having fun?**

Smiling, I type out a response and send it. **Yes. We just drank champagne and now we're going to dinner. I got my hair and makeup done. I look fabulous.**

A giggle takes over, and I stifle it with my fingers. Normally I would never tell a man I look fabulous.

You can't say that and not send me a photo to prove it.

Hmm. I glance around, consider taking a selfie in front of the window wall, but then I decide to ask someone to take a photo of me. So I can get in a full body shot and really drive him wild.

Ha! Clearly, I'm already feeling naughty. He brings it out in me, I swear.

"Stel, would you take a photo of me, please?" I ask.

She lifts her brows as I hand her my phone. "Is this for your new man?"

Nodding, I start walking toward the windows. "Where should we take it?"

"How about with you leaning against the pool table?" Stella suggests.

I almost laugh. No way can I tell her what happened on that pool table last night. But I bet Mitch would appreciate it so I say, "Good idea."

My dress is so freaking cute. It's black. Long-sleeved. High neck. Extra short, flouncy skirt. I'm all legs in it, and while it gives you the illusion of covering everything up, as you get closer, you can see the fabric is kind of sheer. Which means it's kind of see-through. As in, my black bra is on open display beneath the dress.

I don't care. I'm in Vegas, right? We're living it up tonight.

Stella directs me like some sort of fashion photographer and I pose for endless photos. Leg up, leg down. Hair tossed back, hair in front of my chest, covering the bra. Stand to the side, glance over my shoulder, full frontal with my hands on my hips. I'm grateful she's taking so many photos. It'll be nice to have the documentation for later.

"He texted," Stella says as she hands me my phone back. "Something about you taking too long."

"So impatient," I murmur under my breath as I scroll through the endless photos. I don't know which one is my favorite, so I decide to send him three photos.

He responds rather quickly. **What do you have on under that skirt?**

Of course that's the first thing he says.

Pressing my lips together, I answer with the truth. **Black panties.**

He responds: **Take 'em off.**

Should I? He can be rather demanding. And what's funny is that when he makes this demand, I immediately want to do it.

"Hold on. I almost forgot something," I call as I make my way to the stairs. I run up them as fast as I can, which isn't very fast thanks to the high-heeled shoes I'm wearing, and I dash into my room, throwing the door closed.

I slip the scrap of lace down my hips and thighs, kicking off my undies and tossing them into my still-open suitcase before I slam it closed. Tugging my skirt back into place, I stand there, contemplating spending the evening sans underwear.

The cool breeze from the air conditioner makes me shiver. I'm going to feel every draft between my legs tonight, that's for sure. I've never done this before.

I haven't done a lot of things before Mitch.

They're off, I text him.

Prove it.

Uhhh.

My phone starts ringing. He's FaceTiming me.

"What are you doing?" I whisper after I answer.

"Show me," he says with a flick of his chin.

I stare at his face. His hair is damp and his skin is ruddy, like maybe he just got out of the shower? We took one together, but that was a few hours ago and it's hot in Las

Vegas. Lots hotter than where I'm from, and that much easier to work yourself into a major sweat.

"What do you want me to show you?" I ask, talking slow, like I'm having trouble comprehending.

A smile spreads across his face. "You know what I want to see."

Oh God, I do.

Turning to the side, I hold my phone at hip level, then grab the hem of my skirt with my free hand and flip it up for a brief moment. "See? No panties."

"Show me your pussy," he demands, and my entire body catches on fire. It's just like whoosh, I'm going up in flames, thanks to the dark tone of his voice, the thunderous expression on his face.

"Mitch," I start, but he shakes his head.

"Come on. Show me. Touch yourself."

Oh shit.

Sitting on the bed, I prop myself against the pillows and bend my knees, the spike heels of my sandals looking ready to puncture the snowy white duvet cover.

"You look beautiful in that dress," he tells me, making me pause. Making me smile.

"You like it?"

"Yeah. I like everything about you."

Oh, he says the best things.

I readjust my position on the bed, my skirt flipped up, my lower body on complete display. The bed cover is cool and smooth against my bare butt cheeks, and while it's not particularly easy to get my whole body in the shot along with my—*ahem*—pussy, I manage to make it happen.

Mitch sucks in a harsh breath when he can finally see. Lets out a low whistle. "Damn, woman. You're wet." He pauses. "Touch yourself."

"Mitch." It's not a protest. More like a moan.

"Do it."

Kelsey chooses that moment to call my name impatiently. "We're leaving soon. We're leaving *now*."

"Just once. Touch yourself and then suck your finger for me."

This man is so dirty.

But like a woman who's been thoroughly dicktimized, I reach between my legs and drag my index finger through my folds, biting back a whimper. Everything's so sensitive down there, especially my clit.

My gaze glued on the screen, on Mitch—who's watching me very, very carefully—I bring my finger to my mouth and suck it deep, tasting myself. The turned on look on the man's face brings me immense satisfaction, and I smile.

"You like that?" he asks, his voice harsh.

I nod, wondering where my voice went. My entire body feels like it's about to implode.

"That pussy belongs to me. And trust me, I will be fucking it tonight. Text me later." He ends the call, and I'm left sitting there all alone, vibrating with need.

He's pushing my boundaries.

And I like it.

FOURTEEN
MITCH

GOD SAVE me from sexy women.

When she sent me those photos with her in that little black dress, I immediately wanted her. The legs. The boobs straining against that sheer fabric, the long blonde hair with the sexy curls and the smoky eyes. I don't normally care if a woman has makeup on or not. I'm not one for the overly made-up look. Natural beauty gets me every time, and natural curves.

Eleanor's got all that. Everything about her drives me crazy.

Earlier I returned to my mostly empty apartment and promptly fell asleep, exhausted from the previous night's activities. Woke up a few hours later and took a shower. Thought of Eleanor in the shower earlier. The moans echoing off the tile. The way she looked with water raining down upon her naked skin.

Yeah. She's hot. My cock rose to the occasion, but I refused to jerk off. I'm saving it all up for tonight.

At one point, I worried I wouldn't get to see her. I can't be the selfish asshole who demands to be with her tonight when she's there to celebrate her friend. I'm not that guy. We're not in a relationship. If I tried that shit, she should tell me to kiss her ass, and she'd be right. I have no business acting that way.

But once she sent me the photos and I asked her to prove to me that she wasn't wearing underwear, I *knew* I had to see her. And when I FaceTimed her and demanded she touch herself, and then she did? It was on. I *am* seeing her.

As I told her, that pussy is mine. And I'm making my claim.

She's texted me throughout the night like a good little girl. Letting me know where she's at, how much fun she's having, sending me selfies and Snapchat stories of her and her friends dancing at a club. Doing shots together. Grinding on each other at one point, which is hot. Not that I pay attention to any of the other women.

I only have eyes for Eleanor.

Now I'm at Wilder, and I know she is too. They ended up at one of the bars in the casino, and she texted me about fifteen minutes ago to let me know they just arrived. She also gave me the name of the bar. I'm headed there now.

Once I enter the place, I see it's not just a bar but kind of a makeshift nightclub. There's a DJ playing music and a few people out on the tiny dance floor. I spot Eleanor standing near the bar with her friends, and yes, they're all very attractive women. There's one in particular with long dark hair and a face like a movie star's.

That's nice and all, but she's not my Eleanor.

They do another round of shots, and when Eleanor laughs, my body responds. I stare at her, willing her to feel my gaze, to see me, and I watch as she goes completely still, an unsure expression on her pretty face.

She glances over her shoulder, her brows lowered, and our gazes meet.

Lock.

Eleanor parts those pretty peach lips as she watches me, dragging her tongue across her lower lip. I watch her back, keeping my expression impassive, though my body tightens at first sight of her tongue. We're communicating with each other without saying a word.

She turns away from me, resting her hand on one of her friend's arms before she leaves them. Her gaze lands on mine once more, and she tilts her head as if to say:

Follow me.

I do as she silently asks, keeping my distance as we move through the crowded bar, but staying close enough that I don't lose her. She heads to the back of the building, coming to a short, dark hallway before she turns right, and I go after her and find a door. Since she's nowhere in sight, I open it to find a dimly lit bathroom.

And Eleanor standing in the middle of it.

Leaning my back against the door, I reach out and turn the lock—this is the second time today we've done something like this—and remain quiet. She's quiet too, and there's this electric energy that fills the air between us. She can feel it too. I can tell by the sudden nervous look on her face. The way her pretty eyes widen ever so slightly, and her tongue darts out to lick her lips.

Seeing her tongue again is nearly my undoing.

"Having fun?" I finally ask, my voice rough.

She nods. "Yes."

"Did you miss me?"

Another nod. "I did. I do." Her voice is shaky.

I push away from the door and draw closer to her. "I missed you too."

It's crazy but true. It's only been a few hours since we've been together, but I missed her like crazy. I've lived my entire life without her, and now I'm about twenty-four hours in and acting like I can't function without her by my side.

What the hell is wrong with me?

Eleanor tilts her head back to meet my gaze when I stop directly in front of her. "We're going back to the suite soon. We have a little surprise planned."

"What type of surprise?"

Her cheeks pinken. "Strippers."

Jealousy rips through me. I don't want some asshole grinding his junk on my girl.

My *girl?* Where do I come up with this stuff?

"You want to see the strippers?" I ask, my voice even, my emotions chaotic.

She shrugs. "Not particularly."

What a good answer.

"Sounds like you're going to be busy all night." I reach out and rest my hand on her hip, caressing it gently. "Won't have any time for me."

"I will definitely have time for you," she says, her voice firm. "I'm just not sure how I'll get you into the suite."

"You don't want your friends to meet me?" I raise a brow, though deep down, I'm relieved. I don't want to meet her friends either. Not yet. What if one of them is a football fan? What if one of them recognizes me?

Eleanor will think I'm a liar, and technically, I guess I am, which fucking sucks. I feel bad about it, but I don't want her to figure out who I am yet. I want her to know and appreciate me for...me. Not because of who I am or what I do or how much money I make.

She shifts even closer to me, and I can feel her warmth,

catch her honeyed scent. My gaze zeros in on her peachy lips and I watch in fascination as she murmurs, "They know about you, but I want to keep you all to myself."

I swallow hard. My cock reminds me that he's here, and he's ready. Speaking of secrets...

I slip my hand beneath her skirt, resting my palm against the hot, bare skin of her hip. She is naked beneath the dress, and I bet if I touched her pussy, my fingers would come away drenched.

Yep. I think I need to test this out.

"You been thinking about me all night?" I ask, my hand doing a slow glide toward the spot between her legs.

Nodding, she tilts her head to the side, her eyes closing when I make contact. Oh fuck, she's so wet. I stroke her, slow and easy, the juicy sounds filling the quiet air, and I'm hit with the need to bury my face in her.

So I drop to my knees and dive my head under her flirty little skirt, latching my mouth onto her mound. She jerks against me, a sharp *oh* falling from her lips. I grip her ass, holding her to me as I devour her, and she lifts her leg, bending it at the knee. It hangs there in the air downright awkwardly, and I decide to help her out.

I grab her calf and drape her leg over my shoulder, which only opens her up more to me. She's pink and hot and so damn wet. Her clit is throbbing against my tongue. I slip a finger inside her and start to pump, latching my lips onto her flesh and sucking noisily.

"Oh shit." Her entire body goes still, and I know she's close. I can already tell. She starts rocking her hips, rubbing her pussy against my face. "Right—*there*."

The last word chokes out of her, and I suck harder. Fuck her with my fingers. Moan against her flesh. I think it was the moan that did it.

She's coming. Gasping. Her fingers are twisting my hair, her entire body shuddering with her orgasm, and I keep a firm grip on her ass cheeks so she doesn't fall onto the floor and take me down with her.

Damn, this girl is on fucking fire. It is my absolute pleasure to make her come like that.

Jesus.

Once she's come back to herself and we're both standing, Eleanor fussing with her skirt and sounding like a jittery mess, I go to the sink and wash my hands and face. Can't walk out of here smelling like pussy, am I right? Though I doubt I'd be the first guy to do so.

"I don't think any of my friends have as much sex as we do," she tells me as she washes her hands too, our gazes meeting in the mirror.

Her eyes are sparkling. Her cheeks are rosy and those pretty lips are the color of a ripe peach. I realize quick that I made a mistake in not kissing her sooner and I go to her to rectify it.

The water shuts off as I approach and I grab her hand, pulling her in for a soft kiss. She opens beneath me so easily, I swipe my tongue against hers, the kiss becoming deep. Dirty. She moans. I groan.

She pulls away.

"I have to go back to my friends," she says breathlessly. "They probably think I've died in here."

"You kind of did," I tease her, and she smiles.

"I probably shouldn't, um...grind my body parts on you like that," she admits. Aw, she's so cute.

"You mean when you grind your pussy on my face? I don't mind." I stroke my chin, pleased with myself.

Even more pleased with her.

Her cheeks turn redder. "It just feels so good, and you

haven't shaved, so the stubble on your face bites into my skin and creates this friction..." She pauses, gaping at me. "You look really, uh, intense right now."

"You don't say?" I grab her hand and rest it against my very erect cock. "You keep talking like that and this is what happens."

She rubs me, the tease. "I should get back out there."

"Uh huh."

"They're waiting for me." She grips me as best she can through my black dress pants. And she does a pretty good job of it too.

"I'm waiting for you too." I thrust into her palm.

Eleanor laughs and drops her hand, then grabs her purse, which somehow dropped to the floor during our earlier interlude. "I have an idea."

"I can't wait to hear it." My entire body is on high alert. Dying to get inside her. She's acting like it's no big deal, what just happened. Digging in her tiny purse like she's searching for a mint or her lipstick.

Instead she pulls out a keycard and hands it to me. "Go to the suite and wait for me in my bedroom."

My brows shoot up. "Are you serious?"

"I'll be there in a half an hour or so." She bites her lower lip. "Maybe sooner."

I take the key from her and then grab her chin, lowering my mouth to hers. "Better make it worth my wait."

"Oh my God, I don't think we have to worry about that," she whispers after she breaks away from my kiss. "Let me walk out there first."

She turns and I swat her ass right before she starts for the door. I swear she puts an extra swish in her step, her hips moving that little skirt like a tease.

And then she's gone.

FIFTEEN
ELEANOR

I WALK BACK out into the bar on shaky legs and knocking knees, my entire body buzzing from that earth-shattering orgasm I just received. I feel drunk. High. Whatever. And it's not from the alcohol I've consumed tonight. It's from Mitch.

And his perfectly wicked, perfectly wonderful mouth.

When he fell to his knees and dove under my skirt in the bathroom, I'd been scandalized. And then thrilled because seriously, who wouldn't want an orgasm from that man? He's given me so many already. He's going to give me more. When I go back to the suite, I'm going to have to stay with my friends and act like I'm totally into those silly games and the strippers, but honestly? All I'll want to do is go back to my bedroom and get naked with Mitch before he thoroughly fucks my brains out.

You know, I've never thought of it like that before. Fucking. I just think of it as sex. I even tried to call it making love once to a guy I was semi-serious about, but it sounded silly to me then. And it still sounds silly, am I right? At least, it does to me.

But what Mitch and I are doing is straight up fucking. The carnal act at its dirtiest.

I am having way too much fun this weekend. Maybe more fun than Caroline.

"Where have you been?" is how I'm greeted by Kelsey when I make my way back to my group. No one else is paying attention to me. They're all drinking and laughing, a couple of them talking with the very cute bartender.

"Um, upset stomach. Too much rich food." I rest my hand against my belly and offer a wan smile.

Kelsey contemplates me for a moment, and I swear I start to squirm beneath her assessing gaze. "You're lying."

"What? No, I'm not!" I am the worst liar ever.

"Is he here?" Kelsey looks about the room, rising up on her already very high heels. "You just met up with him, didn't you? Your cheeks are rosy and you've got stars in your eyes. Did you two have a secret makeout session?"

I just stare at her, wondering how I can politely phrase what happened between me and Mitch. "Um, sort of."

It's now Kelsey's turn to stare back at me, and I can tell she's trying to figure me out. I play it cool, my expression hopefully indifferent. "What exactly did you two do?"

"I'd rather not say." My voice is calm. Inside I'm praying she doesn't call the rest of the girls over to us for an in depth interrogation.

I can tell Kelsey is trying to keep a straight face, but eventually it gets to be too much for her. She breaks out into a smile, just before she starts laughing. "Did you two *do it* in the bathroom? Gross!"

I don't bother correcting her. I suppose someone could view what we did in the bathroom as gross. I mean, it *is* a public restroom. But the Wilder Hotel and Casino is immaculate. This place is super clean. I don't think I got cooties.

"We get near each other and it's just like...boom." I do jazz hands. I watched "Bring It On" recently, so they seem appropriate for the moment. "Instant sparks. We want each other. It's like this all-consuming thing. I've never experienced anything like it."

"Me either," Kelsey says, gazing at me in wonderment. "Sounds exciting."

"It's so exciting. God, and he's so big. Like, he can just haul me around if he wanted to. It's kind of hot," I further explain, like I can't help myself. Which I can't.

"Sounds really hot."

"Okay, fine, it is really hot." I start giggling. So does Kelsey. She grabs my abandoned drink that's still sitting on the counter and hands it to me, and I take a big slurp, essentially draining it.

Not like I need liquid courage or anything. I've got this. I know what I'm doing.

And I'm about to do Mitch.

All night long.

EVENTUALLY, we take it back to the suite, and I can literally feel Mitch's presence, even though I can't see him. I don't even know if he's actually here, but I swear I can feel his energy. Reaching out to me. Wrapping around me. Sending shivers over my skin and arousal pulsing between my legs.

I'm sure it doesn't help matters that there are literally penises everywhere. Stella whips out bendy straws with little plastic penises at the end and we're all sipping out of mini bottles of champagne—Candice had those special ordered—our lips wrapped around miniature dicks.

Makes me think of Mitch and his not-so-miniature dick.

Caroline is crying-laughing over the idea of having one penis for the rest of her life, demanding that we all take photos of her standing underneath that particular banner. No one pays attention to my "wifey for lifey" balloons, though I'm not insulted. Everyone's got penis on the brain, especially now that we're playing ring toss on the pecker, or whatever the hell it's called.

"Too many dicks," Candice calls out at one point, making all of us pause in shock. Candice is not one to talk about dicks. She's rather prim and proper. More prim and proper than me. Currently those two words can't describe me whatsoever, but you know what I mean.

"There can never be too many dicks," Stella responds, a smug smile curling her lips. "Come on, this is fun!"

"And there's more where this all came from," Sarah adds, both of them bursting into laughter.

Clearly, we've all had a little too much to drink.

I grab my phone out of my bar purse and send a quick text to Mitch. **Are you here?**

He responds quickly. **In bed and waiting for your pretty ass.**

He sends a photo of himself sitting in my bed, bare chested and delicious.

Oh...oh man. I need to get up there.

As if on cue, the doorbell rings—yes, our suite has a freaking doorbell—and Stella rushes to answer it. Two men are standing in the doorway, both of them broad shouldered and tall, clad in obviously phony fire department uniforms complete with red suspenders and mirrored sunglasses.

"Is Caroline Abbott here?" one of the men asks, his

voice crisp and authoritative, like he's not going to take any shit.

I send Mitch a quick text. **Give me a few minutes. The strippers just got here.**

Okay. That's a text I never thought I'd send.

"She's right over here, sir," Stella says, standing to the side as the men enter the suite. Their expressions are like stone, and it's hard to get a read on them since they have those stupid glasses on, but they're not bad-looking. Stella and Sarah must've paid good money to get these two.

My phone buzzes in my hand and I glance down to see another text from Mitch.

You want to hang out with some strippers or do you want some of this?

The next photo he sends is a close-up of the tent his erection makes beneath the white sheet.

I literally start to sweat. I would much rather be with him than these two strippers. No one will notice I'm gone, right?

"Oh my gosh, Stella. Did you hire these guys?" Caroline is squealing. I thought she might be upset, but clearly she doesn't mind. Or she's too drunk to care.

"Ma'am, we're from the Las Vegas Fire Department and we're here because someone reported a fire in the penthouse. No one hired us for anything," one of the strippers says while managing to keep a straight face.

Caroline giggles. "Oops, sorry, Mr. Firefighter. My bad."

"You can call me captain," he says, making Caroline giggle even more.

Deciding I can definitely skip this part, I start typing a response to Mitch. **I'll be upstairs in two minutes.**

He responds fast. **Make it one. I'm dying to get my mouth back on you.**

My knees go weak when I read his response. I am dying for his mouth to be on me too.

"Little lady, we'll have to confiscate your phone." The stripper yanks my phone out of my hands, holding it above his head when I try to reach for it.

"Give it back!" I am yelling in frustration, hopping up and down, trying to grab my phone. I can feel the air swoosh all around my private parts and I immediately stop jumping.

Gotta watch it before I expose my bare ass to everyone.

"No recordings allowed," the firefighter/stripper says, smiling at me.

I glower back. "Please. I'm not going to record you guys."

He grips my shoulder and gently pushes me so I fall back onto the couch behind me, gaping up at him. I glance to my left to see Caroline is sitting in a chair from the dining table, the other cop standing in front of her, his hands resting on his belt like he's ready to drop his pants at any moment.

Freaking great. Looks like I'm somehow the first victim along with the bride-to-be.

Music starts playing, some popular song that gets heavy radio play, but always with equally heavy edits. This is the full-blown explicit version we're listening to, and the lyrics are filthy dirty.

The stripper in front of me starts gyrating his hips, slipping each suspender off before he reaches for the buttons on his uniform shirt. They pretty much tear away, revealing his tanned, well-muscled chest, and while I can admit he's not bad-looking—sure wish he would remove the cheesy aviators—I feel absolutely nothing. No tingling between my legs, nothing.

Not that a stripper has ever made me feel that particular way. All the tingling I'm currently experiencing only happens when I think of Mitch.

God, he's probably getting impatient, wondering where I'm at. Most of the girls are surrounding Caroline, since she's the one this entire show is for, though I spot Candice making a beeline upstairs.

Lucky Candice.

"Hey." I sit up, my gaze locked on the stripper's face. He shifts away a little bit, pausing in his movements. "Go dance on the bride to be."

He frowns. I'm sure he's shocked I'm putting a stop to this.

I hold out my hand. "And give me my phone, please."

He pulls it out of his back pocket and slaps it into my palm. "You're cute."

"I'm taken," I tell him, rising to my feet. "But thanks for the compliment."

He watches me head for the stairs. "You're not going to stick around?" he calls after me.

Aw, he sounds positively disappointed. I'm kind of shocked.

I glance over my shoulder. "I think I've seen enough." I reach into my purse and wave a twenty-dollar bill. "For you."

The stripper hurries over to me and snatches the money from my fingers. Greedy bastard. "You sure you don't want a lap dance?"

Ew. "No thank you," I say breezily, just before I turn and run up the stairs, gripping the hem of my skirt tightly so I don't show the stripper all my goods.

That would be embarrassing.

Once I reach the top of the stairs, I notice Candice's bedroom door is closed. My door is closed too.

Just knowing Mitch is waiting for me in there makes me all jittery inside.

Anticipation rippling through me, I approach my bedroom. Rest my hand on the door handle for a moment before I open it.

There's no light on, but the curtains are drawn back, showing off the fabulous view of the lit-up city. It's just enough light to cast Mitch in perfect, mysterious shadow, his big body sitting in the middle of the bed, a bunch of pillows stacked behind him. His phone is by his side, and I'm pretty sure he's completely naked beneath the sheets.

My mouth waters just looking at him.

"You took longer than one minute," he says, his voice like velvet smoothing over my skin.

"I got distracted by a stripper," I tell him truthfully.

He raises a brow, his mouth tight. I don't think he likes my answer. "Really?"

Nodding, I murmur, "Really," as I start to approach the bed. I am feeling confident. On top of the world. I have a gorgeous man waiting for me in bed. I am looking hot in my little black dress, and I don't have any panties on, which is making me hyper aware of the fact that I'm pulsating with need between my legs.

"Did he wave his dick in your face?" he asks darkly.

I burst out laughing. "You're the only one who does that."

Mitch grins, and it's a sight to see. Be still my heart. When he looks so happy, all that golden scruff on his jaw, the messy light brown hair, the sparkle in his whiskey-colored eyes, he is extra handsome. "Probably going to do it again tonight."

"I don't mind." I rest a knee on the edge of the mattress, standing as close to him as I can get. "I missed you."

His smile fades, his gaze growing serious. "We were together not even an hour ago."

"It wasn't long enough," I admit, crawling onto the bed and into Mitch's lap, spreading my legs wide so I can straddle him. The skirt on this dress is loose, enabling me to move freely, and I settle my bare lower regions right on top of his erection.

His eyes flare and I can only assume it's because he can feel me. All of me, if you get what I'm sayin'. "You're gonna leave a wet spot on the sheet."

With other men, I'm pretty sure this sort of crude talk would've grossed me out. But somehow everything that comes out of Mitch's mouth is sexy.

"I'm guessing we're going to leave lots of wet spots on the sheets tonight," I tell him, curling my arms around his neck.

His hands slip beneath my dress, resting on my bare butt. "Have I told you you're the sexiest woman I've ever met?"

Normal Eleanor would tell him he's confused. Vegas Eleanor throws her head back and laughs. "I think you bring it out of me."

"We make a good pair then." His large hands massage my butt, and his touch makes me shudder.

And—it makes me want more.

My laughter dies and I stare into his eyes. "You really think so?"

Nodding slowly, he hauls me in closer, so I'm pressed against him, chest to chest. "I know so."

I want to say more, but he steals my words with his lips. I'm hungry for him. I would say he's starving for me. We kiss and kiss, tongues tangled, his fingers digging into my flesh. I grind on top of his erection, basically trying to get off, and the sheet is the only thing separating us. I want it gone. I want to feel him inside me. Frustration races through me, so strong I break the kiss first.

We're panting. He's staring at my mouth. His hands are still on my ass, and my fingers are buried in his hair. "What's wrong?" he asks. "Why'd you stop?"

"I have too much clothing on," I say with a little pout.

He smiles, and it's so wicked, so devious, the sight of it steals my breath. "I can take care of that."

SIXTEEN
MITCH

FRUSTRATED ELEANOR IS a sight to see. I can tell she wants out of that sexy dress. Why? So she can rub herself all over me?

Not going to say no to that.

With fumbling, anxious fingers, I feel around her dress, trying to find a button or a zipper, anything to help her get out of it. I eventually find the zipper and I yank it down impatiently, shoving the dress off her shoulders so the front falls forward.

"Don't rip it," she murmurs, batting my hands away when I tug with too much force. "Hold on."

I lean back against the massive headboard and watch in fascination as she disentangles herself from the dress, pulling it off over her head and tossing it on the floor. She's now sitting on top of me with just the black bra on. Nothing else. Those generous tits appear ready to spill out of the lacy bra and I reach for her, my hands cupping her flesh. Thumbs playing with her covered nipples just before I pinch them.

Thrusting her breasts into my hands, she reaches

behind her and undoes the clasp, shedding the bra in a matter of seconds. Now, she is gloriously naked.

Beautiful.

Stunning.

Take-my-breath-away naked.

I study her carefully, taking my time. Last night I was too impatient. Hell, right now I'm real eager to get my hands and mouth on her. More than anything, I can't wait to be inside of her, but I need to look first.

At least for a minute.

Her nipples are the same peachy shade as her lips. They're huge. I love them. I am a tit man through and through, always have been. But she's also got legs. And I bet they'd feel real nice wrapped around my hips while I fuck her into the mattress.

And that pussy of hers, damn. It's covered with a light tuft of dark blonde hair, and I swear to God, the sheet separating us is damp from her juices.

Or it could be from me. I'm probably leaking precome like a motherfucker right now, I want in her so bad.

"Do you like what you see?" she asks coyly, her voice teasing.

Nodding, I say, "Touch yourself."

Her eyes blink wide and her lips part, but she doesn't say anything. Good. I think I shocked her. It's fun, pushing her boundaries. I can tell she doesn't do this sort of thing, and I like that maybe I'm the first to encourage her. Sex should be fun. Sex should be about experimenting and testing your limits.

I didn't realize it could be so much fun with the same woman, though. We haven't even had actual sex yet, and I'm enjoying the hell out of myself.

And Eleanor.

Licking her lips—damn it, she does that way too much—she grabs her breasts in her hands and holds them together, her palms sliding over her nipples.

"Pinch your nipples," I murmur, my dick leaping in response. This girl revs me up like no other. "Rub them."

She does as I ask, her eyes falling closed, her mouth falling open. Her breathing becomes accelerated and so does mine.

Watching Eleanor get herself off is pretty fucking hot.

"Does that feel good?" I ask.

"Yes." Her voice is a breathy whisper, like a shot to my already straining cock.

"Touch your pussy," I urge.

Her hands fall away from her chest and she slides one down her belly, pausing just above her scant pubic hair. Glancing back, she plants her left hand on the mattress behind her, just on the other side of my thigh, and rests her right hand directly over her mound, then spreads her fingers wide.

The way she's positioned, she's giving me quite the view. I can see everything. Her legs are spread, and all that hot pink flesh is on display, just for me. Her fingers rest right at the top of her slit, like a tease, and a low growl escapes me.

She smiles, as if she knows what she's doing to me, and then those fingers are gliding over her folds, rubbing over her clit. I watch with rapt fascination, my gaze never leaving her busy hand, noting how worked up she's getting herself. She's panting. Whimpering. Rubbing harder. Faster. I'm learning all of her tricks, seeing exactly how she likes it, and when I can feel her entire body start to tremble, I bark out, "Stop."

Eleanor goes still. Her eyes pop open to meet mine. "I'm so close."

"I know." I reach for her waist and shift her back at the same time I move forward, until she's lying sprawled at the end of the bed and I'm on top of her. "When you come, I want to be inside you."

Her eyes flare with heat at my words. She likes that. She likes it a lot. "Please tell me you brought condoms."

"An entire box," I reassure her with a smile. "Sitting on the table over there." I wave a hand at the bedside table.

"Thank God," she says, her shaky voice full of relief. She lifts her torso beneath me, trying to rub herself against my dick, I assume. The sheet is gone. There are no barriers between us now. "I want you," she admits.

"I know, baby," I tell her, feeling like a smug ass, but hell. Let's be real now.

It's pretty damn obvious she wants me. And it's extremely obvious that I want her too.

We need to take our time, though. She's leaving tomorrow. She has friends here she needs to spend time with. Tonight is probably my final shot before she's gone.

I have to make it last. Make it good.

Make it so she never forgets me.

I lean down and kiss her. Run my lips down the length of her neck. Lick and kiss her breasts. Suck and tongue her nipples. Rain kisses all over her curved, quivering belly. Press sucking kisses on the inside of her quaking thighs.

Doing my best to drive her out of her ever-lovin' mind.

I go down on her because I can't resist that delicious spot between her legs. She is so damn wet, coating my face in her juices, her body primed and ready for me. I work her into such a frenzy, she's begging for it, saying my name, thrashing about like she can't control herself.

Yet I don't give her what she wants. I don't want her to come yet.

Not like this.

"You're torturing me," she whimpers, and when I finally thrust my face in hers, she kisses me like she's dying, not minding the fact that my mouth tastes like her. "Please, Mitch."

She's asking nicely, so I decide to give in to her.

"Hold on," I whisper, breaking away from her hold so I can grab the box of condoms. I open the box and pull one out, tearing the wrapper off and rising up on my knees to roll the rubber on. My dick hurts, it's so ready to get down to business. I'm afraid to touch it, for fear I might blow early.

But I manage to get the condom on. Of course.

Eleanor lifts up on her elbows, watching me as I finish taking care of the condom, her eyes wide. "Pretty sure you're the biggest guy I've ever been with."

I give my cock a quick stroke before I resume my position, hovering above her, her legs spread and ready to receive me. "Really?"

She nods, looking apprehensive. "Hopefully it fits."

"Oh, it's gonna fit. Don't you worry," I say with confidence, rising up on my knees once more. I grab hold of her hips and pull her in closer, then wrap my fingers around my cock and drag it through her wet folds. She arches her back, her expression one of pure ecstasy as her lips fall open and her eyes close.

"You're the worst," she says on a moan, and I can't help but get off on her sexual agony.

This probably means I'm a sick motherfucker, but I can live with it.

SEVENTEEN
ELEANOR

HE'S DRIVING me out of my mind.

I've never had so much foreplay before in my life. Seriously, he takes me to the brink, only to leave me hanging, gasping for air. Desperate to come. Maybe he's a sadist. Maybe he's into BDSM or whatever. Maybe he's one of those dudes who says, "You can't come until I say so."

Huh. I wonder if that kind of thing would turn me on.

Probably.

Right now he's sitting on his knees between my wide-open thighs, his fingers wrapped firmly around the base of his erection as he rubs just the tip—ha ha—against my folds. My clit. Every little touch makes me twitch, I swear to God, and I'm afraid once he's finally inside me, I'll come immediately.

I hope that doesn't happen. I want to actually enjoy this. Savor it. Not be ready to shove him off me the moment I'm satisfied.

If I say that like I have previous experience, that would be a yes. I do.

Anyway.

"What are you waiting for?" I ask, sounding snappy.

Oops.

"Trying to get you ready," he says, like he has all the time in the world.

"I'm fairly certain I'm ready," I retort, feeling like a smartass, but come on. He's getting off on this.

He smiles, the jerk. The sexy, knows-exactly-what-he's-doing jerk. "You think?"

The music from downstairs gets louder, and though I can't necessarily make out the lyrics, the beat is heavy and slow, and I swear it's making the bed frame rattle. Mitch's expression grows darker as he rests the head of his cock right at my entrance, poised and ready. His gaze is zeroed in on that very spot and I shift beneath him, trying to get him in.

"Impatient?" he asks.

"Very," I answer.

All that apprehension over whether he'll fit or not leaves me the moment he pushes in with ease. It's been a while since I've had sex, and when he's fully inside me I feel very filled up, but it's a good thing.

A very good thing.

Mitch wraps his hands around my hips and starts to move, still on his knees, his gaze still locked on the spot where our bodies are connected. A slow-and-easy, in-and-out glide that sends tingles scattering all over my body. With every thrust, his erection nudges something deep, making me clench, and I wonder if it's the infamous G spot.

Huh. I always thought that was a myth.

I realize he's in time with the music, and it's absolutely blissful. Our bodies move in perfect unison, and I close my eyes, letting the sensations take over. I lift my arms above my head and stretch beneath him like a cat before I blindly reach out, my hands making contact with his sweat-covered chest.

He shifts closer. I can feel his body press atop mine, and then our mouths connect, his lips and tongue claiming me.

Moaning into his mouth, I undulate my body beneath his, sending him even deeper. He grabs hold of my thigh, hitching my leg around his hip, and oh God, that feels so good. He's bumping against something. Hitting me just right. Again and again. Over and over. My body has been primed since the moment I entered the suite, and I'm close.

So close.

He pumps faster. Sending me higher. I'm moaning. Whimpering his name. He grunts with every thrust, the sounds downright animalistic, and I wrap my hand around his neck, bringing his mouth to mine once again.

But it's like I can't kiss him and come at the same time, and I've always prided myself on my multitasking skills. I break away from his lips and avert my head from his, my breaths coming in short puffs, my entire body growing tense. I'm hanging right on the precipice, about to fall over that sweetly sharp edge when his fingers settle on my clit, rubbing and pressing. Driving me out of my mind.

Just like that, I'm coming. Hard. My entire body is shaking as wave after wave of pleasure washes over me. I cling to him, my inner walls milking his cock, and his thrusts turn chaotic. Out of control. Our sweaty skin makes a slapping noise and I've never been so grateful for loud music to mask how noisy we are. Because Mitch is coming too. He's shouting, groaning as he shudders and trembles. I open my eyes to witness him straining against me, his muscles standing out in stark relief as he props himself above me on his hands, a ragged sound escaping from his chest.

Holy shit, I'm impressed.

"Oh God." That's the first thing that comes out of my

mouth when it's over and he's lying beside me on the bed. I can't catch my breath. I'm overwhelmed. I blink my eyes open, staring up at the ceiling as I try to find my voice, but it's gone.

"You okay?" His grumbly deep voice does something to me. Twists me up. Makes me immediately want more.

I turn on my side to face him, finding that he's already looking at me. There's a warmth to his eyes that wasn't there before, and a look of complete and utter satisfaction on his face. It's a good look for him.

"I'm okay," I say. I am more than okay. I am fantastic, thank you very much. "How about you?"

"I feel like I'm about to fall off the bed," he answers truthfully, and I realize we're lying on the end of the mattress.

"Let's move then," I say brightly as I climb off the bed.

He watches me in silent fascination, his gaze roaming hungrily over my naked body while he still lies there. "Come here."

"Move first." I twirl my finger around, indicating I want his head at the top of the bed. "Come on."

Reluctantly he rolls off the mattress, grabbing hold of my waist and giving me a kiss before he murmurs against my lips, "I gotta get rid of the condom."

He heads for the bathroom and I watch his perfectly muscular butt the entire time, disappointed when he shuts the door. Sighing wistfully, I grab my phone out of my bar purse to check the time—dang, it's late—and set it on the bedside table before I climb under the covers. By the time I've settled in, Mitch is back, very comfortable in his glorious nakedness as he approaches the bed, his cock in a semi-erect state already.

I wonder if he always walks around like this. Primed and ready. A girl could grow to appreciate that real quick.

The mattress dips when he joins me, yanking the sheet and duvet cover up to his waist as he rests his head on the pillow, turning so he's facing me. He reaches out, resting his hand upon my cheek and caressing my skin as he stares into my eyes.

This feels like a moment. I can't quite put my finger on why exactly, but this entire night, this entire weekend feels pivotal. Life changing.

Overwhelming.

Oh no. I can feel them. Tears are stinging the corner of my eyes, and I blink rapidly, trying to banish them. He will freak if I start crying. Why wouldn't he? Women who cry after sex scare men on a daily basis. And I'm not one who even cries after sex. Maybe in frustration. One time in anger—the guy was a complete asshole, I don't even want to talk about him. That one's best left firmly in the past.

But I've never cried because I'm so overwhelmed with all the good feelings swirling inside of me. Yes, Mitch and I just had dirty, filthy sex, but he also made me feel so...cared for. He tended to my every need. Even if he was a giant tease who tried to torture me to death, he still made sure I got mine.

And he definitely got his too.

"Eleanor." His voice is soft, carrying a tinge of agony. "Are you crying right now?"

"No," I croak, reaching up to swipe at my eyes with frustration. Stupid, leaking eyes. "Of course not."

He remains silent and I do my best to rid myself of my tears, but it's no use. They are now streaming down my face.

It is super obvious I'm crying after I had sex with this man.

"Oh baby." He hauls me into his arms and holds me close while I just let loose and sob against his bare chest. He runs his fingers through my hair, his mouth at my forehead, murmuring soothing words in between pressing gentle kisses to my temple.

It's the sweetest thing a man has ever done for me.

Once I've composed myself, I'm terribly embarrassed. I can't believe I fell apart like that. "I'm sorry." I pull away so I can look into his eyes. "I don't usually do that sort of thing."

He frowns, his brows lowered. "What? Have sex?"

"No, silly." I gently smack his chest. He is a wall of solid muscle. "Cry after having sex."

The smile curling his lips is nothing short of arrogant. "It must've been a good one. That orgasm I gave you."

Ooh, look, I'm blushing. "It was okay."

"Uh huh."

"You seemed to enjoy yourself," I remind him.

"Being inside your perfect pussy is like heaven," he says solemnly.

He is so crude. But he also called my pussy perfect, so I can't complain.

"We should do it again," he continues, waving toward the box of condoms on the nearby table. "We have lots of protection."

"We do," I agree, my body starting to come alive at the thought of putting all those condoms to use.

He rolls us over so I'm sprawled on top of his big body. And I'm no delicate princess, so that I can sprawl and feel like I'm not crushing him is a huge bonus. *He* is a huge bonus.

"I want you to ride me like a cowgirl," he says, his hands on my hips as he slides me down so I'm settled directly on top of his junk.

Oh my. I like the idea of that. I can feel his erection nudging my backside, and my core is aching for him to fill it again.

"Let me grab a condom," I say, leaning over his face to pluck one from the box on the bedside table. He takes this opportunity to wrap his lips around my nipple and suck and bite it, making me gasp.

"God, I love these babies," he murmurs as he cups them in his big hands, gazing lovingly at my chest. They still manage to overflow his grip, because yes, I have enormous boobs. He sucks the other one in his mouth, nibbling on my flesh, and I sort of just hang there above his head, letting him feast on me.

It feels really good. He is literally worshipping my breasts.

Eventually I push his face away from my chest and slither down his body, putting the condom on his erection myself. It's a really nice penis, and I've never thought that before, but truly, it is. Perfectly proportioned. Nice flared head. Tilts a little to the right.

Pretty sure I've lost my mind, considering I'm sitting here analyzing his dick.

"Hurry up, woman," he says impatiently, like he knows what I'm doing, and I get into position, ready to ride him like a cowgirl, just like he said.

I slide down on top of him, a breathy sigh falling from my lips as he fills me up. It's been a while since I've been on top. I get self-conscious in this position. I've been with lean men before and when we do it like this, I always feel like I'm going to break them. Or there are the men who aren't into boobs swaying in their face, and that happens with me. I don't know, it can get awkward.

I am the queen of awkward, let's never forget it.

Mitch really seems into me. Into this moment. He's watching me, his eyes glazed, his mouth slack, his hands on my thighs. I just sit there for a moment, taking him in, taking in the moment just like he is, and I swear I feel his cock twitch deep within me.

"Did you just do that?" I ask.

"I did." He thrusts his hips up, bucking beneath me. "Whatcha waiting for? Giddyup, sweetheart."

Laughing, I start to move. He's grinning. I'm smiling. We're staring into each other's eyes as I shift above him, but soon our laughter dies. And our smiles fade. I'm sliding up and down his shaft like it's a pole, and he's urging me on with every subtle thrust of his hips. Soon we're in perfect rhythm, no music playing from downstairs to keep time with. There is no sound coming from downstairs at all. I bet everyone's in bed.

Meaning we probably need to keep quiet.

Having sex like this, moving in perfect sync with Mitch, I realize nope. I can't keep quiet. Moans leave me when he hits a particular spot. And he keeps hitting that spot, so I'm moaning pretty much nonstop. He's grunting. The bed, while it's not squeaking or anything, is making noise. Like you can tell someone is having sex.

I really hope no one can hear us.

I also sort of don't care if they can.

EIGHTEEN
ELEANOR

EVER SEE that scene in the movie *When Harry Met Sally* when the characters finally have sex and she's smiling like a loon, looking completely blissed out? I know I'm throwing it way back (#80smoviesforever), but I remember watching it with my mom, and thinking how happy Sally looked after finally doing it. And while I was twelve and really had no concrete information regarding sex, I do know have the memory of thinking, *I want to look that happy someday.*

Well, folks, the moment is here. I woke up smiling like a crazed loon when I found Mitch still in my bed. He's lying on his stomach, his arms above his head as he clutches the pillow beneath him. We kicked the duvet onto the floor at one point last night, so only the sheet was covering us. And the sheet is currently draped over his butt, with his legs sticking out, one knee bent.

Feeling like a deviant, I reach out and gently bat the sheet away so he's fully exposed. I drink him in, still grinning like a fool, remembering all the delicious, wicked, naughty, wonderful things we did last night.

I should be tired. Did I even get actual sleep?

Probably not.

But I'm not tired at all. I'm excited. Ready to bounce off the walls.

"You're starin'," he mutters into the pillow.

I don't even care that I got caught. "You have the perfect body."

He lifts his head, his sleepy gaze meeting mine. "So do you."

Aww. You know what's nice? When he says those things, I one hundred percent believe him.

"Did you sleep well?" I ask.

"When I actually slept, sure." He turns to look at me, his lips curling. No doubt he's thinking about all the things we did too. And how we didn't sleep much at all.

It hits me then that I'm flying out later this afternoon.

"I don't want to leave yet," I say, my mouth forming a little pout.

"Then don't." He rolls over so he's lying on his back, and folds his arms behind his head, his biceps bulging. He's the epitome of a carefree man right now, and I sort of want to jump him. "Stay another night."

I contemplate his suggestion. I don't have to work tomorrow. I could stay. Shoot, I don't have a client scheduled until ten on Tuesday, so I could arrive home late tomorrow night if the flight schedules allow it...

"We could get a room at another hotel," he suggests.

"Why can't we stay at your place?" I ask.

He grimaces. "It's nothing but boxes. The only usable things are the couch and the bed."

"That's all we need, right?" I am grinning but...

He is not.

Huh.

"Let's do a hotel. It'll be more comfortable."

I'm about to protest when my phone dings with a text. I reach over and grab it to see it's our group chat.

And holy hell, there are a lot of missed messages.

Kelsey: **E, where did you go?**

Candice: **Why is no one asking where I went?**

Kelsey: **Because we all saw you run up to the room. Chicken. *insert chicken emoji here***

An hour later.

Stella: **Eleanor is with her man. How do I know this, you might ask?**

Caroline: **How?**

Stella: **I CAN HEAR HER MOANING! HIM TOO!**

Uh oh. I knew they'd hear us.

The conversation goes on for a while, everyone complaining about how loud Mitch and I are while we're having sex. It's mortifying.

I'm also secretly proud.

The most recent conversation is from earlier this morning, concerning brunch, which I forgot about. They're already gone. They left me behind because it's almost noon and the reservation was for eleven. I received a text from Caroline outside of the group.

Our flight is at three. You can just meet us at the airport. The suite has late checkout, so take your time.

I send her a response back, feeling like a shit friend.

I'm so sorry I missed your brunch. I feel terrible.

She responds immediately. **You shouldn't feel terrible at all this morning. We heard you two**

carrying on last night. You should be on top of the world.

Ugh. Seriously, I am the worst friend ever.

"What's wrong?" Mitch asks.

I glance up at him. "I slept in and missed brunch with my friends. They want me to meet them at the airport later."

"What time is your flight?"

"Three."

He rubs his jaw, the raspy sound his stubble makes sends a zing of pleasure through me. I love feeling his stubble on my skin. "You want to call the airline?"

"Do you really want me to stay?"

He nods. "I do."

"Can we stay at your place?" When he opens his mouth to protest, I cut him off. "Please? I want to see where you're living. I want to sleep in your bed."

He stares at me for a moment, and I swear I can see the cogs turning in his brain. He's on the fence about me seeing his apartment, and I don't know why. What's the big deal? Maybe he has secrets after all. But wouldn't they all be packed up, considering his new place is full of nothing but boxes?

"Okay," he finally concedes. He grabs my hand and pulls me in close, dropping a soft kiss on my lips. "Want to take a shower together?"

We're going to have sex in the shower. That's a no-brainer. My entire body lights up just thinking about it. "Yes," I say without hesitation.

He pulls me in closer, wrapping his arms around me. I circle my arms around him. We're completely intertwined. I love it. I love how easy he is with his affection. How generous. How he looks at me like I'm the most beautiful woman in the entire world.

"Should we have sex here first?" he asks. I realize I can feel his erection poking against my stomach.

The man never, ever stops.

"I need to call the airline," I remind him.

"Should we have sex first?" he repeats.

I burst out laughing. "Yes. Then I have to call the airline. Then we can take a shower."

"Sounds good, baby," he murmurs right before he kisses me.

AFTER OUR QUICKIE IN BED—NOTHING wrong with standard missionary, let me tell you—I make a call and I'm able to reschedule my flight for five p.m. tomorrow. This means I won't land in Monterey until almost ten, and I'll probably have to take an Uber home, but that's okay. I get to spend another day and night with Mitch.

We have sex again in the shower before we finally leave the spacious, gorgeous suite. I wish it goodbye, snapping all sorts of photos so I can show some of my clients and also keep as mementos. Then I snap a few photos of Mitch, who's looking ultra-sexy this morning in his outfit from the night before.

Oops. Poor guy should've brought an extra set of clothes to change into.

We're leaving the hotel hand in hand when someone approaches us. Mitch immediately lets go of my hand, the man gaping at him in what appears to be complete disbelief.

Weird. What's going on here?

My phone chooses that exact moment to ring, and I

answer it absently, not bothering to check who's calling while I watch Mitch talk to the flabbergasted guy standing in front of him.

"Eleanor! Where are you?"

It's Kelsey. And she sounds a little...mad.

"Oh my God, I forgot to tell you guys." I turn so my back is to Mitch, lowering my voice. "I'm, uh...staying another night. With Mitch."

Kelsey muffles the phone, but I can hear her say, "She's staying another night, guys."

They all start talking. About me.

"Are you at the airport?" I ask Kelsey.

"Yes. And we were freaking out because you were nowhere in sight. Next time, call us sooner!"

"I'm sorry, I'm sorry." Again, I'm a shit friend. "I feel so bad about missing brunch. We slept in. I didn't even hear you guys when you left."

"I'm sure you were dead to the world, considering how much sex you had last night." Kelsey bursts out laughing, and so do the rest of them. "Girl, you two are loud."

A chorus of "yeah" accompanied by lots of laughter sounds in the distance.

"I am so embarrassed," I mumble.

"Don't be. We're all impressed. This Mitch guy must be a real keeper. At the very least, he'll give you some fond memories to look back on," Kelsey says.

We talk for a few minutes, me reassuring them I'm fine and safe and promising I'll text them later. Once we're finished with our conversation and I end the call, I realize Mitch is...

Gone.

Say what?

I wander around the massive lobby of the hotel, but I

don't see him. And I would. He is head and shoulders above the majority of people. I start for the entrance, wondering if he went outside, when I spot him standing at the curb, talking with one of the valets. The valet is young, very early twenties maybe, and he's nodding repeatedly as Mitch keeps talking, handing over a ticket. The valet takes off and Mitch turns, heading back toward the entrance.

I rush toward him, and we meet in the middle, though still close to the front doors of the hotel. "You did valet parking?"

He nods, looking distracted. "Way easier than dealing with that parking garage."

I've never done valet in my life. I think it's a waste of cash, but maybe Mitch makes really good money. He should, considering he works with professional athletes.

"Why did that guy stop you earlier?" I ask.

"Who called you?" he asks at practically the same time.

"Oh. Uh, it was Kelsey. They're already at the airport. I forgot to let them know I'm staying another night." I offer up a flirtatious smile. "Someone kept me a little too occupied earlier."

He smiles in return before he glances around, tugging on my hand so we end up standing behind a giant plant in a beautiful pot. "Can't help it. I always want my hands on you."

His hand slides to my butt as if to emphasize that fact, giving it a squeeze.

I step out of his hold, not wanting people to catch me getting felt up behind a plant. "How long did the valet say it would take to bring your car around?"

"Ten minutes. I told him if he made it in less than ten, I'd give him a bigger tip," Mitch says. "I want out of here."

I wonder how much he promised the valet. "Tired of

hanging out in a casino?" *Oh God, please don't say you're tired of hanging out with me.*

"Just ready to go home." He sends me a look that's full of promise, and relief hits me, making me relax. "I'm glad we're not staying at another hotel tonight. I want to sleep in my own bed."

"Do you really think we're going to get much sleep?" I ask, raising my brows.

"Probably not, but still." He shrugs, a crooked smile on his face.

My heart trips over itself as I stare into his eyes. We might be moving at a fast clip, but it doesn't feel forced or wrong. It all feels so natural with Mitch. I could fall for this guy.

If I haven't fallen already.

NINETEEN
MITCH

THAT WAS A CLOSE ONE.

The guy who approached me in the lobby of the Wilder Hotel? A Raiders fan. He was dumbfounded to find me there, and right about the same time he started to have a minor freak out, Eleanor's phone rang.

Thank God.

Once I calmed that dude down, I went outside to find the same kid who assisted me Friday night working the valet desk. I gave him five twenties, told him not to make a big deal about me whatsoever, and if he brought my truck to me in less than ten minutes, he could get a bonus tip.

Kid brought me the truck in less than six minutes. Impressive. I gave him an extra sixty bucks for his trouble. I thought he was going to shit a brick, he was so glad to make a $160 tip.

Eleanor was oblivious. When she asked about the fan in the lobby, I asked her about the call at the same time, and once she explained who it was, she forgot all about her question. I somehow managed to get us to hide behind a giant tropical plant for a few minutes so no one would notice me. It worked.

Now, we're in my truck headed back to my apartment, Eleanor glancing around the interior with an impressed look on her face. "This is really nice," she says as she runs her hand over the center console.

"Thanks." I shrug, keeping my eyes on the road ahead of me. Traffic is fucking awful.

"It must've been really expensive."

"Thank God for payments." I'm lying. I paid cash for this thing.

"True that," she agrees with a little sigh as she settles into her seat. I sort of hate it when she makes those sounds, only because they manage to always affect me.

Meaning, they always manage to affect my dick.

This woman has a stranglehold on my libido. I want her all. The. Damn. Time. It's insane. Last night was like—mind blowing. This morning was again, mind blowing. She's so responsive, we fit together perfectly, and it's like we can't get enough of each other.

The entire reason I joined that dating app was to find someone. Someone I could possibly stick with for the long term. I know, it sounds ridiculous. Using a dating app to find lasting love? But hell, people do it all the time. It's normal.

The real reason I used the Rate a Date app was to meet women who wouldn't know who I am. I wanted to lead with me, the regular guy, versus leading with the football player everyone knows. Eleanor doesn't have a clue I play for the Raiders and I'm worth millions. I love that she doesn't know. That she appreciates me for me.

Well, and I think she appreciates me for my talented mouth and dick.

But now I'm stuck. I'm a liar. If and when she finds out what I'm doing, she'll probably think I'm leading her on, and that makes me feel like absolute shit.

I'm not leading her on, but damn it, I'm lying to her. And that sucks. I care about her—yes, already. I do. When she finds out the truth, will she be mad? Will it hurt her?

Probably. And that's the last thing I want to do.

Glancing over at her, I see she's staring out the passenger-side window. She looks pretty in her floral printed sundress. It's this dark yellow color that I wouldn't find normally appealing, with little white flowers dotted all over the fabric. The bodice clings almost lovingly to her chest. The skirt is long and flowy and hides those fantastic legs. She's currently wearing sunglasses, her still-damp hair pulled into a messy bun on top of her head.

I think of our shower earlier. How I fucked her against the tile wall. My body aches from all the sexual acrobatics we've twisted ourselves into. It's been fun.

More than fun, actually.

"How much farther to your place?" she asks.

"It should only take another twenty minutes, but this traffic is awful," I answer, frustration filling me as we inch down the street along with the millions of other cars.

Okay, it's not millions, but you get the idea.

"I don't know if I could ever live here," she says, sounding sad.

"Why not?" I'm immediately hit with the image of Eleanor in my apartment. Sharing my bed. I bet she likes frilly shit. I bet she'd go all out and decorate my apartment, making it look like a woman lived there.

Would that be such a bad thing?

"Las Vegas is so hot." She fans herself, I suppose for emphasis. "And it's so—large. So many people. And it's full of tourists. We get lots of tourists in Carmel, and Monterey too, but it's not so bad. It still feels like a small town. Quaint. And the weather is amazing."

"Yeah." I don't know what to say. I don't know what she's getting at. I'm not even close to thinking about asking her to move in with me, and she has to know that. We've spent actual time together only this weekend. That's it.

But I want to spend more time with her. Definitely.

When she suggested earlier that we stay at my place, I have to admit I panicked. I don't bring girls to my home. Ever. It feels like an invasion of privacy. Plus, I never want to get their hopes up. My past interactions with women were never serious. I was a "wham, bam, thank you ma'am" kind of man.

Now? I want to wham, bam Eleanor on a daily, if not hourly, basis. This means something. A shift in my thinking. In my emotions. I want more Eleanor.

I think she wants more me, too.

WE ENTER my apartment forty minutes later, and I'm pulling Eleanor's suitcase along with me while she follows. She stops short in the entryway, and when I glance over my shoulder, I can see her eyes widen as she looks about the room.

"You weren't kidding," she says.

There are boxes everywhere. I still need to unpack my kitchen—I don't really cook, so what's the point?—and the living room, though the couch is set up, along with an end table and coffee table, and of course the TV, along with my Playstation and Xbox both hooked up.

I have priorities, after all.

"Sorry." I shut the door behind me and turn the lock, then start toward the hall, heading for my bedroom. "Come on. I'll give you a quick tour."

I wave my hand toward the kitchen and the living room. Throw open the door so she can check out the empty spare bedroom, and the equally empty bathroom. I point at the hall closet door, and then we're in my bedroom. I leave Eleanor's suitcase by the wall and walk inside, opening the blinds on the window to let some light in.

"It's roomy," she says as she walks around the end of the bed. She turns to look at me. "You don't have bedroom furniture?"

"Nope." I shrug. "I've always just used the closet."

"What about for your underwear and socks? You don't fold anything?"

"Oh, I've got a couple of these." I open the closet door and flick on the light, Eleanor following right behind me. I point at the three-drawer plastic cube storage thing I picked up at Walmart a couple of years ago. "They work just fine."

The look she sends me is one of pure sympathy. I had no idea my lack of furniture would make me look like a poor man. It's more like I'm a man with no time to shop for a dresser or bedside tables. I don't need 'em.

Not now, at least.

"I like your place," she tells me once we leave the closet. "You have a connecting bathroom?"

"Oh yeah." She goes to check it out and now it's my turn to follow her. The bathroom in this apartment is actually pretty spacious, and she looks impressed as she stares at the giant glass-walled shower.

"That's nice." She points at it.

"We could test it out later if you want," I suggest, wagging my eyebrows at her when she meets my gaze.

A teasing smile curves her lips. "By the time our extended weekend is through, we're going to be some of the cleanest people in Las Vegas."

"You know it." I approach her, settling my hands on her waist. She's leaning against the counter, her head tilted back, her gaze meeting mine. "I like seeing you in here."

I'm speaking the truth. Despite all the boxes and the fact that I've lived here all of a handful of days, it's still nice to have her here. To see how well she fits in my apartment. How easy I could make this a habit.

Me and Eleanor. Eleanor and me.

Her cheeks turn the faintest shade of pink. I think what I just said pleased her. "You didn't want me to come here at first." I'm about to deny it, but she lifts her hand, her fingers resting on my lips, silencing me. "Don't bother spinning some tale. I know you didn't want me here."

Parting my lips, I draw her fingers into my mouth, giving them a little nip. She starts to remove her hand, but I circle my fingers around her wrist, keeping her there. I bite each fingertip, putting enough pressure behind it that there's probably a bit of a sting, but not too bad. Then I pull her hand away, lacing our fingers together.

"I never let women visit my place. This is mine. It doesn't belong to anyone else. It feels—sacred," I start, keeping my fingers firmly gripped in hers.

She says nothing. Just continues to watch me.

"It scared me when you suggested coming here," I explain. Here, I can tell the truth. "But now here you are, and I'm so fucking glad."

A smile blooms on her pretty face. "I'm glad too."

Somehow, without even meaning to, I lift her up so she's sitting on the edge of the bathroom counter. Her legs separate and I stand in between them, my hands resting on her waist once more. "Everything about you drives me out of my mind."

Her eyes darken. She licks her lips. I let my hands slide up, rest them just beneath her perfect tits before I smooth them over her abundant flesh, my thumbs pressing into her skin. The fabric of her dress is thin, and the bra she's wearing must be really thin too, because I can feel her nipples.

And they're hard.

Without thought, I tug on the front of her dress. When nothing really happens, I reach for the thick straps on her shoulders, pushing one down, then the other. Now the fabric gives, and when I pull once more, it slips down, resting below her breasts, revealing that she's wearing some thin, nude-colored tube top thing.

"What's this thing?" I pluck at the edge of the stretchy fabric.

"A bandeau. It keeps everything in place." She glances down at it for a moment before she lifts her head, her gaze once again meeting mine. "Why? You don't like it?"

"It's hiding my favorite part of you." I yank it down and just like that, her breasts are exposed. Those hard, peach-colored nipples are pretty much begging me to take a taste, so I bend my head, swiping first one nipple with my tongue.

Then the other.

Her hands are immediately in my hair as she holds me to her. I feast on her breasts, unable to contain myself. I pretty much worship up at the altar of Eleanor's perfect tits, and she knows it.

Even better? Pretty sure she likes it.

"All we ever do is—this." She says the last word on a gasp because I bit her nipple.

"You don't like doing this?" I gather the fabric of her

skirt, pushing it up so it exposes her from the thighs down. I reach between her legs, brushing my fingers against the front of her panties.

What a surprise, they're already damp.

"It makes me worry," she admits.

I pause my exploration, our gazes locking, and I see the concern in her pretty face. "Worry about what?"

"That our relationship is only based on this." She waves her fingers in the space between us. "Sex. That's it." I'm trying to come up with the right words to say when she confesses, "I want more than that, Mitch. With you. You want me to be real with you right now? I'm a hardcore romantic. I'm not usually into the sex thing so much. Until —you."

Her voice is the slightest bit shaky, and the vulnerable expression on her face tells me she's being honest with me, and it scares her.

I'm all about the sex thing. Hell, that's all my so-called relationships ever were. And while yes, Eleanor and I have terrific chemistry, I also know there's more to us than just chemistry.

Can she feel it? See it? Or is she too blinded by the sex?

I remove my hand from beneath her skirt and take a step closer, grasping her hip and cupping her chin. Tilting her head back, I stare into her eyes as I say, "You want me to be real right now?"

Eleanor nods, but otherwise says nothing.

"I'm usually all about the sex thing. I don't have serious relationships. Ever. But for the first time, I've met a woman who makes me think. Who makes me feel."

"Really?" she whispers.

"Really," I say firmly. "I want the same thing as you do. With you. I want to take care of you. I want to make you happy. I want to protect you. I don't think you realize just how much you twist me up inside."

She blinks up at me, remaining quiet, and I can't help but continue.

"Every time I touch you, I want more. You make me fuckin' crazy, Eleanor. Every time we have sex, I'm plotting the next time I get to be inside you again. It's like I'm a man possessed. I just want to bury myself deep, and feel you tremble all around me. It's my new favorite thing. *You* are my new favorite thing."

That was probably the most amount of words I've ever said to a woman at one time, no joke.

She studies me, shock slowly registering on her face. I wonder if I overstepped. Maybe I shouldn't have said all that.

But I've never been one to take anything slow. That goes against my very nature.

"That is the most romantic thing a man has ever said to me," she says, her voice full of wonder. She slides her hands up my chest, her fingers going to the buttons of my shirt. She starts undoing them, her fingers fumbling, and I can tell they're shaking. "It's okay that we want to have sex all the time, right?"

"It's perfectly natural," I reassure her, my hands going to her tits yet again. I massage them. Press them together, all while she unbuttons my shirt and then tries to shove it off me. "I think I'm addicted. To you."

"Me too," she says just before she pulls my head down and kisses me.

We somehow manage to make it back to my bed. Our clothes fall off and we're naked. Thank Christ I remembered to bring that box of condoms home, and I suit up, just before I slide home and start fucking her in earnest.

This time, there's no foreplay. It isn't necessary.

This is a quickie.

I feel greedy. Consumed with her. I just take and take. Fuck and fuck. My hips are moving uncontrollably, my balls are slapping her ass with every deep thrust inside her always-welcoming body, and she's clinging to me, moaning like she's never been fucked that thoroughly.

Maybe she hasn't.

I come fast. So fast, I think I beat her to the gate, and regret hits me hard when it's over and I've calmed down some. Once I come back from the bathroom after getting rid of the condom, I settle back into the bed. She curls up by my side, her fingers sliding all over my skin, and I ask her an important question.

"Did you have an orgasm?"

She shakes her head. "It felt good, though."

Oh no. That won't stand with me.

"Are you still sensitive down here?" I cup her mound like I own it.

Eleanor shivers. "A little."

Her clit is swollen. I can tell. I rub my thumb over it and she sucks in a breath, her legs parting, allowing me better access. I test her folds and they're swollen too. She's so hot. Creamy. I wish I could fuck her bareback. Maybe later, but not now.

"That feels good," she says after a few minutes of me stroking.

I suck a nipple between my lips and continue to play between her legs. That's how I finally make her come. A couple of quick strokes, concentrating on her clit, all while I lick and bite her nipple.

Damn, this girl is sexy. I don't want to let her go.

But she might leave me once she finds out the truth.

TWENTY
ELEANOR

"WE NEED TO HAVE A CONVERSATION," I say as I go through the box labeled *kitchen shit*.

No joke. That's what he wrote on the side of the box.

"About what?" His expression is full of apprehension.

"Your favorite foods." I pull a giant pan out of the box, admiring it. Looks like it's never been used. "What do you like to eat?"

He's leaning against the counter, watching me. I finally convinced him that we couldn't spend all afternoon in bed —he was disappointed, poor guy—and now we're in his kitchen, and I'm thinking about making a very late lunch.

I'm absolutely starving. I checked his food situation, and there's nothing in this place. I think we might have to make a grocery run, but that's okay. It'll be fun.

I want to make him something. But...what?

"I like everything." He grins. "Especially you."

The man can eat me like no other, I will give him that.

"I'm not talking about my vagina," I say breezily, which makes him burst out laughing. "I'm talking about actual food. You're a big boy. Surely you eat a lot."

"Yeah. I try to keep it healthy."

"I'm craving an omelet. How about you?" I rise to my feet and settle the pan on top of the stove.

"We can find a restaurant around here. I'm sure there are ones that serve it all day," he suggests.

"No, I want to *make* you an omelet. It's my specialty." I'm limited on my cooking specialties, but an omelet is definitely one of them.

"You can cook?" He rubs his jaw.

"Yes." Sort of. "Can you?"

"Not really." He shrugs. "Why cook when you can just buy whatever you want to eat, whenever you want it?"

"You said you like to keep it healthy."

"I'm not always buying McDonald's or whatever. You can buy healthy takeout too," he says.

"Right." I cross my arms, contemplating him. "But I want to make you a meal. So let's go to the supermarket."

"Why?" He is honestly perplexed, which is kind of funny.

"So I can buy some eggs and cheese and milk, silly. Oh, and butter. And bacon. Or maybe you'd rather I put ham in the omelets? Maybe some green onion, a little bit of spinach?" My mind is a whirl with ideas.

"Is that what you really want to do?" he asks calmly.

Nerves eat at my insides. Why is he looking at me like that? So intently. All I want is to make him an omelet. What's the big deal?

"Yes." I lift my chin. "I do."

"You are too good to me." He pulls me into his arms and buries his face against my neck, his lips tickling my skin when he speaks. "Wanting to make me a meal. No girl has made me food since I lived at home."

"Really?" I'm shocked. But then…

"How many relationships have you been in?" I ask warily.

Slowly he pulls away from me, his brow furrowed. "Uh." He says nothing else.

That's his answer. Uh.

"I'm guessing the answer is none?" Now I'm the one frowning.

"How many relationships have *you* been in?" he asks.

"I had one serious boyfriend in high school. There was that one guy I dated off and on who I met at beauty school. Turns out he's gay." I wince a little. That had been so embarrassing. I made a fool of myself over that man, all for nothing. He didn't even like women. He just didn't know how to tell me he was gay. "He had the prettiest face I'd ever seen on a man. He was beautiful. Like a statue."

Mitch's jaw goes tight and he averts his head, staring off into space. He looks almost...jealous?

No. That's crazy.

"And that's it. I've gone on lots of dates. I've even gone on multiple dates with one man, but they never worked out. We just never...clicked." My voice is full of sadness as I mourn the dating ghosts of my past. Some of those guys were nice.

Most of them were not. Meaning, my mourning period is very short lived.

"I guess my last relationship was in high school," he says. "Danica Allen was her name. Cutest thing ever. Cheerleader to my football player. She had a great rack." He pauses, sending me an apologetic look.

It's fine. But I am definitely sensing a theme here.

"Danica was always down for a good time. And I don't mean that in a nasty way. More like she just always knew how to have fun. We dated through football season my senior year," he explains.

Now it's my turn to be jealous. Over a girl who was in his life in high school. I'm being ridiculous. Danica is long gone.

So why do I feel the sudden need to pull pretty, fun Danica's hair out?

"After Danica, and once I got into college, I just looked for fun wherever I could get it," he says. "Always temporary fun. One-girl-after-another fun. I didn't want anything serious. That wasn't my thing."

He gets quiet once again, and I know he's lost in memories. Which is nice and all, but considering I'm still dealing with my jealous feelings, we need to keep this conversation moving.

"It's been a long time then," I say. My words seem to snap him out of his thoughts, and he stands at attention.

"Yeah."

"You're not one to do relationships."

"That's why I got on the app," he reminds me. "I thought it might be a good place to find a serious relationship."

"Right." I nod, putting on a bright smile. I'm faking it a little, but he doesn't need to know that. It's weirdly awkward, talking about our past relationships—or lack thereof. Normally I'm feeling awkward every step of the way with a new guy.

This time, with Mitch, it was never awkward. The entire weekend has been awkward-free.

Until now.

Plus, his explanation about using the app makes no sense. They're not where people normally go to find a serious relationship. Some are used for hookups only.

Well, whatever. I'm just glad I snagged him up before someone else did.

"Should we head to the store?" I ask.

"Let me get my shoes on and we'll go."

We relax a little in the car ride over. The supermarket that's closest to his apartment building is teeming with cars and people. I guess everyone's shopping on a Sunday afternoon. As we drive by the storefront, I notice there's a giant display of beer that spells out *Welcome, Raiders!*

"I forgot that the Raiders moved to Las Vegas." I turn to look at him, ready to say more, but I clamp my lips shut.

Wow. He looks—annoyed. Nervous.

Why?

"Do you work with any of those guys?" I ask.

"A few," he says with a little shrug. "I'm going to drop you off right here, okay? I'll find a parking space and meet you inside in a few."

I hop out of the giant truck, staring after him as he roars away. I don't understand what's happening between us right now, but it doesn't feel...right.

Shaking my head, I head into the supermarket, admiring the giant display of beer. Not sure what brand it is, but the twelve-pack boxes are black-and-white, perfect for a Raider display. They were able to switch the boxes around to spell out the words, plus there are black and silver balloons. It looks good. There's a guy standing in front of the display wearing a black polo shirt with a tiny Raiders emblem on it, and he smiles at me as I walk by.

"You a Raiders fan, miss?" he asks.

"I prefer the Niners, actually," I tell him, and he rests his hand against his chest, making me laugh.

"My heart is offended," he tells me, but he's grinning, so I know he's teasing me.

"It's a family thing," I say with a shrug, as if that explains everything. "My dad loved Joe Montana."

We chat a little bit more about football and I don't mind, because I'm waiting for Mitch to join me. Eventually, I just grab a cart and head for the aisles. It's busy, but he can find me. Or he can text me if he can't.

But I find everything I'm looking for and still no Mitch. It's been at least fifteen minutes. No way did it take him that long to find a freaking parking spot. Frustration rippling through me, I yank my phone out of my bar purse—yes, I'm still stuck with it—and call him.

"Where are you?" I ask when he answers.

"I had to take a business call," he says, his voice casual, like no big deal. "I just got off the phone."

"I'm finished with my shopping," I tell him as I pull into the self-checkout line.

"Perfect. I'll pull up in the front and pick you up," he says, like that was his plan the entire time.

I'm tempted to growl into the phone, but I keep myself in check. He's being kind of—annoying. Why wouldn't he shop with me? Do grocery stores scare him? What's the big deal?

"Give me a few minutes. I'm still in line," I mutter.

"No problem. I'll wait for you," he says cheerily.

I end the call, pleased that I sort of hung up on him, which is silly. Why am I so annoyed? Or is it why is he being so annoying?

This entire afternoon has slipped right into the toilet. It's such a bummer.

Within a few minutes, I'm exiting the supermarket clutching a shopping bag, and Mitch pulls that giant truck right up beside me, rolling his window down so he can flash me a smile. He has really nice teeth.

Oh, who am I kidding? He has really nice everything.

I scowl at him as I round the front of the truck and open the door, climbing inside.

"Hey!" I hear someone shout from in front of the store. "Isn't that Mitchell—"

The truck roars away from the curb, sending me backward, the tires squealing. I send Mitch a look, but he's not even paying attention to me. He's gripping the steering wheel so hard, his knuckles are white, and his jaw is tight. I can see a ticking muscle there.

"Are you okay?" I ask.

"I'm fine." He's distracted. Clearly.

I decide to remain quiet. Maybe he had a bad phone call about work. Maybe he's stressed out. Why did that person yell his name right before we left the store? I'm sure that's Mitch's full name: Mitchell. Not that he's ever told me that. It's such an old-fashioned name. I like it. It's very manly.

Did he see someone he knows? I'm not sure how, considering he's not from Las Vegas, but what do I know? I want to ask him about it, but tension is radiating off him in big, heaping waves, so I leave it alone.

We can talk about it later.

Once we arrive at his apartment, I go right into prep mode. Mitch leaves me be, settling in on the couch and turning on the TV. He puts it on ESPN, and they're giving some sort of recap about football. The moment they mention the Raiders, he changes the channel.

Huh.

Fifteen minutes later and with a giant mess all over his beautiful kitchen, I'm finished.

"It's ready," I call to him as I plate the food.

"Want to eat in here?" he asks, indicating the living room.

"Sure," I say, because really, where else are we going to eat? He doesn't have a table in here.

I bring him his plate, steam still drifting from the very hot omelet. He gazes at it gratefully for a moment before he glances up at me. "Thank you," he says appreciatively.

I hand him a fork and a paper towel he can use as a napkin. "You're welcome. You need something to drink?"

He waves at the water bottle sitting next to him. "I'm good, thanks."

I go back to the kitchen and grab my plate, along with my fork, napkin and a bottle of water, before I make my way back to the couch. Once I'm settled in, I see that his plate is freaking empty.

"You ate all your food," I say incredulously.

"It was delicious." He pats his very flat stomach.

"I made you a giant omelet."

"And I appreciate that. It was good." He leans over and drops a faintly greasy kiss on my lips. I'm guessing that's from the bacon he stuffed into his mouth at a rapid pace. "Thank you, baby."

"You're welcome." I hand him a piece of bacon, which he doesn't hesitate in taking it from me. "I'm glad you enjoyed it. I feel like I should've made more."

He munches on the bacon thoughtfully, his lips curving into a smile. "We'll order pizza later."

I finish my omelet and take my plate and Mitch's back to the kitchen. He follows after me, making a tsking noise when he sees the mess I made, but he doesn't hesitate in helping me. We both go through the various boxes stacked nearby to find kitchen towels and a scrubber to clean off the plates with before we put them in the dishwasher.

Once that's taken care of, I rinse off the plates and pans while Mitch puts away the leftover ingredients. He's wiping down the counters with a damp paper towel when I ask him, "Do you have dishwashing detergent?"

His expression turns sheepish. "No."

"How about dish soap so I can hand wash everything?"

"Yeah." He scrubs the back of his head. "I don't think so."

This man is clearly not domesticated.

Well, I cleaned off everything as well as I could. "You'll need to run the dishwasher soon."

He salutes me. "Whatever you say, ma'am."

I'm grinning as I go to him and he wraps me up in a big hug, dropping a kiss on my forehead. "Thank you again for the omelet."

"Thank you for helping me clean up," I say as I press my cheek against his warm, solid chest.

A girl could get used to this kind of treatment.

We enter the living room and both plop down on the couch, sitting right next to each other. He grabs the controller and hits a button, and I realize the video game he was playing earlier was on pause. The volume is turned up super loud, and the room seems to rumble and shake every time a bomb goes off or a shot's fired. The men in the game are all yelling and cursing at each other, and Mitch is sitting poised on the edge of the couch. He's got the controller in his hand, clutching it tightly, his intense focus on the game and nothing else. I scoot away from him and grab my phone from the coffee table and start scrolling, wondering what the hell are we doing.

I mean, this isn't so bad, hanging out together. But I thought we could actually...you know. Hang out. With each other.

Not me cooking him food and him playing video games. He helped with the kitchen so he's not a total fail, but still. I would rather he pay attention to me versus play his video game. I'm leaving tomorrow. We're on limited time here.

Though I guess this is what real life would be like if we were in an actual relationship, right?

Is that something I want? Frowning, I contemplate our situation. We live in different cities, so it would have to be long distance, and that's kind of tough. I love it back home. I don't want to leave.

Eleanor, you are clearly jumping the gun. You hardly know this guy.

Right, I tell my know-it-all inner voice. *Right, right, right.*

"Fucking GO!" he suddenly yells, making me jump. I rest my hand over my chest, watching as he's tapping away at the controller, growling under his breath as his character on the video game is getting the shit shot out of him.

It's rather violent. And excessively graphic.

He loses. It's game over. Frustration radiates from him as he tosses the controller onto the coffee table, where it lands with a loud clatter. Glancing over at me, he offers up a grim smile before grabbing the TV controller and turns the TV and game off.

"Sorry about that," he mutters, sounding contrite. "I paused the game so we could eat and thought I could finish it real fast. Took longer than I thought."

I shrug. "It's okay." This is what men do, I suppose. Well, not all of them. But I know many of them like to get out their aggression playing violent video games. I'm not bothered by it. It's a different side of him, and I appreciate seeing it.

Mitch contemplates me for a moment, and I want to

squirm under his assessing gaze. What is he thinking about right now? What does he see when he looks at me? And does he *like* what he sees?

Ugh, I hate it when my old insecurities flare back up. Always at the worst times, too.

"You want to go out tonight?" he asks.

My brows shoot up. "And do what?"

"Go see a show at one of the casinos? Go to the movies? Gamble our lives away? Go to a strip club? Do that zip glide thing downtown?"

What a variety of interesting suggestions. Sadly, none of them sound good. I think I'm too tired. Sex will do that to a person. "Maybe we should just stay in."

"Netflix and chill?" Now his brows are shooting up. His expression is hopeful. He has sex on the brain.

No problem, so do I. It's what we do.

"Let's do that. And order a pizza later," I say.

"Hey." Somehow, he grabs hold of me, those big hands landing on my waist and pulling me to him. His face is in mine, and his eyes seem darker. More serious. "Thank you for making breakfast. Or lunch. Whatever you want to call it. I appreciate you making me a homecooked meal. No one ever does that sort of thing for me."

Aww. The sincerity ringing in his voice, that look still glowing in his eyes...all the earlier tension between us just melts away and I'm left with a warm, fuzzy sensation filling me.

"You're welcome."

"I also want to apologize."

I'm about to protest and tell him it's not necessary but he holds up his hand, silencing me.

I'm sorry, Eleanor. I was a complete dick just now with the video game thing," he confesses, his voice low, his gaze sincere. "I'm not used to sharing my space with someone else."

"I get it." I smile. "If we're being real right now, I'm not used to it either."

"We could get used to it." He brushes a few stray hairs away from my face, his touch gentle. "Together."

"That sounds nice." I pat his shoulder. Run my hand down his chest. Silently marvel at his muscular deliciousness.

I do that for a while. Touch him. My fingers exploring. Soon his hand is wrapped around my nape and he's guiding me backward onto the couch, his mouth landing on mine, devouring me. My dress is shoved up and his shorts are shoved down and then he's inside me. No condom. Just Mitch's bare cock, filling me completely.

"Shit." He drops his forehead to mine, panting heavily as he remains completely still. "I forgot to grab a condom. I'll go get one."

He's about to pull out but I keep him where he's at, my hands firm against his back. "Just..." My voice drifts and I shift beneath him, resting my hands over my face. I'm on the pill. I don't usually have sex with men without condoms, so I'm taking a chance here. Or maybe not. "When you're about to come, pull out."

He moves my hands away from my face so he can look into my eyes. "Can I come on your chest?"

I start to laugh. He sounds so eager, so hopeful. I nod my answer.

Within a few minutes, I'm coming. And then he is too.

All over my breasts.

TWENTY-ONE
MITCH

IT'S Monday afternoon and I'm driving Eleanor to the airport. The air is hot outside. Stifling. The sun is so damn intense, I feel like I'm going to melt, and I have the air conditioner on high, for Christ's sake. This weather is going to take some getting used to.

We had a few bumpy spots yesterday, but eventually Eleanor and I found our groove and had a good time together. It didn't help that I silently freaked out over the fan spotting me at the supermarket. Oh, and the giant *Welcome, Raiders* display in the front of the store, made out of a wall of beer boxes. I know the city is excited to have us there, but I wasn't prepared. It threw me off guard.

And made me act like kind of a dick toward Eleanor.

She's not picking up on the clues, and I'm grateful for it. I'm always able to dodge the many bullets shot at me, but this won't last for long. I need to come clean and tell her the truth.

I should tell her right now.

But it's like I can't. The lump in my throat won't let me.

The tightness in my chest definitely won't let me either. I chicken out.

As usual.

Instead, I think about what we did last night. We watched a couple of movies on Netflix. Ordered a pizza that was pretty decent. At one point, she got on her knees on the floor while I sat on the couch and I watched her suck me off, my hands in her hair, her shiny peach lips working my dick over.

That was hot. No surprise there.

We had lots of sex throughout the night. Again, as usual. I'm exhausted, running on empty, but I still feel good. On top of the world, really, and the reason is because of the woman sitting next to me in my truck.

I glance over at Eleanor to find she's on her phone, typing away as she texts someone. I don't ask who. It's none of my business, right? Who am I to want to know her every move? I'm just the guy she had a hot weekend with, that's it.

Yet it seems like so much more. For me it does. I'm halfway in love with her, I think. Big words from a dude who's never really done this thing before, but yeah. I'm feeling it. I'm feeling *her*. I want her to be a part of my life. Does she feel the same way?

We don't talk much on the drive, and I think it's because she's sad. I'm sad too. I didn't work today. They're giving us a few days off to get settled after everyone's big move, but later this week, we start training, in preparation for preseason.

I'm ready for it. I need the distraction.

When I finally pull up in front of the airport drop-off, I put the truck in park and look over at her. If I can't be honest about who I really am, I can at least tell her how I really feel. "I don't want you to leave."

Her big blue eyes meet mine, her lower lip trembling. Oh shit, she's going to cry. Don't know if I can handle that. "I don't want to leave either. But I have to work tomorrow."

"I know. You have a life. I get it." I nod, pretending that I do, but deep down I just want to keep her. Not let her out of my sight. That's crazy. I know it is.

But it's how I feel, so...

"Maybe I could come back and visit you? In a couple of weeks?" she suggests.

"Definitely," I say, sounding way too eager, but I don't care. I want her to know how I feel. How much she already means to me.

"This is moving so fast," she admits, her expression shy, her gaze cast downward. "Probably too fast."

"It's perfect," I tell her, reaching out and settling my hand on her knee. I give it a squeeze. Remind myself I can't do anything inappropriate in front of the airport. She has a plane to catch. "Really. This weekend was—perfect."

We smile at each other, and then we both get out of the truck. I grab her suitcase and bring it to her. We stand on the sidewalk, surrounded by all sorts of people, the Vegas heat seeming to shimmer in the air around us, and I stare at her, never wanting to forget this moment.

The time I dropped off my future girlfriend at the airport.

Yeah, I'm a complete sucker for this woman. It's cool. I've got this.

Hopefully she won't hate me when I confess the truth about my profession.

Pulling her into my arms, I give her the tightest, biggest hug I can. She clings to me, her face buried against my chest, her arms stretching around my middle. I slip a couple of fingers beneath her chin and tilt her face up, pressing a soft, sweet kiss to her lips, and she goes in for another one. Then another one.

"I have to go," she whispers shakily, her lips tickling mine when she speaks.

"Text me when you get on the plane. And when you land," I tell her.

She nods. Presses her lips together, like she's trying to contain herself. Like she might break out in tears.

"Let me know you make it home safe, okay?" I cup her cheek. Stroke her skin. Memorize her face with my eyes and fingers.

"I will," she says once she releases a shuddery breath.

We kiss again, like there are magnets in our lips and we can't resist each other. Finally I break away and she grabs the handle of her suitcase. I remain standing where she left me, watching her enter the airport, the doors sliding shut the moment she walks through them. I stand there and wait and wait until finally...

I can't see her anymore.

She's gone.

"I'M HOME," Eleanor singsongs, her sweet voice filling my ear and making me feel instant relief.

I'm lying in bed, going in and out of wakefulness as I waited for Eleanor to call me. So freaking tired after the wild weekend we had, but I knew I wanted to hear her voice one last time before I fell sleep.

"Your flights were okay?" She mentioned she had to fly to Los Angeles first, then Monterey.

"Yes. And luckily enough, Stella came and picked me

up at the airport, so I didn't have to catch a ride home with a crazy Uber driver," she explains.

"Wait a minute, you were going to take an Uber home this late at night?" I don't like the sounds of that. Too many scary stories about freaky drivers on the Internet.

"My flight was so late, I figured I didn't have a choice. But Stella came through," she says.

"Thank God for that," I mutter.

"Worried for my safety?"

"Always," I answer quickly.

"Aw, that's so sweet." She hesitates for only a moment before she says, "I had a really good time this weekend."

"Me too."

"My thighs are sore," she admits.

I chuckle. "Guessing your pussy is too."

"Mitch," she chastises. "You can't just—say things like that."

"What do you mean? I say things like that all the damn time." It's true. I talk crude to her and while she puts on a bit of a to-do over it sometimes, I think secretly, she likes what I say.

"I know, but not over the phone."

"Get used to it, baby. This is how we'll have to communicate when we're not actually together." I smile when an idea strikes me. "Maybe we could FaceTime each other naked tomorrow night."

"Whaaat?" Ha, I scandalized her.

"Yeah. I'll call you and we can give each other a full body scan and show off our best parts. In fact." I find myself warming up to this idea. "Maybe I could watch you touch yourself, and you can watch me touch myself, and we can get each other off. I wonder, do other people do that? Have FaceTime sex?"

She's quiet for a moment. Long enough that I thought I lost her. "I have no idea," she finally says.

"You want to do it?"

"Um..."

"Just say yes. You know by tomorrow night you'll be dying to see my giant cock," I tease her.

"Mitch." She gasps. "You shouldn't talk like that. It's—shocking to hear."

"Like I said, get used to it. This is what you do to me." I lower my voice. "I miss having you lying next to me."

"I miss you too," she says on a sigh.

"We need to figure out when you can come back and see me."

"It might be a while. Plane tickets aren't cheap," she protests.

"I'll buy your ticket. I've got money." Loads of it.

"I couldn't do that..."

"You will. Don't protest. Two weeks. What do you think?"

"I'll have to come on a Sunday then. Saturday is my busiest day of the week and I can't miss it. I've already missed too many this summer. Like this one, and the one a couple of weeks ago when we had Caroline's bridal shower. And I'll miss one next week too, when Caroline gets married," she explains.

"The day doesn't matter. I just need you here soon," I tell her.

"We'll make plans." I can hear her yawn. "But I need to go to sleep. We'll talk tomorrow?"

"Tomorrow for sure. Good night, Eleanor."

"Good night."

"Sweet dreams," I murmur.

I can tell she's smiling. "Same to you."

"I'll be dreaming of your sweet pussy, so that's guaranteed."

She bursts out laughing. "Good night, Mitch." She ends the call.

I fall asleep smiling.

TWENTY-TWO
ELEANOR

I'M SWEEPING up hair off the floor while I'm between clients when Kelsey comes bursting into the salon, a frazzled expression on her gorgeous face. She always seems to do this, and when she does, she's usually bringing bad news with her.

Warily, I stop what I'm doing and wait for her to say something.

"What's your new boyfriend's name again?" she asks.

"Um, Mitch?"

"Mitch what? What's his full name?" She sounds very impatient.

Just hearing his name makes me feel hot inside. We've been talking and FaceTiming non-stop since I returned home. We've even naked FaceTimed, and it's been pretty—enjoyable. He watched me touch myself, saying such encouraging, dirty words I couldn't help but come. He liked that.

A lot.

I had a difficult time saying dirty words to him—it's not in my wheelhouse like it is his—but I watched him jerk off, and wow, he was so rough with that thing. I thought he might yank it right off his body.

Men can be a little weird sometimes. But I really, really care about this one, and I can be weird too, so maybe we're a perfect match.

I wish he would come with me to Caroline's wedding. I asked him if he could, and he apologized profusely, saying he had a big work thing that he couldn't get out of.

I told him I understood, but honestly, I was so disappointed. I want to show him off as my wedding date.

"Eleanor," Kelsey snaps, bringing me out of my Mitch-induced thoughts.

"Mitchell Anderson," I finally tell Kelsey as I sweep the hair into the stationary vacuum the salon has set up for us.

"Oh. My. *God.*" Kelsey's eyes look like they're ready to bug right out of her head. "Why didn't you tell us your boyfriend plays for the Raiders?"

I gape at her. Shake my head like I'm trying to clear my ears. "What now?"

She thrusts her phone in my face. There's Mitch. He's wearing a Raiders jersey. Number 96. He's got a serious expression on his face. He looks mean.

But that is definitely my Mitch.

Wearing a football jersey.

Because he's a professional football player.

And the motherfucker...

Never.

Bothered.

To.

Tell.

ME!

I take the phone from Kelsey and start tapping, scanning the images and links Google brought up. Oh look, there's a video of him. One of those short introduction clips they play at the beginning of a game. There he is in all of his football playing glory.

I hit play.

"Mitchell Anderson. Texas A&M."

Serious, serious face. No smiling allowed, I guess. His hair is shorter. His face, leaner. I'm guessing it's from a year or two ago.

But that is my Mitch. Those lips have been in very intimate places on my body, and I have heard that voice whisper crude, filthy things in my ear. Sweet, adorable things too.

That lying scumbag!

"Wait a minute. You knew, right?" Kelsey's voice is weak. And full of worry.

Lifting my head, I meet her gaze. I'm sure she can see it written all over my face. "Uh...no?"

"That asshole!" She covers her mouth with her hand, her eyes wide and full of horror. "He didn't tell you? Why would he keep such a big thing from you?"

How am I supposed to know? I'm the one he kept in the dark this entire time. "He said he worked in fitness, remember? Then he told me he trained professional athletes." I guess that's not exactly a lie...

Oh, who am I kidding? It's a total lie!

"I'm so, so sorry, El. I thought you were keeping it from us on purpose, that you didn't want us to know. I would've never just burst into your work and thrown something like that at you as a surprise," Kelsey says, as if I might be angry with her, but that's not the case. I'm not mad at all. Not at her.

But I definitely think I'm in shock.

"It's okay," I say as I collapse in my chair, staring at my

reflection in the mirror. Yep, I am dazed and confused.

"Where is everyone?" Kelsey asks as she looks around the mostly empty salon.

"They're done for the day. I'm waiting for my last client," I tell her, my mind racing. Mitch *lied* to me. He's a professional football player. He's like...famous or whatever. He probably makes millions of dollars.

I'm such an idiot. Yet again duped by a man. A man who is really sexy, who made *me* feel really sexy, and also touched my heart.

"What are you going to do?" Kelsey settles her hand on my shoulder and gives it a comforting squeeze. I tilt my head back, meeting her gaze, and I see all the sympathy there. She feels bad for me.

Same, girl. Same.

"Cut my client's hair and go home I guess," I say with a shrug.

She drops her hand. "You have to confront him, you know."

"How?" I ask hopelessly. I catch my own gaze in the mirror again, and all I want to do is call myself names.

Stupid.

Gullible.

Dumb.

"Call him up and call him out, that's how," Kelsey says firmly. She's always so tough. Tougher than I could ever be.

"But..." My voice drifts. So do my thoughts. I like this guy. Can I forgive him for such a big secret? Yes, I probably can. There has to be a reason he hid this from me, right? This wasn't a trick on his part.

Right?

We spent three days together. We had sex multiple times. I repeat, multiple times. I gave everything to him. Did things I've never done with another man before. We talked and we laughed and we watched movies together. He brought me into his home. I cooked him food. This wasn't some casual weekend fling.

This was real. It still is.

Maybe that's why this revelation hurts so much.

"But what? You have to confront him, Eleanor. You can't let him get away with this," Kelsey stresses.

"I know. You're right. What he did was wrong. Terrible," I tell her, my gaze meeting hers. She's angry on my behalf. Her face is flushed and her eyes are blazing. She looks all fired up. "But I want to hear him out first. See what he says."

"You're going to let him talk you into forgiving him?" Kelsey asks incredulously.

"If he has a valid enough reason, maybe." Reaching out, I grab hold of both of her hands. "I've never connected with a man like that before. Mitch and I—I can't explain it."

"It was just really good sex."

"No, it was more than that." I'm about to further explain myself when Bonnie the receptionist appears in the doorway that leads into the salon, my client standing right behind her. I hop out of my chair and start walking toward them. "Oh hi, Sandie."

Bonnie smiles and heads back to the reception desk. Kelsey remains rooted in place. I shoot her a look. "We'll talk later," I tell her.

She hesitates for a moment but then dashes out of the salon, leaving me alone with my client.

And my turbulent thoughts.

"...AND I was so distracted, I almost snipped off the top of my client's ear," I say with a moan, covering my face with my hands.

Kelsey pushes the freshly refilled pitcher of beer toward me. I feel some of it slosh onto the table in front of me. "Drink up, girlfriend."

We've been at Milligan's for about a half hour already, the bar down the street from where I work. It's me, Kelsey, Sarah and surprisingly enough, Amelia. We used to be closer to Amelia—she hung around with me, Stella, Caroline and Sarah a lot back in the day. Back before some of us met men and ended up engaged to them. But she's so off and on with her jerk ass boyfriend and consumed with their toxic relationship, she doesn't make much time for us anymore.

It's nice having her here tonight, even if I'm feeling like absolute garbage.

"Were you so distraught after what Kelsey told you that you couldn't focus?" Sarah asks, her gaze full of sympathy. I know she feels bad for me. All of my friends sitting at this table do. I know Stella and Caroline and Candice would be here too if they could, but there are wedding preparations keeping Stella and Caroline occupied, and Candice is at some fancy-schmancy fundraiser event with her boyfriend, so it's just us.

"So distraught. My focus was just gone," I say as I pour myself another glass of beer. I shouldn't drown my sorrows in alcohol. This is a recipe for disaster. I say stupid stuff when I'm drunk.

Drunk and upset? I'll probably say something I'll regret.

I filled them all in on what Kelsey told me once we were all seated at the table. What's nice is when I put the text out in our group chat that I needed them, they didn't hesitate. If they could, they all showed up for me. And I love that.

I love my friends.

"Why do you think he kept such a big secret?" Sarah asks.

"I don't know. He kind of hinted around it. Said he worked in fitness, but that sounded like a lie—too vague, right?" They all nod their agreement. "When I questioned him further, he said he trained professional athletes and he couldn't talk about it because of some NDA he signed."

"Wow," Amelia says, slowly shaking her head. "He's good at this. I wonder if he's done it before."

"What do you mean?" I ask, slightly annoyed. It's not like I want to feel like a special case, but...

Yeah. Maybe I do want to feel like a special case. Which makes no sense.

"Maybe this is his MO. He gets with women, lies to them about who he really is, spends a little time with them and then disappears," Amelia explains.

"I don't know. He hasn't disappeared on me." As a matter of fact, he keeps texting me, but I haven't mentioned that little fact to my friends yet. They'd probably want me to confront him right now, while they all could watch.

No way. I'm not doing that in public. Not even in private with them listening in.

This problem is between me and Mitch.

"Give him time," Amelia says, the rest of them nodding their agreement.

I can't agree with Amelia. Not right now. She claims she broke up with her boyfriend for good, and she's a bit of a Bitter Betty when it comes to men, not that I can blame her. But if she just cut the cord once and for all, she'd feel better about herself.

We're not here to discuss Amelia tonight, though. It's all about me and my troubles. And while I appreciate their help and need their support, I also don't want any negativity aimed at Mitch.

Damn it, I really care about the guy.

The TVs are on at Milligan's, and of course they're all tuned in to sports. Either the Football Network or ESPN. My gaze catches on one of the screens when I spot the Raiders emblem, and I watch as my friends talk all around me, my jaw dropping open when I see my Mitch appear on the TV.

"Shush!" I tell my friends, my gaze glued to his face, which is like four times its normal size, thanks to the enormity of the big screen.

Thankfully, they all go quiet. And I can actually, sort of hear what he's saying.

"...it's going to be a good season. We did well last year, and I think this season, we're going to be even stronger, especially with Clay leading us," Mitch explains.

"That's him," Kelsey hiss-whispers to everyone else at the table.

The interview switches to someone else, the reporter talking about spending time at the team's practice earlier today and I can only sit there, completely dumbfounded. Feeling like a fool. I knew Kelsey was telling the truth. Google doesn't lie.

Well, most of the time.

But there were so many articles listed. And photos. Lots and lots of photos. His name on the Raiders team roster. It was all right there, in black-and-white or full color, telling me that yes, indeed, he's a pro football player for the NFL.

None of it felt real, though, until seeing him in that interview just now. His hair curling around his head, like he was a little sweaty. Wearing a Raiders T-shirt and grim determination. Talking on a national television network like he doesn't have anything to hide, while he's texting me at this very minute, asking where I am.

Who does this guy think he is?

Yes, I really care about the guy, but now I'm even angrier.

"He acts like he's just living life," I say, waving my hand at the TV screen. "All the while, he's lying to me. Who does that?"

"Psychopaths," Kelsey answers, making Sarah choke on her beer.

"I doubt he's an actual psychopath," Sarah says once she's stopped coughing.

"Egomaniac then," Amelia suggests.

"That makes no sense," Kelsey says. "If he's an egomaniac, he would've led with the pro football thing. He would want women to know he's the big-time football player so they'll lose their minds and panties for him in an instant."

Now there's an image. One I don't want put into my head. Mitch is a very—sexual man. He likes sex. He's really good at it. Meaning, he's probably had a lot of it. With lots of women. Fans of his. Groupies. They probably throw themselves at him on a regular basis. He could have as much pussy as he wants, whenever he wants it.

God, look at me. I'm thinking just like him.

"Maybe he wanted to find a woman who appreciated him for who he is, not what he does," Sarah suggest.

We all go quiet. Especially me.

"I'm sure he meets plenty of women, but they all just want him because of his fame, or his money, or because of what he does for a living. And I bet that gets old," Sarah further explains. "Maybe he went on that Rate a Date app to find a woman he can connect with on a real level."

"What a bunch of horseshit," Amelia starts, but I send her a look, silencing her.

"Go on," I encourage Sarah.

She sits up straighter, and I can tell she's getting into it. I like the direction she's taking. But could it be true? Or is it just me being hopeful?

"There was nothing about professional football mentioned on his profile, right?" she asks.

I shake my head. "Not at all."

"And he never brought up anything related to football when you guys talked?"

"Never. I practically had to pry it out of him that he works with professional athletes," I say.

"That's not necessarily a lie," Sarah starts.

"Oh, give me a break. Stop making excuses for this guy. He's a total douche, leading you on like this and not being truthful," Amelia says, sounding thoroughly disgusted. Her nose is wrinkled and her eyes are narrowed, like she just smelled something bad. She's pretty in an understated, elegant way. She comes from money, unlike some of us. She works at her family's jewelry store, and hopes to run it someday, though her father is bit of a tyrant. Oh, and sexist.

"What else could he be lying about?" Kelsey asks.

All the things they're saying are swirling in my head, making me confused. The beer is too. "I should go home," I say.

"I'll drive you home," Sarah suggests.

"But my car is still here," I protest.

"It's fine. Just leave it here. I'll pick you up tomorrow and take you to work," she says, like the good friend she is.

"Okay." I give in easily, because first, I don't want to get a DUI, and second, I don't want to drive home alone.

It'll be nice to have Sarah with me, at least for a little while longer.

We leave Milligan's and I ride home in Sarah's car, both of us pretty much silent the entire ride.

"The rehearsal dinner is tomorrow," I say at one point.

"I know." Sarah hesitates. "Are you going to talk to him tonight?"

"I have to."

"Are you going to be okay?"

"No, but eventually I will be," I say morosely, staring out the window. This is not how I thought this weekend would play out. I'm going to be a sad bridesmaid instead of an on-top-of-the-world bridesmaid. I'm the romantic of the group, remember? I believe in true love and heart eyes and passion.

I was ready to throw myself into the wedding festivities with everything I've got. I was going to embrace the notion of love and celebrate Alex and Caroline. I have always firmly believed there's someone for everyone, and thought I might've found my someone.

It sucks to find out he's someone else.

TWENTY-THREE
MITCH

I'M GOING out of my mind tonight, trying to get Eleanor to talk to me via text. But she won't. Not really. She's not very responsive, and she keeps me hanging for twenty, thirty minutes at a time before she finally says something. And when that happens, it's usually just one- or two-word sentences. At one point she tells me she's at a bar having a couple of beers with her friends, and I know the wedding is getting closer, but why is she at a bar, drinking beer?

That doesn't sound like my Eleanor.

Of course, do I really know her that well? In the sexual sense, hell yeah. But in other ways?

Not yet.

Finally, my phone rings, and her face lights up my screen. I snapped that photo Sunday night, right before she got on her knees and gave me a BJ. There's a glow in her eyes that she only seems to aim right at me, and the smile stretching her peach-colored lips is so bright. So beautiful.

Just seeing this photo makes my entire body ache with wanting her.

"Hey," I greet her when I answer.

"Hi," she says glumly.

Unease settles over me, making me sit up straighter. "You all right?"

"No. As a matter of fact, I'm not."

Fear has circled around my heart, gripping it in a stranglehold. "What's wrong?"

There's a hesitation there. I can hear her breathe, and it sounds shaky.

Fuck. This can't be good.

"I know who you are. Or more like what you do."

I'm silent. She's silent. My heart is racing. The blood is roaring in my ears. I actually feel a little faint. This is the moment I've been dreading, and it is happening.

Right now.

"Why didn't you tell me?" she asks when I still haven't said anything. "I wouldn't care what you do. But you kept it from me. Why?"

"I—" I clear my throat, hating how scratchy my voice is. "I didn't want you to know at first."

"Why the hell not?"

I wince at her tone. She is super pissed. Not that I can blame her. "I just wanted to get to know a woman without all the shit that comes with me being who I really am, and what I do. I'm not that guy, Eleanor. I never really was."

"What do you mean?"

"The arrogant football player. The guy who goes out with his friends and spends money and gets with all sorts of women and does whatever the fuck he wants."

Wait a minute. This all feels like a lie. A denial. And that is the very last tactic I want to take with Eleanor. I need to be one hundred percent truthful with her.

"I guess I *was* that guy." Yeah, I really can't deny it, all the evidence is out there on the internet. "But I'm not that guy anymore. I haven't wanted to be him in a long time. I was trying to find something real."

"Real? You wanted something real, yet you built it all on top of a lie?"

She has a valid point.

"I didn't know how to tell you." There. That's also the truth. "I got in too deep, and I couldn't figure out what to say next."

"So you built a lie on top of a lie then." She sighs, the sound full of so much disappointment. I swear to God I just felt my heart crack wide open. "I gave you my trust, Mitch. I thought what we had was special."

Her using the past tense about what we had is freaking me out. "It *is* special, Eleanor. You mean a lot to me. Our weekend was—everything. Our talks every night, they get me through the next day."

"Right. The next day when you're out on the football field and conducting interviews on ESPN or whatever the hell," she says snottily.

My heart drops. Did she see me on ESPN?

"Yes, I saw you," she says, confirming my internal question. "My friend found you on the internet. I told her your first and last name, and she looked you up. I can't believe I didn't think of it sooner. I guess I'm just too trusting."

The imaginary knife in her hand just keeps stabbing me directly in the heart. "Eleanor, please. Know that I never meant to hurt you."

"Well, you did." She sounds like she's holding back a sob, and holy hell, that sort of makes me want to cry too. "Goodbye, Mitch."

The call ends.

My phone slips from my hands, landing on the floor with a thunk. I sit on my couch, staring into space, going over what she said to me. What I said to her. What I could've said that might've made a difference.

I come up with nothing. I'm a liar. I lied to her. I hurt her. This woman, who matters to me more than any other woman I've met in my life, I hurt her. Destroyed her trust in me. So stupid.

Running my hands through my hair, I leap to my feet and start pacing. How can I fix this? I need to fix it. I can't let her go. No way. No fucking way. She's mine. Eleanor's going to learn real quick...

I don't give up that easily.

TWENTY-FOUR
ELEANOR

IT'S Caroline's wedding day and I look like I've been crying for the last forty-eight hours straight.

Oh, maybe that's because I *have* been crying for the last forty-eight hours. Well, maybe that's a slight exaggeration, but that's what it feels like. The crying started Thursday night after I ended the call with Mitch. He never apologized. He never once said he was sorry for lying and hurting me. Seriously, what a jerk.

Friday was tough. I worked all day, and I was grateful for the distraction, even though I felt like I was in a semi-daze most of the day. Then I had to go to the wedding rehearsal and dinner afterward. The wedding is being held at the Wilder Hotel in Pebble Beach, of course. It'll be an outdoor ceremony, the reception afterward in a giant tent constructed on the grounds, all of it overlooking the ocean. It's going to be beautiful.

The rehearsal went smoothly. I'm a bridesmaid, and I'm walking with one of Alex's college friends. He's nice enough. Single. Very friendly. Probably looking for a wedding hookup.

Pass.

The dinner afterward was held in a ballroom at the hotel, and the food was amazing. At least, that's what everyone said.

I could barely eat.

Late Saturday morning and we're in a suite at the hotel, getting ready. The ceremony is at four, with photos immediately afterward and the reception kicking off at five. Caroline is sitting in a chair in front of a mirror, clad in a pale pink robe that is butter soft. I know this because we're all wearing matching ones. The back of Caroline's robe says *Mrs. Caroline Wilder*.

Just seeing those words scrawled across her back earlier when I first arrived made me tear up. Made me realize that this is actually happening. One of my very best friends is getting married today, and I couldn't be happier for her.

But I'm also filled with so much melancholy, it's hard for me to smile. Hard for me to feel joy. All the joy has been sucked right out of me, thanks to Mitch.

I miss him. I want to be able to forgive him, but I can't worry about that. Not today. He's tried to text me, but I ignore him. He's tried to call me as well, but I ignore those too. I can't talk to him right now. There's too much going on.

What I really need to do is put my own issues aside and focus on Caroline. This day is about her. And Alex. Their wedding. Everything is in place, and though she was extremely stressed last night during the rehearsal dinner, this morning our bride-to-be is serene. Calm. It's so nice to see. I need to take a lesson from her and find some inner peace.

Kind of difficult, though, when all I want to do is talk to Mitch.

We're all getting our makeup and hair done in the suite,

including Caroline's and Alex's mothers, other family members, and of course, the bridesmaids. Our dresses are beautiful. The color is a dusky blue, with a crossover front and thin straps that crisscross in the back. The skirt is gauzy, covered with delicate pearl-and-rhinestone embellishment that looks like vines.

I wish Mitch could see me in it.

One of my gifts to my friend is doing her hair for the wedding. This is why she's in the chair and I'm standing behind her, trying to focus so I don't screw up. She found a hairclip that matches the embellishment on the bridesmaids' dresses almost perfectly, and I'm going to create a loose curl updo, with soft tendrils framing her face and the clip in the back of her hair.

It's going to be fabulous. I've done this hairstyle before on other brides, so this should be a piece of cake. But considering this is for one of my best friends and I'm in said friend's wedding, I'm nervous. My hands are literally shaking.

Clearly, I need to calm myself down.

"Do you need some coffee?" Caroline asks, her gaze meeting mine in the mirror.

"No thank you." I shake my head. "That'll just make it worse. I'm worried I'll screw up your hair."

"No way. You can't do that." She smiles, her expression gentle and full of love. "You are the best hairstylist I know. I've seen some of the styles you've done for other brides and for proms. You're amazing."

I hear what she's saying, but it's like it doesn't compute. I just stand there frozen in place, my hands resting on her shoulders. "I don't feel very amazing right now," I admit softly.

"Here." Stella appears out of nowhere, a champagne

flute in her hand. She holds it out toward me. "Have a mimosa. It'll steady your nerves."

I gladly take the glass from her and sip. Oh, it's delicious. The orange juice is icy cold and with that crisp bite of champagne, it goes down smoothly. Too smoothly. As a matter of fact, I drain my glass within minutes, making an "ahh" sound when I finish.

Caroline just watches me in the mirror, her eyes wide. Crap. I probably just scared the bride.

"I'm better," I tell her after I set the glass on a nearby table and smile at her. Funny how the alcohol steadied my nerves, just like Stella said. "Okay, let's do this."

It takes me almost an hour and about a million bobby pins, but I finally finish Caroline's hair, and it's like a freaking masterpiece, if I do say so myself. Everyone comes over to her chair when I'm finished to admire my handiwork, all of them making the appropriate noises and offering gushing compliments. I bask in their praise. It's just what I need to hear to fuel my confidence and make me feel better about today.

See? I know what I'm doing. I'm a competent, in-demand hairstylist. I am surrounded by friends who love me, celebrating Caroline's special day. The wedding and reception will be magical. My life is full.

So why do I feel like I have a hole in my heart? And that it is somehow the exact same size and shape of Mitch?

Stella pulls me aside once I'm finished thanking everyone for the compliments and hands me another mimosa. "Girl, I think you need this."

I of course filled everyone in on my Mitch-lied-to-me news. They were all perfectly pissed on my behalf, which I appreciated greatly. I gave the quickest rundown to Caroline, only because she's getting married and has too many things on her mind already.

"Thank you," I tell Stella as I sip from my glass. I didn't eat much breakfast—a couple of apple slices—and I probably shouldn't drink so much on a mostly empty stomach, but screw it.

"Are you okay?" she asks, her voice gentle, her gaze full of concern. I love Stella for her no-nonsense approach to everything. How she doesn't hold back when she feels like something is wrong. She's blunt and honest and gives it to us straight.

I need her bluntness right now more than ever. I need someone to tell me to shape up and forget that man. I know Stella can do the job.

"Not really," I say miserably. "I miss him."

"I can tell," she says, her voice quiet.

I meet her gaze. "What should I do?"

Stella shakes her head slowly. "I can't tell you what to do. This is too big of a moment for you to listen to all of us."

I'm frowning. "What do you mean?"

"You need to listen to your heart. Your mind," she says. "What are they telling you to do?"

Who is this person and when did she abduct my friend? She looks like Stella. She sounds like her too. But what she's saying is...

Kind of romantic.

She sounds like me.

"He hurt me," I admit, my voice hushed as I glance around the hustle and bustle that is currently filling this room. But no one is paying any attention us. I can be one hundred percent truthful right now. Stella is open-minded to my plight, and I need that. "Keeping his career hidden feels like he might have other secrets too, right?"

"We all have secrets, and when we're with someone we care about, we slowly expose them, vulnerable and raw the entire time. By keeping that from you, he made you feel vulnerable," Stella explains.

"And raw," I add with a humorless laugh.

"Right." She smiles faintly. "I know what Sarah told you. She told me about your conversation. And I have to agree with her. Maybe he kept it from you because he didn't want you to fall for the illusion of him. He wanted you to appreciate the real him. The man beneath the career, the money, the fame."

"Yeah," I say, my voice raspy. I chug the rest of my mimosa and tell myself I can't drink anymore until the reception. "He kind of said the same thing. I just wish he'd told me before the weekend was up."

"I don't think he knew how," Stella says. "It's hard, coming clean from a lie. It just gets more and more difficult as time goes on, you know? I'm guessing that's what happened. He got to a certain point where he didn't know how to tell you without looking like an absolute asshole."

"He couldn't win," I say, shaking my head. "He looks like an asshole no matter what."

"Can you forgive that asshole?" Stella asks.

Yes. That's the first word that comes to my mind.

Yes, I want to forgive him.

Yes, I want him back in my life.

Yes, I want us to pursue this relationship and see what happens.

But how?

She must see something in my expression, because she forges on. "It doesn't matter what I think or what anyone else thinks either. What do *you* want, Eleanor? What's going to make you happy? *Who* is going to make you happy?"

"I can make myself happy no matter what," I say automatically. "I don't need a man to complete me."

"Good, that's good," Stella says, nodding her encouragement.

"But I want to give him another chance," I admit, my voice so soft, I'm almost whispering. "We fit together perfectly."

"You two seem very compatible sexually," Stella says, her expression serious.

That makes me laugh, and my face heats up. "I am so embarrassed you all had to listen to that."

"We were actually really happy for you. You've tried dating a variety of guys over the years, and they never work out. They always end up making you feel bad about yourself, and that sucks." Stella grabs my hand. "You are nothing short of fabulous. You're funny and smart and you're an amazing hairstylist. You are a loyal friend. You love unabashedly. And you're beautiful, both inside and out."

I am flat-out crying. I have never heard Stella say such sweet things before, and it's making me emotional.

"You deserve a man who sees all of those things and more. You deserve a man who puts you on a pedestal and worships the ground you walk on. One who treats you like an equal, and doesn't think your quirks are awkward or weird," Stella continues.

"That was Mitch," I say, nodding fiercely as the tears stream down my face. "I barely knew him, but that's exactly how he treated me."

"My nonna always says, 'When you know, you know.'" A mysterious little smile curls Stella's lips. "I think you know, Eleanor."

I absorb everything Stella said to me, thinking on it as I get my hair curled by one of the stylists who works with me at the salon. Laci loves to chat, and she's chattering away, not even paying attention if I'm listening to her or not, which is perfect. Her nonstop talking gives me time to think.

Stella's right. I deserve everything Mitch was willing to give to me. He worshipped me. Made me feel like the most beautiful woman in the world. The way he touched me, looked at me, kissed me...

No one has ever made me feel like that before.

I can't let him go. I have to talk to him. And I don't want to do it over the phone either. Or even FaceTime. I want to stare into his eyes and listen to what he has to say. And then when he's finished, he's going to listen to me too.

Maybe we can make this work.

"Okay, I'm done," Laci says, and I blink my vision back into focus, staring at myself in the mirror. Laci stands above me, a giant smile on her face. "What do you think?"

My hair is down, wavy at the ends, and she clipped up one side, where eventually a fresh white rose will be tucked behind my ear. "It looks great," I say, smiling in return. "It's so nice not to have to worry about my own hair for once."

"You have beautiful hair," Laci tells me, giving my shoulders a quick squeeze. "Wonderful texture. It can do just about anything."

"Thank you." I'm feeling good. Better than I did when I first arrived, that's for sure. I need to hold on to this feeling and carry it with me throughout the rest of the day.

Positivity is the name of the game this afternoon, and I'm going to own it.

Even if it kills me.

TWENTY-FIVE

ELEANOR

"WORK IT, WORK IT!" I am yelling at the top of my lungs, encouraging Stella to shake what her mama gave her, and Stella is giving it as good as she can, pretty much twerking in the middle of the dancefloor, her boyfriend Carter—and Caroline's big brother—watching her with complete and utter amazement.

I bet he didn't realize his girlfriend could throw her ass back like that.

The reception is in full swing, and I am having the time of my life. I let go all of my Mitch-induced sadness and throw myself fully into the moment.

The ceremony was gorgeous. There was a breeze, the sun was shining but it wasn't too hot—it's never too hot this time of year here, so that's always a bonus.

Caroline and Alex's vows were solemn and powerful. I teared up. A lot of people did. I could hear sniffing throughout the crowd, even among the women standing at her side. Once the endless photos were finished being taken—that went on forever—we finally made our way to the reception tent.

When we first entered, I couldn't help but think it looked like something out of a dream. Caroline kept the vine theme throughout, with tendrils of greenery and fresh flowers wound around every available space. The lighting was subtle, casting everything in a gentle, golden glow. There are twinkling fairy lights draped in the middle of each table. Bright, fragrant flowers everywhere you look. You could even smell them, fragrant and sweet.

My bouquet is beautiful and I can't wait to take it home and stare at it for the next few days. My dress fits like a dream, which I'm thankful for considering I haven't ate much these last few days and was worried I lost weight.

My boobs still threaten to fall out of it, though. Like right now, while I'm dancing and pointing at the twerking Stella. Everyone's laughing and clapping, encouraging her bad behavior. More women start twerking. I can't manage it. I've tried before, but failed. This is not my time to shine. I'm giving it up to Stella and Co. for tonight.

Once the song is over, the DJ starts talking, announcing that it's time to cut the cake. We all make our way over to the table where the giant cake sits. It's a beautiful thing, three round tiers with white frosting and topped with real flowers. I can't imagine the florist bill for the wedding.

Caroline and Alex are kind as they feed each other cake. No shoving cake in each other's faces, which I'm sure was discussed beforehand. There are sounds of disappointment, but for the most part everyone claps.

And then it's back to the dancefloor.

I beg off, going over to our table so I can sit down for a minute and rest. My feet ache. The sandals I'm wearing are beautiful, with thin silver straps, but painful after so many hours of being on my feet. I'm a little sweaty around my hairline and between my shoulders, and I grab a napkin, dabbing my forehead with it to take the shine off.

"Tired?"

I turn to find Sarah has slid into the chair next to mine. She appears as tired as I feel.

"Yeah." I smile. "This has been the best day."

"I can tell you're enjoying yourself. I'm so glad." She reaches out and squeezes my hand. "I was hoping you could forget about Mitch for a few hours."

Just like that, he's forefront in my thoughts. And that's okay. It doesn't hurt so bad right now. Maybe because I have a plan.

"I'm going to talk to him," I tell her, hoping she doesn't berate my choice. "Probably tomorrow. I want to hear what he has to say."

"I think that's a good idea. Maybe he deserves a second chance."

"He has to grovel." I smile. "A lot."

"Make him beg!" Sarah crows, just before we start laughing.

"I need to go to the bathroom," I tell her as I rise to my feet. "Want to go with?"

"Sure."

We make our way to the bathrooms that are in the ballroom section of the building. There's another wedding reception happening inside, and I can hear the music carry in the hallway, along with the dull roar of lots of people talking all at once. Sarah and I slip into the bathroom, and I'm grateful there's a stall available and I don't have to wait in line. I really have to pee.

Once we're finished, Sarah and I wash our hands and fix each other's hair. I dab at the streaks of mascara beneath both of my eyes. We stand up straight, shoulder to shoulder, studying ourselves in the mirror.

"This dress is so fabulous," Sarah says with a wistful sigh. "It looks good on all of us. And we all have distinctly different body types."

"Right? I mean, look at my boobs." I gesture toward them. They look ready to fall out, but they're constrained pretty well. I just have really great cleavage. "Plus it hides all my flaws." Like my generous hips and thighs.

"You have zero flaws. You're beautiful," Sarah says earnestly.

I almost can't deal with all the compliments my friends are doling out. They're making me feel so appreciated.

Loved.

"So are you," I tell her just before we turn toward each other and hug.

We are having a total moment here. I feel like my friends all talked among themselves and decided it was going to be nothing but positive reinforcement where I'm concerned.

I'm not complaining. It's been really good for my crushed ego today.

"Okay, let's go," Sarah says. "I don't want to miss the bouquet toss."

"You don't think they're having it yet, do you?" I ask as we both make our way to the door.

"You never know. This DJ seems to be moving everything along at a pretty good clip," Sarah says as she holds the door open for me.

We both exit the building, heading toward the tent when I spot a very tall man in the distance, hovering right at the tent's entrance.

A very familiar tall man.

My heart starts thumping extra hard as we draw closer. He's broad. Muscular. Clad in a black suit and a white shirt, no tie. His golden-brown hair is neatly trimmed, like he just got a cut, and I'm filled with disappointment that I didn't get to give him one.

Because I know that hair. That man. It's freaking Mitch.

And he's *here*.

In Monterey. Pebble Beach. At Caroline and Alex's wedding.

How did he find us?

Freezing, I stand there like an idiot and gape at him. He spots me almost immediately, as if he could feel my presence, and now he's gaping too.

Oh God. He looks so, *so* good. I want to run to him.

But my feet refuse to move.

"Why are you stopping? What's going on?" Sarah looks from me to where Mitch is standing, her eyes going wide when she realizes who he is. How does she know? I'm sure they've all Googled him now and know exactly what he looks like. "*Oh.*"

"He's here," I whisper. I sound excited. I *am* excited. My heart is beating so hard I'm afraid it might fly out of my chest and my entire body is covered in tingles.

It's the way he's looking at me, like I'm the most beautiful woman he's ever seen. I see it all in his eyes. The regret. The apology. The reverence. The wanting.

Every single emotion is shining in his gaze for me to see.

I feel the same exact way—though I'm not saying sorry, no, sir. I'm not the one who did anything wrong here.

"I'll leave you two alone," Sarah says just before she walks off.

I barely acknowledge her leaving. I'm too wrapped up

in the man who is now approaching me. His steps are sure. His gaze is direct. But I see the worry in his expression. The tension in his jaw. Is he afraid I'll tell him to leave? He should be.

He has no idea I've had a slight change of heart.

"I had to come find you," he finally says, his deep voice washing over me, making my knees weak. "I've been looking for you for hours."

"Really?" I squeak. I clear my throat. Stand up a little straighter. Note the way his gaze drops to my chest for the briefest moment.

My skin catches fire there. He has such a thing for my breasts. What a perv.

I want him to be my perv.

He nods. "Traffic is hell on a Saturday afternoon in Pebble Beach."

"There was some sort of car show," I tell him.

"Yeah, and a golf tournament," he grumbles, making me smile.

I banish my smile away. This feels so normal, talking with him. Looking at him. Wishing he would just pull me into his arms and never let me go.

Nope. Not yet. I can't think like that.

"I missed you," he says. "So damn bad. I'm sorry, Eleanor. That I lied to you. That I didn't tell you who I really am, or what I really do. I love what I do. I'm a lucky motherfucker, and I know it. But playing pro ball also comes with a lot of restrictions. It's hard for me trust anyone. Every woman I meet, I never think she'll actually like me for me. Some women only seem to care about how much money we make, or how much airtime we get during a game broadcast. I've seen it happen time and again to other guys I play with, and it sucks."

I could care less about any of those things he just mentioned. I had no idea he even played football for the NFL, so none of that matters.

All I care about is him.

"You liked me for me. None of that mattered. You thought I was funny. You wanted to spend time with me, and you didn't even know who I really was, or what I did. And that felt good. It felt great." His hungry gaze rakes over me. "Damn, woman, you're gorgeous in that dress."

"Thank you," I say with a smile, soaking up his compliments.

"I want another chance with you." He takes a step closer, reaching for my hands and clasping them in his own. They're big and warm and cradle me gently, and I know without a doubt that's how he'll always hold me. Carefully. Securely. He's got me. "If I have to get down on my knees and beg for your forgiveness, I'll do it. Just please, Eleanor. Give me another chance."

"Go ahead," I tell him. "Get on your knees then."

He doesn't even hesitate. Just crouches down and gets on his knees on the damp grass in his expensive-looking trousers, still holding onto my hands. He's so tall, he's almost at eye level, but not quite. Actually, he's at tit level. And he's staring at them for a too long moment, as if he's in a trance.

Then he shakes his head and tilts it back, his warm gaze meeting mine, and it takes everything within me not to burst out laughing.

"Do you forgive me?" he asks.

I squeeze his hands. "I don't like that you kept such important information from me, but I understand your reasoning behind it. I don't know what that's like, having to deal with being a celebrity."

He rolls his eyes. "Baby, I'm not a big time celebrity. I'm no Kardashian."

"Oh I know. But you still deal with fame. Women throwing themselves at you because of what you do, not who you are." I smile. "I like you for you. I don't care what you do. Well, I do, because how freaking cool is it that you play for the Raiders? But that doesn't make a difference in how I feel about you."

"How do you feel about me?" he asks.

"Like I'm falling for you," I tell him with the utmost sincerity. "I forgive you."

"Thank God," he mutters. "Can I stand now?"

Laughing, I pull him back up, though I really had nothing to do with that. He's solid as a rock. "Can you kiss me?"

There's no hesitation as he pulls me into his arms and presses his mouth to mine. A shiver moves through me when he parts my lips with his tongue, and we're full-blown making out in front of the tent, while the party still carries on inside.

Minutes later I'm finally extracting myself from his embrace, my entire body flushed and shaky. "We need to calm down."

"I can't help it." He grins. "I'm so glad to see you. And that dress. Goddamn. Turn around." I do a little circle and he whistles low. "You're trying to kill me."

"I didn't even know you'd be here," I tell him as I hook my arm through his and lead him toward the tent entrance.

"I had to come get you, Eleanor. I don't give up on what I consider mine." He stops me, dropping another kiss on my lips. "And you're mine. Just like I'm yours."

Oh shit. I am beyond giddy at his words, at that wondrous glow shining in his eyes.

We enter the tent and I start introducing him to everyone I know. The men stare at him slack-jawed for a moment, because they all pretty much know exactly who he is, which is such a thrill. Mitch handles it all with ease, smiling and shaking hands with everyone, putting on the charm on every single one of my friends. He tells Caroline and Alex he's sorry for crashing their reception and they both forgive him easily.

Maybe I forgave him too easily as well, but I'd be a fool to let this man go.

And I know it.

"All right, single ladies, gather around! The bride is going to toss the bouquet!" the DJ announces a few minutes later.

My friends and I all go to the designated spot a few feet away from where Caroline stands. Candice sits this one out since she has a fat diamond on her finger, but the rest of us are there. Even Amelia, who's still currently split from her jerk of a boyfriend. I'm so proud of her for keeping away from him. He's toxic and I think she finally realizes it.

"Your Mitch is cute," Stella says, nodding toward where he's standing. I glance over to find him watching me as Carter speaks to him. "He seems totally into you."

"He *is* totally into me," I say with a giant grin. "I can't believe he showed up here tonight."

"I can," Stella says with confidence.

I stare at her. "Did you know?" How could she?

"Nope, but I had a feeling he'd come for you eventually. And look, he did." She gives me a brief hug. "I think he might be good for you."

"I'd like to think I'm good for him too," I say.

"Oh, I'm sure you are. And by the way he's staring at you, I'd guess he can't wait to you get alone. I'm sure you two will cause a ruckus in your hotel room tonight. Again." She nudges me in the side.

We all have rooms at the hotel this evening. Alex made sure we wouldn't have to drive home. In fact, I sort of forgot all about that tasty little fact.

"Better hope your room isn't next to mine. We'll keep you awake all night," I tell her, just before we start giggling.

"Okay, ladies, here we go! Our bride is ready to toss the bouquet. Who's ready to catch it?" the DJ asks over the microphone.

We all start shouting and jumping up and down. Caroline's laughing at us, aiming the bouquet at Sarah, then me. Then Stella. Kelsey. Amelia. We all give each other a look, and I know it's going to be a fight.

But I don't want it. I'm just pretending I do. Come on, do you really think I'd battle it out for that bouquet and then show it to Mitch? He'd probably quietly lose his mind. I know we're moving fast, but not *that* fast.

So I put on a bit of a show, acting like I'm going to leap over all of them to get that bouquet. Caroline sizes us up over her shoulder before she turns away and tosses it.

Right at...

Stella.

The flowers fall into her hands as if it's meant to be. We all start pointing and looking over at Carter, who appears a little surprised. He and Stella are madly in love, but I don't believe he's thought about marriage.

Yet.

Poor dude.

Anyway.

The garter toss happens next, and lo and behold, it's Jared, Sarah's boyfriend, who catches it. Stella and Jared take photos together—never a missed photo opportunity at this wedding, that's for sure—and then I find myself back out on the dancefloor, swaying to the slow music in Mitch's arms.

"I feel like a jackass for crashing their wedding," Mitch says as he tightens his arms around my waist. "But I don't regret it."

"Good." I smile up at him, thrilled that my dreams actually came true. I got to show off my boyfriend to my friends. I got to be the happy bridesmaid with a hot date after all.

But you know what? I would've been perfectly content being just me tonight too. I don't need a man.

I sure do like this one, though.

"I have a surprise," I say as I gaze into his eyes. I look my fill, enjoying his handsome face, the possessive way he holds me, his hand splayed across my bare back, his fingers playing with the straps of my dress.

His gaze darkens. "Tell me."

"I have a hotel room here tonight."

"So we can go to it now?" he asks hopefully.

"Um, no. Not yet." I slowly shake my head.

His gaze wanders all over my upper body, settling squarely on my exposed chest. "I can't wait until we can leave."

"You're the worst," I say, laughing.

"It's been almost a week since I've had my hands on you like this," he reminds me, just as he slides his hand over my butt, nice and slow. My skin turns hot. I feel like I'm burning up. "I can't wait to get you naked."

"I thought you liked my dress."

"I do. I love it. You're fucking beautiful in it." He bends his head, his mouth at my ear. "But you're also pretty fucking beautiful wearing nothing at all." He presses his lips to my neck in an open mouthed kiss.

My knees wobble. This man knows just how to undo me. "We have to stick around for at least another hour."

"Maybe we could manage a quickie in the bathroom."

"Absolutely not."

He pouts. He is so adorable. "I guess I can wait."

"It'll be worth it," I tell him.

"Oh trust me." He grins. "I know."

TWENTY-SIX
MITCH

THE MOMENT we enter the hotel room, I've got Eleanor pinned against the door, my hands at her waist, my mouth fused with hers. I kiss her hungrily, my tongue searching, swallowing those pretty little gasps and moans.

My entire body aches for her. I still can't believe I'm here with her. I earned Eleanor's forgiveness. We're together.

I'm a lucky man.

Unable to resist, I cup her breast, my thumb teasing her nipple. The fabric of her dress is thin, and somehow she's not wearing a bra. I don't know how she gets away with it, because her tits are huge. They should be falling out of her dress.

In fact, I test that theory, tugging aside the fabric, exposing her skin. Breaking the kiss, I look down at her, watching her peach-colored nipple harden under my gaze. Swooping in, I draw her nipple into my mouth and start sucking.

Her hands land on my head, fingers threading through my hair as she holds me to her. I suck and lick and bite, then do the same thing to her other breast. I can't get enough of this woman. I want to consume her. Knowing that she was so angry with me, worried that I lost her, I about fell apart.

I had no idea a woman I only just met could matter so much to me in such a short amount of time?

I shift away from her chest, needing to kiss her again. "I missed you," I growl against her cheek, just before my lips land on hers once more. We kiss and kiss, tongues circling, teeth nibbling. My hands are everywhere, and so are hers. At one point, she's cupping my dick, and I thrust against her palm, wanting more.

Wanting all of her.

We move across the darkened room, shedding each other's clothes, until we're both naked. The curtains are open, letting in light from the moon outside. Otherwise it's dark, but I can see enough of Eleanor to get my blood pumping. She has the most beautiful body. Skinny waist, flared hips. Curvy. Womanly. I grab hold of her and we fall onto the bed, until at one point she's on top of me, her breasts swaying as she rubs her wet pussy against my cock.

"You feel so good," she says on a moan, her eyes falling shut, her mouth falling open. She's completely focused on driving me out of my ever-lovin' mind, dragging her wetness all over my dick. Up and down she slides, making my eyes cross, my hands gripping her waist tight, fingers digging into her skin.

I rear up, latching my mouth around her nipple as she grinds against me. Next thing I know, I'm inside, and she's sliding down, down, until I'm fully in. She goes completely still, her head dropping, and I pull away from her chest, our gazes locking.

"I'm on the pill," she admits.

"I've never fucked a woman without a condom before you," I tell her earnestly, my voice ragged.

It just feels so damn good, being inside her with no barriers. Her inner walls grip me tight, and I can tell she's flexing and squeezing those muscles down there. I lift my hips, trying to get her to move with me, and she starts riding my cock, her movements slow, her moans getting louder and louder.

I barely move. Just watch her in complete and utter fascination. She's beautiful. And she's mine. All mine. She's working herself into a frenzy, her hand dropping between her legs as she touches herself, and my gaze fixates on that spot. I start moving faster, gripping her hips and pounding inside her and then she's coming, her molten hot pussy milking me into my orgasm that about wrings everything I've got out of me. I just come and come, groaning her name and sounding like I'm about to die.

Damn. Pretty sure she's trying to kill me.

"Wow, that was good," she says minutes later, once we've both caught our breath and calmed our racing hearts and shuddering bodies.

"Not much foreplay," I say woefully.

"Dancing at the reception was like foreplay," she says with a little laugh. She clings to me as she sits in my lap, my cock still inside her, her hands resting on my shoulders as she presses her face against my neck. "I missed you so much."

"It's only been a few days," I remind her.

"How are we ever going to survive a long-distance relationship?" she asks, lifting away from my neck so she can look into my eyes. "I don't like not having you around."

"I'm here. For the rest of the weekend," I tell her,

cupping her cheek with my hand as I lean down and drop a kiss on her perfect lips.

"You fly back tomorrow?"

"Yeah." I kiss her again. "We'll make this work, baby. I know we can. Maybe eventually you can...move to Vegas?"

Swear to God, my heart's lodged in my throat as I wait for her reply. She stares down at me with those big blue eyes, like I just stunned the crap out of her with my suggestion, until finally she says, "Maybe I will."

My heart feels light. Like it might float right out of me. "Really?"

"We have to give this some time, but...I can see it happening." She wraps her arms around my neck and squeezes me tight. "I want to be where you are," she whispers against my ear.

Just hearing her voice so close to my ear drives me wild. I attack her with renewed gusto, kissing her soundly, repositioning us so she's lying on the bed and I'm hovering above her, racing my mouth all over her skin. She giggles when my lips land on certain spots, and I'm sure I'm tickling her, but once I place my mouth on her pussy, all that giggling stops and she starts moaning. Wiggling. Rubbing herself against my lips and chin.

This woman loves it when I go down on her.

I cradle her ass in my hands and basically devour her, licking and sucking her clit until it's swollen and throbbing beneath my tongue. At one point, her eyes crack open and meet mine, and it's my turn to put on a show for her. I draw my tongue across her, my gaze never leaving hers as I lap at her folds.

"Oh God," she chokes out, and I know she's close. We both get off on watching each other. It's like we're compatible in every way. As if she were made for me.

I can't believe I almost lost her.

HOURS LATER, we're still awake. Makeup sex is a great thing, though I don't want to put us in the place we were in a few days ago. That about destroyed me.

"You think we're moving too fast?" Eleanor asks at one point. She's draped her naked body across mine, our hands wandering as usual. We can't stop touching each other. I actually crave her skin. The scent of her. The feel of her.

It's kind of nuts.

"No," I say firmly. "Others might say that, but it feels right to me."

"It feels right to me too." She presses a kiss on my pec. My cock makes a halfhearted attempt at rousing, like it might be down for some action, but my muscles feel like jelly. I don't think I can physically have sex with her again tonight.

I'm a professional athlete who's expected to go nonstop, and I need to rest after having too much sex. I don't understand what's happening to me.

But I'm not complaining.

"I have a question," Eleanor suddenly says, her voice hesitant.

What's that about.

Frowning, I glance down at her to find she's already watching me. "What?"

"Did you actually rate me? On the dating app?"

I chuckle, giving her shoulders a squeeze. "Nope. I guess I should. Ten out of ten. Five stars. Superior status. Whatever scale they use, you're at the top."

"So are you." She laughs as she rests her cheek on my

chest. "Tomorrow we should look over a calendar and compare each other's schedules."

"And delete all dating apps from our phones," I add.

"Most definitely." She's quiet for a moment before she says, "I'm sure you're going to get super busy with football."

"Very busy," I agree. "And I want you to come to some of my games."

"I totally want to go to them!" She lifts her head, smiling at me. Her hair is a mess. Her eyelids are at half-mast and she looks exhausted.

And happy. So happy.

"Good." I give her a squeeze. "Have you ever been to a NFL game before?"

"No, we never got around to it, though we always meant to." She makes a face. "My family...we're all Niner fans."

"We?" I lift my brows.

"Joe Montana is the king," she whispers.

"Overrated," I say, though I'm teasing her.

Her mouth drops open. "Those are fighting words."

"Please. Claiming you're a Niner fan when I play for the Raiders? Them's fighting words, lady." I start tickling her, my fingers wiggling against her ribs, and she bats my hands away, both of us laughing.

Soon our laughter stops and my mind drifts. My eyes close. I got my woman in my arms and I've never felt so content.

Life is good.

EPILOGUE
ELEANOR

SEVEN MONTHS LATER...

A NEW YEAR means new beginnings, and I'm in the throes of creating beginnings all over the place. I quit my job. Just moved out of my apartment. Packed up all my stuff—and do I have a lot of stuff—and hired a moving company to take my belongings to Las Vegas.

Yep, Mitch and I are moving in together.

I know I said I never thought I could live in Las Vegas, but when a woman finds a good man and falls in love with him? She'll do just about anything to make it work. And since Mitch is the one who's stuck in Las Vegas due to his profession, I happily agreed to live with him.

Plus, come on. Las Vegas is like the marriage capital of the world. So many places to get married at! This city is right up my alley.

Anyway, Mitch bought a house a few months ago, and oh my God, it's so gorgeous. Four bedrooms, three bathrooms, with an open-concept kitchen and a beautiful backyard with a pool. It's brand new—everything inside is white and gleaming and perfect and we're going to make this place ours.

We're headed to the house now to meet the movers. Mitch took most of his belongings in almost a week ago, right before he had a playoff game. He came back a few days ago after his team won, and he's been on a perma-high ever since. I arrived in Las Vegas last night on a one-way ticket.

This is my town now, and I'm so excited. Beyond ready to create this new life with Mitch. Of course, I'm going to miss my friends terribly. We had a big cry fest together a few nights ago. We all gathered at Tuscany, the restaurant Stella's brothers own, and ate delicious Italian food and drank a lot of wine. We cried and laughed and talked about fun times together, and at one point I told them this wasn't a funeral. I'll be back. And they can come visit me in Sin City whenever they want.

They all cheered when I made that offer.

And I mean it. I want them to visit me as much as possible. It's going to be weird, not being able to see my friends on a regular basis, but that's what texting and FaceTime is for. Living in Las Vegas isn't forever either. Mitch told me he doesn't see himself lasting beyond a couple of more seasons in the NFL. His position is tough. Hard on the body. He doesn't want to hurt himself and be forced to retire. He wants to leave on his own terms.

After that, he wants to go back to California. That's his native state, and it's mine too. It might be expensive to live there, but with what Mitch makes, money is no object.

Isn't that exciting? I remember thinking I would never know what it's like, to not have to worry about money, and now I'm living the dream!

Oh, I'm still working, though. Mama has to make her own money, am I right? I found a job at a high-end salon in the Wilder Hotel, of all places. The salon is part of their renowned day spa. The timing couldn't have been more perfect. Caroline mentioned the position since she knew I was moving to Las Vegas, I went in for the interview a few weeks ago, and got a job offer on the spot.

Despite missing my close friends, my life is somehow... perfect. I want to pinch myself, just to make sure I'm not in the middle of a dream.

Nope, this is my real life.

We arrive at our house to see the movers are already there, and they've started unloading the truck. Most of my furniture is sitting in the driveway, and it's not the most high-quality stuff. IKEA has been my favorite place to shop, especially on my budget.

"My stuff looks shabby," I say on a sigh as Mitch parks next to the curb and shuts off the engine.

"We'll get new stuff." He grabs hold of my hand and pulls me in close for a kiss. "Come on, let's get this going."

Mitch opens the garage and we start going to work. I'm directing movers and Mitch is helping them. They're all dazzled to be in his presence, and I get it. He's rather dazzling to me too. He takes photos with them. Signs autographs. Speaks to them in low, hushed tones so I can't tell what he's saying, but whatever it is, they kick into high gear and start unloading that truck at a rapid-fire pace. They're done in less than sixty minutes.

Once the truck is gone and we're standing in the garage, eyeing the many boxes that are now filling the space, I have to ask him, "What did you say to those guys?"

"I gave them each an extra hundred bucks if they could

get it all unloaded in less than an hour," he explains with a shrug.

"That cost you like...four hundred dollars."

"Worth it, because now they're all gone." Smiling, he walks over to where I'm standing and pulls me in for a bear hug. I snuggle against his chest for a moment, savoring his warmth, his scent. I can never get enough of his hugs.

"We still have to move most of this stuff into the house," I murmur.

"I'm gonna buy you all new stuff. Furniture, clothes, knickknack shit. Whatever you need," he says.

I pull away so I can look into his eyes. "Knickknack shit?"

"Whatever you want." He kisses my forehead. "I love you."

We've only just started saying that to each other, and a thrill moves through me every single time I hear those words. "I love you too."

"Want to go have sex on the kitchen counter?" He waggles his brows at me like some sort of lecherous perv. Which I suppose he sort of is.

But he's all mine. And I wouldn't want him to be anything else but what he is.

"Are you wanting to do it in every room of the house?" I ask.

"Eventually."

"That granite countertop is going to be cold on my butt," I tell him as he grabs my hand and leads me inside.

"Don't worry. I'll keep you warm," he promises with a wicked smile.

I know without a doubt Mitch Anderson will keep his promises.

Especially when it comes to me.

WEDDING DATE SNEAK PEEK!
CHAPTER ONE

Kelsey

As time goes on and I only get older and somehow not wiser, I recently made a secret vow with myself. None of my friends know this, though I've said it out loud a few times around them. Problem is, none of them take me seriously. They all just laugh and think I'm kidding.

I'm not.

Anyway, my vow is this:

I've sworn off men.

It sounds extreme, I know, and this is a temporary situation but come on. Let's be real right now. They're all terrible. And I know I'm painting with a wide brush by saying that, but it's true. The last few guys I've tried to go out with, the dates ended spectacularly—and not in a good way. A while ago, I convinced my friend Eleanor to get on that Rate A Date app with me so we can find someone, and she meets the man of her dreams who just so happens to be a pro athlete.

While I meet a jerk who treated me like garbage and harassed me for weeks afterward.

Yeah. See? Terrible.

One good thing that came out of meeting the harassing jerk (his name is Paul, though that really doesn't matter) is that I have become friendly with his friend, Theodore Espino. Theo. He's sweet. Kind. He just got out of a serious relationship—engaged serious—after he found out she cheated on him.

With his cousin.

He's anti-dating as well. In fact, he's given up on women. He made that declaration to me a few weeks ago, when we went out for drinks together.

Yes, we're just friends. That's all I want from Theo, and that's all he wants from me, and it is positively liberating.

How did we meet up again after the disastrous double date I had with Paul and Theo had with my friend, Eleanor? Picture this:

I'm at a business mixer on a Wednesday evening at the Wilder Hotel in Pebble Beach, where I work. I'm already bored and wondering when I can leave when I hear someone say my name in this wondrous, questioning tone. I turn to find Theo approaching me, his big brown eyes drinking me in as if I were the best thing he's ever seen.

It was flattering, don't get me wrong. But considering I associate him with one of the worst first dates I've ever been on, at first I was reluctant to chat with Theo. Plus, I remember him being so sad. He'd only been separated from his ex-fiancée for a few months when I first met him, and he was still in a major funk.

But he was *so* fun that night at the business mixer. Talking nonstop and making me laugh. Telling me funny stories. Reminding me that if I was interested in investing money, he could help me.

I took him up on that offer and made an appointment with him. He took me to lunch. He convinced me to invest the five grand in savings I had and I've seen some growth, which makes me happy. Since then, we've gone out for a few dinners, mostly for business-type stuff. We cross paths frequently at community events. I like Theo.

A lot.

But not enough to want to have a relationship with him. I have my guard up. A wall that is solid steel and no one can penetrate it. Like I mentioned, I've given up men, and while I know it's not a forever type of thing, I am making myself do this for the betterment of my soul. So I won't settle. I need to find a good man. One who'll take care of me. One who won't have a wandering eye. One who'll treat me as an equal. One who'll give me multiple orgasm.

I might have high standards, but shouldn't we all?

Theo understands me. He understands what I want right now, and all I want is friendship. Same with him. I don't think he's interested in me at all. He doesn't act like he is, and that's perfect.

Perfect.

We're meeting for lunch right now, as a matter of fact. He's coming to the hotel because he has a business meeting here at two. We're going to have a long lunch and he's meeting me at one of the hotel restaurants that has a patio outside with a gorgeous view of the beach. The weather is perfect for outdoor dining. The sun is shining, the water is a deep, dark blue and there's a slight breeze.

"Sorry I'm late," Theo calls in greeting.

I lift my head to find him making his way toward me, winding his tall, trim body through the tiny tables scattered on the brick patio. He's got a smile on his face and his brown eyes are warm and friendly as they meet mine.

He just instantly makes me feel comfortable, and that's rare.

Rising to my feet, I give him a quick hug. He briefly kisses my cheek. We settle in at our tiny table and he picks up the menu, though I already know what he's going to order. I always get a salad and he gets a cheeseburger. While we eat, I secretly salivate over the juicy burger he eats and when he spots me making puppy dog eyes at his food, he always cuts off part of it for me.

Theo is very generous.

"I have news," Theo says gravely after he sets the menu down.

I study his face. When I first met him, I thought he looked like the saddest version of Ross from "Friends" and Eleanor totally agreed with me. Now, I don't get that vibe at all. He's got the dark hair and the dark eyes, but the glum expression has completely disappeared. He smiles a lot, and he has a nice smile with straight, white teeth. Those warm brown eyes that seem to dance every time he looks at me, and the thick dark hair that's a little too long on top, though he can carry it off. He's tall and fit and he wears impeccable suits that look expensive because they *are* expensive.

He's a successful investment manager at one of the local banks in Monterey. He makes a lot of money. He's not Alexander Wilder—my boss—level rich, but he does very well for himself.

"What's your news?" I ask when Theo hasn't volunteered any more information.

Uh oh. Unease settles over me, making me wary. He's giving me those old, sad vibes right now, which I haven't seen in a while.

Blowing out a harsh breath, he tells me, "I received an invitation this morning. To Jessica and Craig's wedding."

I blink at him for a moment. "Jessica? *The* Jessica?"

As in his former future wife.

He nods, his gaze flickering with an unfamiliar emotion. "Yes. That Jessica."

"They invited you to their wedding?" I'm so outraged on his behalf, my voice just rose about ten decibels.

"He's my cousin," Theo says with a shrug, seemingly unaffected. I wish I could be as cool as he's currently acting. "We're family."

"Don't forget Craig stole your girlfriend. The woman you were going to marry," I tell him.

"Oh trust me. I remember." His face is an emotionless mask, and my heart is heavy for him.

The server appears at our table and takes our order. Not only does Theo order his cheeseburger with fries, he also orders a beer. Something he never does.

"A beer, huh?" I ask once the server leaves.

"I need it to get through the rest of my day," he says. "I have to admit, seeing that invitation kind of rocked me."

I would assume so. "So you just received the invitation in the mail?"

"Jess sent it to my work address." I kind of hate how he just called her Jess, as if she's an old, intimate friend, which I suppose she is.

Thinking of her fills me with murderous images. I don't know what she looks like, but I imagine tearing her hair out at the roots and kicking her over a cliff, never to be seen again.

See? Murderous. I hate that she hurt Theo in such a cold, callous way.

"You're not going to go, are you?" I lean back in my

chair, contemplating him. The breeze sweeps over us, ruffling his hair and sending it into his eyes and he pushes it back in annoyance.

Look, I can admit that Theo is somewhat...attractive. Okay fine, he's really attractive. He's definitely a catch for a certain woman. But that woman is not me. He's my friend.

Nothing more.

"I have to go to the wedding," he says, his voice deadly serious.

I balk at him. "Why? What does it matter if you show up or not? Everyone would understand why you don't. She was your fiancée. She practically left you at the altar."

"Not quite," he says with the faintest smile. "Our breakup wasn't that pitiful."

"You found them in bed together," I remind him. "Naked." I hesitate before I forge on. "That's pretty pitiful, don't you think?"

He winces. "Kelsey, you always have this...way of always keeping things extremely real between us."

I sit up straighter, my demeanor solemn. "Some say it's my best trait."

"Who says that?" He grins and I can't help but laugh a little. "I'd say sometimes it detrimental."

"I just don't want you to forget what they did to you," I say, unable to ignore how heavy my heart currently feels on his behalf.

"I will never forget," he says, and I can tell from the serious way he's watching me, he means it. "Right now though, I'd prefer not to dwell on the horrendous details of when my future marriage went up in flames."

Pressing my lips together, I nod once. "Sorry."

"Hey. It's all good," he says easily.

The server returns with our drinks. Theo gratefully

reaches for the beer and takes a sip, leaving a thin line of foam on his upper lip. He licks it away quickly and I experience a weird dip in my stomach.

Yeah no. I'm not ready for weird dips. I'm off men, remember? Especially ones I consider an actual friend.

"The main reason I wanted to meet for lunch with you is that I was hoping I could convince you to..." His voice drifts and he glances down at the table for a moment before he lifts his head, his gaze meeting mine once more.

But he doesn't say anything.

I shake my head a little, giving him a confused look. "Convince me to what?"

"Be my date. For the wedding," he says softly, suddenly looking bashful.

My mouth drops open. "You want me to go with you to your ex-fiancée's wedding?"

"Yeah, I do. I definitely do." He nods eagerly.

"I don't know if that's a good idea," I start, trying to choose my words carefully, but he cuts me off.

"Honestly, Kels, what's the big deal? I need a date, we're friends, you're gorgeous, Jess will take one look at you and realize I made a major upgrade and I'll look like I am on top of the world," he says, his words coming out all at once, like one long string of consciousness.

I'm guessing he's been thinking about this situation a lot. And he wants me in on it.

I'd love to help but...

"I just worry about you," I admit, reaching out to rest my hand over his. "Have you seen her lately?"

He slowly shakes his head. "I was invited to a family get together recently and when I found out they were there, I didn't go."

"Right. Because you didn't feel ready to see her."

"Well, I feel ready to see her now." He flips his hand up so now our fingers are interlaced, and he gives them a squeeze. "Come on, Kels. Go with me. Be my wedding date. We'll show everyone I'm completely over Jessica once and for all."

I don't know why, but the idea of going to Theo's ex-fiancée's wedding to his cousin fills me with dread. Like this is a bad idea.

Perhaps even the worst idea ever.

But have I mentioned how hard it is for me to resist Theo when he's looking at me like that with those big brown eyes? I'm suddenly filled with the overwhelming need to make him smile, make him happy, and so of course I say:

"Sure. All right. Let's go together."

Preorder Wedding Date now! Coming December 1st!

ALSO BY MONICA MURPHY

Dating Series

Save The Date
Fake Date
Holidate
Hate to Date You
Rate A Date
Wedding Date

The Callahans

Close to Me
Falling For Her
Addicted To Him
Meant To Be

Forever Yours Series

You Promised Me Forever
Thinking About You
Nothing Without You

Damaged Hearts Series

Her Defiant Heart
His Wasted Heart
Damaged Hearts

Friends Series

One Night
Just Friends
More Than Friends
Forever

The Never Duet

Never Tear Us Apart
Never Let You Go

The Rules Series

Fair Game
In The Dark
Slow Play
Safe Bet

The Fowler Sisters Series

Owning Violet
Stealing Rose
Taming Lily

Reverie Series

His Reverie
Her Destiny

Billionaire Bachelors Club Series

Crave
Torn
Savor
Intoxicated

One Week Girlfriend Series

One Week Girlfriend
Second Chance Boyfriend
Three Broken Promises
Drew + Fable Forever
Four Years Later
Five Days Until You

Standalone YA Titles

Daring The Bad Boy
Saving It
Pretty Dead Girls

ABOUT THE AUTHOR

Monica Murphy is a New York Times, USA Today and international bestselling author. Her books have been translated in almost a dozen languages and has sold over two million copies worldwide. Both a traditionally published and independently published author, she writes young adult and new adult romance, as well as contemporary romance and women's fiction. She's also known as USA Today bestselling author Karen Erickson.

- facebook.com/MonicaMurphyAuthor
- twitter.com/msmonicamurphy
- instagram.com/monicamurphyauthor
- bookbub.com/profile/monica-murphy
- goodreads.com/monicamurphyauthor

Printed in Great Britain
by Amazon